"A fun, insightful romp . . . we'~~...~~ not
– and this witty, sceptical book ~~...~~ got
here"

"It's a remarkable journey we humans have been on . . . The heights of self-aggrandisement Burton encounters are dizzying . . . she does not condemn outright the modern urge for self-expression. Bounding from one historical anecdote to the next, she reveals the human ingenuity that is unleashed when God's plan for us is taken out of the equation"

*New Statesman*

"A fast-moving train of a book . . . Burton is a confident conductor"

*New York Times*

"This funny, startling, insightful story of the selfie, from Dürer to the Kardashians, is a must-read if you want to understand how we reinvent ourselves every time we reveal ourselves"

Peter Pomerantsev, author of *This Is Not Propaganda*

"*Self-Made* takes the reader on an incredible journey that begins in the Renaissance and ends with the Kardashians, Donald Trump and Silicon Valley's extropians, tracing the peculiarly modern phenomenon of people who make themselves the objects of their life's work. It is both revelatory and a warning about the ways that focus on the self distorts our individual lives and the broader society"

Francis Fukuyama, author of *The Origins of Political Order*

"Burton is that rare cultural critic who delivers insight with sass and wears her deep knowledge of history and philosophy with a lightness and grace. A dazzling cast of characters struts across these pages, but Burton is always fully in control; every case study and example accretes to build her argument, for we are not merely self-stylists but shapeshifters, not just makers, but gods"

Marina Benjamin, author of *Insomnia*

"Tara Isabella Burton's thoughtful, beautifully written book charts the engrossing history of the self-made man (and woman) from the geniuses of the Renaissance to present-day reality TV stars. Philosophical, ethical and pragmatic by turns, Burton urgently interrogates the culturally dominant myths of individualism and self-realisation, asking what we lose when we gain what we think we really want: when we make ourselves into gods"

Carolyne Larrington, author of *The Norse Myths*

"Ranging from Aristotle to OnlyFans by way of the Marquis de Sade and Frederick Douglass, Tara Isabella Burton delights, infuriates and instructs while offering some of the sharpest and most insightful social commentary being written today. This is a book you will not forget"

Walter Russell Mead, author of *The Arc of a Covenant*

"Looking around at the strange terrain of American politics, religion, culture and media, almost everyone is asking, 'What happened?' and 'What's next?' This book tells us the story behind those questions. Those who wonder why almost every aspect of life seems to be, at best, a reality television series and, at worst, a dark science fiction drama will need this important work. This book will shift the conversation, at perhaps just the right time"

Russell Moore, author of *Losing Our Religion*

"What does the Marquis de Sade have to do with David Bowie? Oscar Wilde with Oprah Winfrey? Montaigne with Donald Trump? Learn the fascinating historical and philosophical connections over the past five centuries in this erudite and wildly entertaining study on the fine art of self-creation, one of the modern era's defining cultural traits long before Instagram made it a daily universal habit"

Tony Perrottet, author of *The Sinner's Grand Tour*

"In the spirit of Kurt Andersen's *Fantasyland* and Barbara Ehrenreich's *Bright-Sided*, Tara Isabella Burton delivers a fascinating intellectual and cultural history of our never-ending quest to reinvent ourselves. She masterfully balances high and low culture, ranging from Renaissance sculptors and Parisian dandies to American hucksters and Instagram selfies. *Self-Made* clears through the fog of our current moment and lets us see the methods behind our collective madness. An essential read for our era of Late-Stage Everything"

Jamie Wheal, author of *Recapture the Rapture*

"Since the rise of Instagram and Facebook, how we present ourselves to the world has become a contemporary obsession. But as Tara Isabella Burton shows in her new book, *Self-Made*, it has a long history, from Beau Brummell to the Kardashians. The result is a fascinating, deeply researched and entertaining tour de force"

Simon Worrall, author of *Star Crossed*

Tara Isabella Burton is the author of *Strange Rites: New Religions for a Godless World* and the novels *The World Cannot Give* and *Social Creature*, which was a book of the year for the *New York Times*, *Vulture*, the *Guardian* and more. She regularly writes on religion, meaning-making, digital self-creation and the internet for the *New York Times*, *Washington Post*, *Wall Street Journal*, *Aeon*, *The Economist's 1843*, *City Journal* and more. She has a doctorate in theology from the University of Oxford.

# SELF-MADE

### CREATING OUR IDENTITIES
### FROM DA VINCI TO THE KARDASHIANS

## Tara Isabella Burton

sceptre

First published in the US by PublicAffairs, an imprint of Perseus
Books, LLC, a subsidiary of Hachette Book Group, Inc.

First published in Great Britain in 2023 by Sceptre
An imprint of Hodder & Stoughton Limited
An Hachette UK company

This paperback edition published in 2024

1

Print book interior design by Linda Mark

A CIP catalogue record for this title is available from the British Library

Paperback ISBN 978 1 529 36473 6
ebook ISBN 978 1 529 36471 2

Printed and bound in Great Britain by Clays Ltd, Elcograf S.p.A.

Hodder & Stoughton policy is to use papers that are natural, renewable
and recyclable products and made from wood grown in sustainable
forests. The logging and manufacturing processes are expected to
conform to the environmental regulations of the country of origin.

Hodder & Stoughton Limited
Carmelite House
50 Victoria Embankment
London EC4Y 0DZ

www.sceptrebooks.co.uk

*For Dhananjay, who challenges
and delights me daily*

# Contents

# Contents

# INTRODUCTION:
# HOW WE BECAME GODS?

I N JANUARY 2020, HIGH-END FITNESS CHAIN EQUINOX DEBUTED one of its most lavish advertising campaigns, titled "Make Yourself a Gift to the World." Produced by marketing studio Droga5, the billboards and posters featured implausibly beautiful, artistically rendered young men and women evoking mythological demigods of ages past. In one poster, a powerful-looking woman easily lifts two men, Samson style. In another, a shirtless man lies on a funeral dais, attended by frenetic worshippers. According to Droga5, the campaign is supposed to depict "divine characters as god-like 'gifts to the world' in moments and situations that reflect their self-worship as serving a larger purpose to humanity."[1]

The campaign's commercial takes this theme of divine self-obsession even further. Retelling the story of Narcissus—the infamously beautiful Greek demigod who fell in love with his own reflection in a pond and subsequently drowned trying to reach him—the film turns the myth's moral warning on its head. Self-obsession, a campily costumed narrator tells us, turns Narcissus into "a gift not just for him to treasure, but a gift that brought the whole world pleasure." (This Narcissus survives and starts a dance party.) With a wink to the viewer, the narrator asks us: "Does that not make self-obsession the most selfless act of all?"

The message of the advertisements is clear. Join an Equinox gym—where prices start at $250 a month and members are locked into yearlong contracts—and you too can become God's gift to the world, or maybe even a kind of god yourself. "We're targeting individuals dedicated to becoming the very best they can be," Equinox's chief marketer told one skeptical journalist. "We believe that when you become the best version of yourself, you radiate outward and contribute more to the world around you."[2]

The ad campaign—like many of Equinox's high-fashion-inspired commercials—is, of course, deliberately transgressive and more than a little tongue-in-cheek. But the worldview it represents—that shaping yourself, through both muscular discipline and aesthetic creativity, is the highest calling imaginable—is not limited to Equinox or even to the wider boutique wellness culture. Rather, the idea that we are self-makers is encoded into almost every aspect of Western contemporary life. We not only *can* but *should* customize and create and curate every facet of our lives to reflect our inner truth. We are all in thrall to the seductive myth that we are supposed to become our best selves.

In the economic sphere, we valorize self-made men and women. Entrepreneurs like Apple founder Steve Jobs and media mogul Oprah Winfrey rose from humble or deprived backgrounds to become billionaires or celebrities. These figures—our culture tells us—took control of their destinies through some combination of skill and good old-fashioned grit. Refusing to accept the circumstances into which they were born, they decided for themselves the lives they would lead. The narrative of the man (or woman) who pulls themselves up by their bootstraps, and who therefore deserves the fortune and fame they achieve, is a foundational part of the capitalist American dream. This myth, in turn, has shaped how Americans—and those across the globe whose ideologies are shaped by American cultural hegemony—think about, and legislate, our wider economic system.

But the fantasy of self-creation is also integral to our wider culture. We live, after all, in a social-media-saturated era where more and more of our most notable celebrities are "influencers." They present not only their work but their meticulously curated personal lives for public consumption and private profit. Even those of us who aren't necessarily looking to land a brand partnership or to post sponsored content on our Instagram pages are likely to have encountered the need to create or cultivate our "personal brands." More and more of us work to ensure that our social media presence reflects the way we want others to see us, whether we're using it for professional reasons, personal ones, or a mix of the two.

Our cultural moment—in the contemporary English-speaking world, at least—is one in which we are increasingly called to be self-creators: people who yearn not just to make ourselves a gift to the world but to make ourselves, period.

Our economic, cultural, and personal lives are suffused with the notion that we can and should transform ourselves into modern-day deities, simultaneously living works of art to be admired by others and ingeniously productive economic machines. If we have ultimate control over own lives, after all, why not use this to our advantage?

At the core of this collective project of self-creation lies one vital assumption. We can find it everywhere from Equinox's clarion call to become divine narcissists to the now-ubiquitous life coaches and personal growth classes that claim they can help us self-actualize or "become who we really are."

That assumption? That who we are—deep down, at our most fundamental level—is who we most *want* to be. Our desires, our longings, our yearning to become or to acquire or to be seen a certain way, these are the truest and most honest parts of ourselves. Where and how we were born, the names, expectations, and assumptions laid upon us by our parents, our communities, and our society at large? All these are at best incidental to who we really are, at worst actively inimical to our personal development. It is only by looking inward—by investigating, cultivating, and curating our inner selves—that we can understand our fundamental purpose in this life and achieve the personal and professional goals we believe we were meant to achieve.

Taken to its logical conclusion, this assumption means that we are most *real* when we present ourselves to the world as the people we most want to become. Our honest selves are the ones we choose and create. We can no longer tell where reality ends and fantasy begins. Or, as one of history's most famous self-creators, the writer and consummate dandy Oscar Wilde, notoriously put it: "Give [a man] a mask, and he will tell you the truth from another point of view."[3]

From this perspective, self-making isn't just an act of creativity, or even of industry. It's also an act of self-expression: of showing the world who we truly are by making the world see us as who we want to be. Self-creation, in other words, is where artificiality and authenticity meet.

The story of *Self-Made* is the story of how we got here.

IT IS THE story of some of modern history's most famous and eccentric self-makers: from Renaissance geniuses and Civil War abolitionists to Gilded Age capitalists and Warhol's Factory girls. These luminaries didn't just transcend their origins or circumstances; they also charted a new path for others to do the same. But the history of self-making was also written by some of the modern era's most notorious charlatans: unscrupulous self-help gurus, con artists, and purveyors of what circus impresario P. T. Barnum called "humbug." These charismatic upstarts understood one of self-making's most fundamental principles: that self-invention was as much about shaping people's perceptions of you as it was about changing anything about yourself.

*Self-Made* is also the story of how the social upheavals and technological transformations of the early modern period helped usher in two parallel narratives of what self-making looked like. In one—largely European—narrative, self-making was something available to a very particular, very special kind of person. A natural "aristocrat," which is to say not necessarily someone of high birth but rather of graceful wit or bulging muscles or artistic creativity, could use his innate ability to determine his own life to set himself above the common bourgeois herd. In another—predominately American—story, self-making was something anyone could do, so long as they put in sufficient amounts of grit and elbow grease. Conversely, if they failed to do so, that meant they were lacking on an existential as well as pragmatic level. These two narratives, more similar than they might at first glance appear, converged in the twentieth century, with the rise of Hollywood and a new image of what mass-market stardom—simultaneously innate and self-taught—could look like.

AS WE SHALL see, both of these narratives ultimately come from the same place: a radical, modern reimagining of the nature of reality, humans' place in it, and, even more significantly, of who or what "created" humanity to begin with. Our faith in the creative and even magical power of the self-fashioning self goes hand in hand with the decline in belief in an older model of reality: a God-created and God-ordered universe in which we all have specific, pre-ordained parts to play—from peasants to bishops to kings—based on the roles into which we are born.

The philosopher Charles Taylor famously characterized this intellectual transition as a shift into a secular age. We have moved away from spiritual belief and enchantment and toward (perceived) rationality. We have entered an era of what he calls "expressive individualism," or the sense that our internal image of ourselves has become a kind of compass for who we really are. And I agree with Taylor's ultimate diagnosis that expressive individualism dominates how we think about ourselves in modern life. But I disagree that this shift represents a move from a religious worldview to a secular one.

Rather, I believe we have not so much done away with a belief in the divine as we have relocated it. We have turned our backs on the idea of a creator-God, *out there*, and instead placed God *within us*—more specifically, within the numinous force of our own desires. Our obsession with self-creation is also an obsession with the idea that we have the power that we once believed God did: to remake ourselves and our realities, not in the image of God but in that of our own desires.

This sense that there might be something magical, even divine, about our hunger to become our best, wealthiest, or most successful selves is not a new one. Even the most atheistic accounts of human existence, like those of Friedrich Nietzsche, make room for something special, something distinct, even something enchanted in the human will. Yet plenty of other accounts—like the New Thought spiritual movement that animated and legitimized so much of Gilded Age capitalism with the idea that thinking hard enough could bring you wealth or riches—treated human desire as not just a powerful force but an explicitly supernatural one. It was a way in which human beings connected with a fundamental energy in the universe, one directed toward our own personal happiness and fulfillment. In each version of the narrative, however, our human desires—to strive, to seek, to have, to be—double as the animating power: that against which our material and social reality is judged.

In this way, we might say, we have become gods, no less than Equinox's Narcissus. And, as the guilt-tripping, get-off-the-sofa-and-into-the-gym subtext of Equinox's advertisement suggests, self-creation has become something that all of us are not just encouraged but required to do. All of us have inherited the narrative that we must shape our own path and place in this life and that where and how we were born should not determine who and what we will become. But we have inherited, too, this idea's dark underbelly: if we do not manage to determine our own destiny, it means that we have failed in one of the most fundamental ways possible. We have failed at what it means to be human in the first place.

FROM ONE PERSPECTIVE, this story of human self-divinization is an empowering tale of progress and liberation from tyranny and superstition. It is the story of the brave *philosophes* of the European Enlightenment who dared to stand up to the abuses and the excesses of the Catholic Church and corrupt French monarchy. It is the story of the rise of liberal democracy in Europe and the founding of the United States on the ideal that all of us have a right to liberty and the pursuit of happiness. It is the story of the American dream—espoused by figures like Frederick Douglass and Benjamin Franklin—that with enough hard work and a bit of grit anyone from any race or class could become a self-made man. It is the story, too, of the liberation of other marginalized people, particularly of the queer writers and artists, from Oscar Wilde to Warhol muse Jackie Curtis, who found in the promise of artistic self-creation relief and reprieve from a world that all too often deemed them unnatural.

This narrative is true, at least in part. Certainly, many of the writers, artists, and thinkers profiled in this book have made heroic efforts toward making a better and more equal world.

But it is also true that this new idea of self-creation has, as often as not, been used by its proponents to divide those who had the "right" to shape their identities (generally speaking, white, middle-class men who sought an upper-class life) from those who did not (minorities, women, the genuinely poor).

In Europe, where what I call the "aristocratic" strain of the self-making myth took hold, the power to self-create was largely understood as something innate. Special people—the dandies and possessors of bon ton, or grace—were born with it, but most of the ordinary rabble did not possess it. This strain found its zenith in the personality cults of twentieth-century protofascist and fascist leaders like Gabriele D'Annunzio and Benito Mussolini, who peddled the fantasy of superhuman specialness to a population all too willing to treat their neighbors as subhuman. In America, where the "democratic" strain of the myth took hold, self-creation soon became a handy way to discount the poor and suffering for simply not working hard enough.

In both cases, the promise of self-making functioned less as a straightforward path to liberation than as a means of preserving the status quo. It helped to legitimize the uncomfortable truth that, even as society was changing to allow some people to define their own lives, others were relegated to the status of psychic underclass: incapable of self-making due to either innate inferiority or else plain moral laziness. It will not be lost on the reader that the majority (though by no means all) of the prophets and paradigms of self-making featured in this book—at least until the twentieth century—are white and male.

ULTIMATELY, OUR HISTORY of self-creation is not an inspiring tale of unremitting progress. But I do not think it is a tragic narrative about cultural decline and the dangers of modernity, such as we have seen in the accounts of recent cultural critics from Philip Rieff to Carl Trueman. Rather, *Self-Made* is an account of how we began to think of ourselves as divine beings in an increasingly disenchanted world and about the consequences—political, economic, and social—of that thinking. These consequences have both liberated us from some forms of tyranny and placed us into the shackles of others. It is a story, in other words, about human beings doing what we have always done: trying to solve the mystery of how to live as beings both dazzlingly powerful and terrifyingly vulnerable, thrust without our consent into a world whose purpose and meaning we may never be able to truly know.

"What a piece of work is a man!" Shakespeare's Hamlet mused, sometime around 1600. "How noble in reason! How infinite in faculty! . . . In action how like an angel! In apprehension how like a god!" And, at the same time, he is nothing but a "quintessence of dust."

More than four hundred years later, we're still wrestling with Hamlet's contradictions, asking ourselves what it means to be our "true self" anyway.

*Self-Made* is the story of one of our still imperfect answers.

- one -

# "STAND UP FOR BASTARDS"

O N APRIL 8, 1528, A WORSHIPPER STOLE A SACRED RELIC FROM
a Nuremberg corpse. The act was not an uncommon one. All
throughout medieval Europe, devotees had often gone to extreme
lengths to secure the bones or other body parts of favored saints. There had
been the twelfth-century British bishop who had allegedly bitten off a piece
of Mary Magdalene's hand while genuflecting before it on a visit to a French
monastery. A French monk, three centuries earlier, had spent a full decade
undercover at a rival monastery to secure the skull of Sainte-Foy.

But the luscious, S-shaped lock of golden hair one mourner surreptitiously
sliced that April belonged not to any saint, or even to anyone particularly holy.
Rather, it belonged to the notorious painter, printmaker, and devastatingly
good-looking bon vivant Albrecht Dürer.

By the time of his death, Dürer had become one of the most famous artists
of the European Renaissance. And his funeral proceedings were worthy of the
celebrity he had become. Within three days of Dürer's death, his body was
exhumed, allowing his many admirers to cast a wax death mask of the alluring
face one contemporary had lauded as "remarkable in build and stature and not

9

unworthy of the noble mind it contained."[1] The lock of hair—cut by an anonymous mourner—was ultimately delivered into the hands of Dürer's friend and sometime rival Hans Baldung, who held on to it until his death.

The writers, too, were honing their elegies. German humanist poet Helius Eobanus Hessus had started work on a series of funerary poems, declaiming of the late painter that "all who will be famous in your art will mourn / this is the honor that they owe you."[2] Admirers began to make and disseminate copies of the unremarkable family history that Dürer—like many members of Nuremberg's merchant class—had composed. And Dürer's close friend (and possible lover) Willibald Pirckheimer composed an epitaph for the grave: "Whatever was mortal of Albrecht Dürer," he wrote, "is covered by this tomb."

What *wasn't* mortal about Dürer, though, was the image he projected. Dürer didn't just have an astounding talent for painting and printmaking. He also possessed an extraordinary knack for self-promotion. Alongside his myriad saints and expertly rendered Madonnas, Dürer made a habit of painting, and promoting, himself.

In medieval Europe, such self-aggrandizement would have been unthinkable. Medieval artists were traditionally anonymous. They were craftsmen, often working in collective guilds, whose output—the stonemasonry above a (church) door, the stained glass of a (church) window, the images of saints on (church) wall frescoes—was designed to reflect not individual glory but rather the majesty of the earth's true creator: God. Credit for one's work was superfluous at best, suspiciously prideful at worst. One early "copyright" case from 1249, in which two competing Dominican friars claimed authorship of a popular theological tract, was settled by stripping both authors' names and publishing the text anonymously.[3] Self-portraits were exceedingly rare. At most, an artist might depict himself as a humble worshipper in the background of a religious scene. Then Dürer came along.

Dürer's self-portraits—he produced thirteen, a mixture of paintings, drawings, and prints—are masterpieces of self-veneration, luxuriating in the beauty, and the glory, of his own finely rendered image. In each, Dürer appears in elegant, even aristocratic raiment (never mind that he was born a middle-class goldsmith's son). In each, he lingers with every careful brushstroke on the delicate shape of those spiraling curls, an aesthetic so central to Dürer's public persona that contemporaries joked that he might be too busy to take commissions because of the amount of time he spent on his hair.[4] Even when Dürer depicted himself in the background of religious scenes, he called attention to his presence, taking the then-unprecedented step of adding to the scene a *cartellino*, a little sign, to make sure the viewer knew exactly who he was.

Dürer didn't merely present himself as an aristocrat, however. Rather, he evoked something even more ambitious: a god. Drawing on the iconography of religious art in which he had been steeped, Dürer created self-portraits that depicted himself as, essentially, Jesus Christ. For example, in *Self-Portrait at the Age of Twenty-Eight* (1500), Dürer reveals himself not in profile but facing straight on, a pose traditionally reserved for God the Son. His hair, golden in other portraits, is here rendered a dark hazelnut to match a then popular (if forged) "eyewitness" account of Jesus's own coloring.[5] Dürer's index finger and thumb are raised, as Jesus's would traditionally have been. But while Jesus's fingers often spelled out the letters ICXC, an acronym for Jesus Christ, Dürer's seem to be spelling out his initials, AD, as his own substitute *cartellino*. Those same initials appear alongside the painting's date to the left of the head, making a distinct visual pun: "1500 AD." Anno Domini, the year of our Lord, is also the year of Albrecht Dürer, coming into his own.

Dürer's "AD" wasn't just his signature, however. It also became his professional calling card, an early attempt at what we might today call personal branding. Dürer used his initials to sign not only his paintings but also, more importantly, the prints he designed. He cautioned would-be plagiarists against claiming credit for his work: "Beware, you envious thieves of the labors and ingenuity of others; keep your thoughtless hands from this work of art."[6] Unlike other printmakers at the time, Dürer eventually took the extra step of purchasing his own printing press, giving him creative control over the whole operation and allowing him to share his work far more widely than ever before.

From design to implementation to dissemination, Dürer was in complete control of how he presented himself and his work to his audience. And that audience, furthermore, wasn't just God or even the clergy and worshippers of a specific church paying for his pieces. Rather, Dürer knew he had the opportunity to command the attention of the whole world. When, in 1507, a patron pressured Dürer to speed up work on a time-consuming Nuremberg altarpiece, his reply was dismissively curt: "Who would want to see it?"[7]

Albrecht Dürer has been hailed as many things: one of the Renaissance's finest artists, the inventor of the selfie, the world's first celebrity self-promoter. But what he truly pioneered, in his life and his work—and the two were never easily separable—was a new and ambitious vision of the self. That is, at least, for selves that resembled Albrecht Dürer. Dürer recognized, as few earlier artists had done, the potential for conscious self-creation, the place where creative self-expression and pursuit of profit might meet. Dürer didn't just make art; he transformed *himself* into a work of art. He forged a personality that sustained and advertised his work, even as his work—constantly emblazoned with his trademark—advertised the man. Dürer-the-artist, Dürer-the-portrait, and Dürer-the-advertiser all mutually reinforced one another.

But Dürer recognized something else, too. To create yourself, to fashion your personality and your public image and your economic destiny—and Dürer never doubted that these were all inextricably linked—was to adopt a kind of godliness, to displace a God-centered view of the universe with one that saw the individual, and particularly the creative individual, as divine. Whatever magic, whatever enchantment existed in the world—whether it came from God or nature or some nebulously defined being in between—it was up to the cunning genius to harness it and make it serve his purpose.

<hr>

IT WOULD BE easy to conclude—and no doubt he would want us to—that Dürer was a singular genius in this regard, that he and his knack for personal branding had sprung up, fully formed, in fifteenth-century Nuremberg to rock the Renaissance world. The truth, however, is a little bit more complicated. Dürer's talent for self-invention—and his understanding of himself as a divine self-inventor—was inextricable from the changing society in which he lived.

Dürer was, after all, a Renaissance man in the most literal sense of the term. He was an artist working in a thriving mercantile city at a time when thriving mercantile cities all over Western Europe were rethinking—at least for certain relatively fortunate classes of people (that perpetual caveat)—what society might look like and what new kinds of people might forge paths to success and splendor in it. Throughout the fifteenth and sixteenth centuries all over the European continent, artists, philosophers, scholars, and poets were wrestling with profound cultural, social, and economic changes.

Most of these changes will be so familiar to graduates of any elementary school European history curriculum as to border on narrative cliché: Johannes Gutenberg's invention of the printing press in the 1450s and the subsequent widespread proliferation of literacy; the rise of trade and craftsmanship and the re-centering of European cultural life from church-adjacent farmland to newly prosperous cities; the burgeoning development of an urban, middle, mercantile class and the social mobility that went with it; the renewal of interest (by people other than monks, at least) in Greco-Roman thought and with it the optimistic worldview traditionally called "humanistic," as theology and philosophy alike turned away from the profound suspicion of worldly attainment that marked so much of medieval thought. Hoarily familiar (and in some cases overly simplistic) though these narratives may be, they nevertheless are helpful to contextualize Dürer as a man of his time. More important, they illustrate why and how our history of self-making starts here, with a single question, one that not just Dürer but a whole host of Renaissance artists, philosophers, poets, and statesmen were wrestling with together, a question that would come to revolutionize, and perhaps even define, the modern world.

The question? How do we understand, let alone explain, men like Dürer? Or, more broadly, how can we make sense of men (and it was usually men) who seem not to fit into society's rigid existing hierarchies? How do we, as a society account for the *self-made man*: the man whose destiny came not from birth or blood, but rather from some mysterious, and perhaps even magical, quality within himself?

In an era of unprecedented social mobility, this question was particularly relevant. All through Europe's flourishing city-states, particularly on the Italian peninsula (here, the German Dürer was something of an outlier), there could be found men who, if not quite as flamboyant as Dürer, were nevertheless using their creative and intellectual talents to transcend the social strata into which they had been born. They were peasants turned craftsmen, or else craftsmen whose skill had propelled them into even higher social spheres, perhaps even into the company of royalty or popes. Leonardo da Vinci—the illegitimate son of a notary and a peasant—found himself patrons among the dukes of Milan and king of France. Goldsmith's son Dürer produced commissions for Holy Roman emperor Maximilian I. Plenty of Renaissance Italy's most prominent artists—da Vinci, of course, but also architect Leon Battista Alberti and painter Filippo Lippi—were bastards: men with no legal parent and thus no clearly defined social place.

And it wasn't just artists either. Clever would-be scholars like Poggio Bracciolini—born virtually penniless as an apothecary's son—could show up in Florence with five silver soldi in their pockets and be "discovered" by wealthy patrons in need of librarians or court scholars, working their way up through secretarial ranks to become wealthy and well-connected in their own right. By the time of Bracciolini's death in 1459, he had become one of Florence's wealthiest men, having married, at the age of fifty-six, an eighteen-year-old heiress.

This new class of men was not merely self-made in the colloquial sense— the one we most commonly use when we talk about a "self-made billionaire" or a "self-made entrepreneur" who has, despite the absence of family wealth or privilege, succeeded in becoming an economic success—although, in many cases, they did indeed do just that. They were also *self-makers*: people whose personal creative qualities seemed to give them license to mold not just the art (or poetry, or philosophy) they produced but also their public personality and, through it, their destiny. Self-making was always a double act, simultaneously the construction of a self to move through the world and a shaping of that self's fortune.

~~~∽∾~~~

THIS RISE OF these self-made men wasn't just a social question, however. It was also a theological one. Self-creation—as Dürer's cheeky rendering of himself as Jesus rightly suggested—was a challenge to a deeply rooted religious view of the cosmos, steeped in centuries of medieval Christian thought. After all, was not the act of creation—of the natural world, of human beings, of their lives and destinies—the foundational prerogative of God himself?

Certainly, to the medieval Christian mind, God was not just the creator of the natural world but also the creator and sustainer of the social world. Indeed, the distinction would have been unthinkable. The natural world and the world of human life were considered to be one cohesive whole, in which each being had its God-given place and God-given role. Animal life, peasant life, the life of kings—all these echoed and reflected one another to God's glory, sustained by the God-ordered natural law that bound all things together. The thirteenth-century philosopher-saint Thomas Aquinas, for example, character-ized human government and artistic production alike as merely an instantia-tion of the natural principle that "the power of a secondary mover flows from the power of the first mover." The "plan of government is derived by second-ary governors from the governor in chief," while "the plan of what is to be done in a state flows from the king's command to his inferior administrators." He wrote that the act of craftsmanship "flows from the chief craftsman to the under-craftsmen, who work with their hands," for "all laws, insofar as they par-take of right reason, are derived from the eternal law."[8]

What that meant, practically speaking, is that God had also determined the shape of human life, including rank, blood, and station. Medieval life and law, by and large, treated human beings not as isolated individuals but as members of the family, the class, the community, and the land into which they had been born. Self-making, of any kind, would have been a nonsensical proposition to the medieval mind. Human beings had already been made, fearfully and wonderfully, by their creator, as part of a holistic and complex unity, working toward a divine purpose that transcended anything an individual human could understand. A man could no more create himself than he could create a frog, a flower, or a tree.

⁓⁓

HOW, THEN, TO account for the self-made man, a figure who seemed to not just shatter societal expectations but overthrow the law of nature itself? Over the fifteenth and sixteenth centuries, Renaissance discourse about the self-made man—the artist, the scholar, and the lowborn upstart alike—began to coalesce around an answer, one that preserved the vision of a God-ordered universe and yet made room within it for a special kind of person. This individual could at once leapfrog the social order and yet remain safely within the consoling paradigm of a society God had determined. Different writers and thinkers used slightly different terminology to describe such a person—the "true noble," the "maker of virtue"—but the one in most common use today, and the most apt for our purposes, is the genius.

Genius, as it was used in the Renaissance by figures from Petrarch to Boccaccio to Erasmus, already denoted two vital qualities of the self-made man the term sought to define and explain. First, the word itself suggested that such a person's power had a divine or supernatural origin. The Latin word *genius* originally referred to a guardian that might attend or inhabit a human being. A person possessing genius wasn't just intelligent or talented, in other words. Rather, they were touched by something far greater.

Second, genius suggested a connection to the faculty of creative thought, that very *ingenium*, or ingenuity, that Dürer was so anxious to defend. Whatever made the genius a genius—whatever power animated a Dürer or a da

Vinci or a Poggio Bracciolini—it had something to do with, specifically, the human power to reflect, or imitate, that divine faculty of creation.[9]

How could Renaissance society incorporate such a novel, forceful figure? The answer was a specific rhetorical move that gave the genius a determined place in society, not as a self-made self exactly, but as a special scion of God, someone who could claim a higher and purer lineage than that provided by their earthly father. Those who transcended the social order had to be understood as a coherent part of, rather than a transgression against, a world in which God had ordered all people and all things.

The apocryphal stories of Renaissance genius—whether told by self-declared geniuses themselves or by their hagiographic biographers—tend to follow a similar pattern. Geniuses were coded, metaphorically and rhetorically, as the contemporary equivalent of Greco-Roman demigods: mythological figures like Hercules or Achilles conceived by a liaison between a god and a mortal woman. They belonged, in other words, to a higher aristocracy.

The genius might have a humble father—or, indeed, in the cases of so many Renaissance genius bastards, no legal father at all—but his "real" father, morally and spiritually speaking, had to be understood as divine. The genius's social mobility, therefore, like that of the fairy-tale peasant who discovers he is secretly a prince stolen away from the castle of birth, rested upon the assumption that he had already been marked out by God's transcendent authority. His success was not because he had transcended or transgressed against societal order but simply because he was acting according to his superior nature and being recognized as a result.

The genius as demigod became a common rhetorical trope in Renaissance life. The Mantuan painter Andrea Mantegna, most famous for his depictions of life at the court of Gonzaga, often referred to himself in Latin as "Aeneas"—another famous demigod and hero of the *Aeneid*. In one memorial portrait of Dürer, the Danish artist Melchior Lorck added a caption lauding the artist as "one whom Minerva [Roman goddess of wisdom] brought forth from her own bosom."[10] And, in a rare Christianized example of the trope, the

Nuremberg sculptor Adam Kraft was apparently so fond of promoting himself as a kind of second Adam—the biblical one, that is—that in order to please him, his steadfast wife started referring to herself as Eve.[11] Though the idea of a "second Adam" had traditionally been one used to describe Jesus Christ, Kraft—like Dürer—hinted that the Renaissance genius might well deserve to appropriate such a title.

Narratives about the precocious childhoods of perceived geniuses were also often preposterously embellished, heightening the sense that these figures' overwhelming talent was supernatural in nature. Just as the infant Hercules famously slew snakes while still in his cradle, the painter Leonardo da Vinci was said by biographer (and noted exaggerator) Giorgio Vasari to have so overwhelmed his mentor, Andrea del Verrocchio, with the force of his talent that the older man gave up painting entirely. (Vasari also tells a similar story about Michelangelo and his mentor.) Lorenzo Ghiberti's fifteenth-century biography of the thirteenth-century lowborn painter Giotto di Bondone follows a similar narrative: an older painter, Cimabue, is so impressed by the young farm boy's drawing of a sheep on a slab of stone that he whisks the boy away at once to serve as his apprentice. Central to each narrative is the notion that the genius's power is totally innate and entirely unteachable. Indeed, human mentors who try to teach these boys skills are usually shown up by the force of their pupil's naive power. Genius must come from something outside, and beyond, human endeavor.

Now, writers of these accounts did not literally believe in liaisons between the Greco-Roman gods and human beings, or indeed in the existence of Greco-Roman gods at all. We are still, after all, discussing an era strictly defined by a Christian worldview. But the Christianity of the Renaissance was a rather different, and perhaps more fluid, one than the medieval worldview that preceded it. The more explicitly theological language of God as creator was often used side by side with metaphorical language depicting either Nature or Fortune—mysterious and impersonal forces—as a goddess, one who imparts her will directly by imbuing geniuses with some of her power.

Renaissance geniuses were a little bit like Renaissance bastards, liminal figures of mysterious parentage who could not be easily slotted into an existing social system. In England, one of Shakespeare's most magnetic villains, *King Lear*'s illegitimate upstart Edmund, made the parallels explicit. He excoriates the "plague of custom" that condemns him to inferiority to his legitimate brother, declaiming that "thou, Nature, art my goddess." He concludes: "Stand up for bastards."[12] The language (metaphorical or otherwise) of divine origin solved some of the problem of the genius. By understanding geniuses as analogous to aristocrats, Renaissance thinkers were able to incorporate these seemingly anomalous figures into a world still governed by divine law.

A MAJOR FEATURE of Renaissance debates and dialogues—one that reflected just how fraught the question was at the time—was the relationship of what we might call traditional aristocracy to that new aristocracy of genius. As the Renaissance scholar Albert Rabil Jr. points out in his extremely worthwhile book on the theme, the question of true nobility became a mainstay of humanist dialogues; throughout the fifteenth century, at least eleven treatises were published on that point, each one featuring heated debate between proponents of the older model of nobility and of this new one. In Buonaccorso da Montemagno's 1429 "Dialogue on True Nobility," for example, the lowborn advocate for genius argues that "the proper seat of nobility is in the mind, which nature, that empress of all things, bestows on birth on all mortals in equal measure, not on the basis of the legacy derived from their ancestors, but on the basis of that high rank that is peculiar to divinity."[13] Nobility, he insists, "does not come from family but from innate virtue." His own "desire for knowledge was infused in me . . . by nature, so that nothing seemed more worthy of my talent than pursuit of the knowledge of the good."[14] Montemagno leaves the question open—the dialogue ends before it is formally decided—but it's the flashy upstart who gets the last word. A contemporary poem on the topic, by Carlo

Marsuppini, celebrates those "well-born noble though they eat off earthen-
ware / and belong to an unknown family."[15]

We find similar imagery in another treatise by the lowborn Greek bishop
Leonard of Chios, himself a self-made man. For the characters in Leonard's
dialogue, the ideal man is born "with wisdom as his mother and free will as his
father," possessed of the nobility that "arises from the root of virtue as though
its strength had sprung from innate principles of nature."[16] Commenting on
the Greek philosopher Aristotle's argument that desirable qualities for happiness include "good birth," Leonard's interlocutor insists that Aristotle could
not possibly have been referring to aristocratic lineage but "rather moral birth,
because the former involves corruption of blood, the latter the most graceful
character."[17]

Notable in each of these texts is the delicate balance the authors must
strike between affirming the status quo—a world largely defined by aristocracies of birth—and accounting for this new class of people finding their place
in it. The language of "true nobility" and the imagery of the demigod serve a
useful double purpose. Geniuses have the capacity to make themselves precisely because they have been chosen by God to do so. They are a special few,
a favored few, and their self-authorship is limited and proscribed by divine will.

Even more ambitious and explicit about the superiority of the aristocracy of
genius was the 1440 dialogue "On True Nobility," written by Poggio Bracciolini, the Florentine arriviste we encountered earlier. Bracciolini uses "virtue"
to describe the quality we've elsewhere discussed as genius, but it is clear from
his context that virtue does not simply mean a capacity for right moral action.
Rather, Bracciolini treats it as something innate and embedded in the personality of the "true noble," regardless of the circumstances of his birth. "Virtue,"
Bracciolini writes, "must be grasped by a kind of divine power and favor and
by the hidden movement of fate, and cannot be gained by parental instruc-
tion."[18] Human parents, in other words, are of little use when it comes to this
divine inheritance. As Bracciolini insists, "Children do not inherit either vices

or virtues from their parents; the author and maker of virtue and nobility is the person himself."[19]

In this, Bracciolini goes even further than his contemporaries, pointing to a question that will continue to underpin the entire history of self-creation. Is the self-made man merely lucky, blessed, chosen by either a personal God or impersonal nature to make his fortunate way in an otherwise orderly world? Or is he, as Bracciolini's language suggests, the author of his selfhood, someone whose free choice, will, desire, and effort all work together to create his identity and destiny? Is the self-made man like a Hercules or an Aeneas, a demigod child under the paternal authority of a stronger deity? Or is he like the Christ of Dürer's infamous self-portrait, fully, splendidly, and dangerously divine of his own accord? Does he have a preternatural, even magical, ability to achieve the economic and artistic goals God has preordained for him, or does his magic lie in his ability to choose his goals himself?

⌇

BY AND LARGE, Renaissance authors dealing with the twin questions of self-creation and genius tended toward the former, more conservative approach. The genius is a special kind of person, to be sure, but he is a rare case: an accounted-for exception to the general rules that govern the social order.

But one Renaissance humanist, Giovanni Pico della Mirandola, went much further, taking an ambitious approach to the project of self-creation that would prefigure much later, and more explicitly ambitious, models of self-making. A thoroughly unorthodox figure, Pico blended his Christian humanism with Jewish kabbalah, Arab philosophy, Classical learning, and a healthy dab of the occult. Pico didn't just argue that human beings were capable of self-invention, or even that self-invention was a morally desirable thing. Rather, in his "Oration on the Dignity of Man," composed as an introduction to a longer philosophical lecture, Pico argues that self-creation—the active, willed imitation of God—is precisely the quality that makes us human. The ability to determine who we are and to decide our own place in the divine cosmos is God's gift to us.

Pico makes his case by retelling the creation story of the book of Genesis. As in the Bible, God creates various elements of the world in order. But in this version, the act of creation is so taxing that God, in essence, uses up his mental "seeds." So, he decides to create a singular creature without any kind of seeds, and thus without any kind of inheritance or obligation. He makes man. In Pico's telling, God, in creating Adam, is essentially making another god to take over. "Adam," God announces, "you have been given no fixed place, no form of your own, so that you may have and possess, according to your will and your inclination, whatever place, whatever form, and whatever functions you choose. Divine law assigns to all other creatures a fixed nature. But you, constrained by no laws, by your own free will, in whose hands I have placed you, will determine your own nature."[20]

Pico's "Oration" was never delivered. The longer project it was planned to precede—a full nine hundred theological theses he intended to present to his philosophical contemporaries—proved controversial. Seven theses were deemed outright heretical, six more of concern, and Pico promptly fled Rome for France. But the sentiments the "Oration" contains would have represented among the most striking and potentially transgressive visions of the self-made man in the Renaissance world. Pico wasn't just allowing for true nobility, or moral birth, or other mechanisms within which to fit human will into a God-ordered system. He was saying that human beings should decide the system for themselves. And while that gift, in his telling, does indeed come from God, Pico suggests that God—who has, after all, used up all his energy creating the world—is no more powerful than we might ourselves become. In Pico, no less than in Dürer, the power to fashion ourselves holds within it the promise of dethroning God himself.

Pico and Dürer both anticipate one of the major tensions that will recur throughout this history of self-creation: the relationship between human self-creators and God, or at least our ideas about God. Already, this first flowering of ideas about modern self-creation coincides with a period in history marked by a growing suspicion of organized institutional religion and the idea of an authoritative creator-God. In the centuries to come, the idea of the self-creator as a kind of successful Lucifer—overthrowing God's creative power and seizing the throne himself—will come to the forefront even as belief in such a God, and the political system predicated on that belief, recedes. Pico and Dürer are extreme among Renaissance theorists of genius, but their vision of the self-maker as a new god for an increasingly godless age will outlive them.

∼∽

BUT A SECOND set of unresolved questions lurks at the margins of this narrative: questions about authenticity, truth, and performance. It's all very well and good to say that some people are geniuses, chosen by God to have special fates that transcend their economic station. But how exactly do we tell who these geniuses really are and whether we might ourselves be one? Can it be ascertained from how they carry themselves, how they present themselves, how they behave in public? And, if so, can genius be imitated by those who wish to improve their station in life? And if genius can be so successfully imitated by those who are willing to fake it until they make it, then what is the difference between the divinely chosen self-maker and the arriviste who decides to dispense with God and nature altogether and simply choose himself?

From the Renaissance to the Regency era, from the stages of fin de siècle theaters to the trading floors of the American Gilded Age, whenever we find a cultural obsession with "divine" self-makers, we are likely to also see an equally fervent obsession with what we might today call the cult of self-help: manifestos and guides that purport to help ordinary people convince their peers that they belong to the ranks of the favored few.

But defining genius was only one piece of the puzzle. At the same time that many Renaissance writers were negotiating the genius's precise social status, they were also working out a different question: how to make people *think* that you were a genius. Among the most notable handbooks to this kind of art is Baldassare Castiglione's 1528 book *The Courtier*: a guide for those who wished to serve in aristocratic courts like Castiglione's own duchy of Urbino. The book—an extended series of dialogues between characters who double as stand-ins for a variety of Renaissance views—features a number of debates, including several on the nature of true nobility and whether the virtuous and talented lowborn are as desirable as courtiers as the biological aristocrats. Yet one of the most significant passages in the book doesn't deal with birth at all. Rather, it deals with another mysterious—and difficult to translate—quality, one Castiglione refers to as "sprezzatura," often translated into English as "lightness" or "nonchalance."

Sprezzatura, we learn, is one of the most important qualities a courtier can have. As Count Ludovico, one of Castiglione's interlocutors, puts it, sprezzatura "conceal[s] design and show[s] that what is done and said is done without effort and almost without thought."[21] The figurative talents of a Giotto or an infant da Vinci may be obvious from the time they're out of the cradle. For the rest of us, Castiglione suggests, it is necessary to simply give the impression that whatever we do is as easy for us as it would have been for one of life's more favored few. Looking like you tried too hard was as unfashionable at Castiglione's court as it would be today at a modern Fashion Week party, a surefire sign that you weren't one of God's noble bastards.

Ludovico goes on to be even more explicit about the conscious imitation of genius. "We may affirm that to be true art which does not appear to be art; nor to anything must we give greater care than to conceal art," he insists, praising the example of "very excellent orators" who "strove to make everyone believe that they had no knowledge of letters, and . . . pretended that their orations were composed very simply, and as if springing rather from nature and truth rather than from study and art."[22] Lying—at least the delicately artful, little-white-lie kind—is integral to self-making. In order to become who we want to be, we first have to convince other people that we are what we are not.

*The Courtier*, therefore, represents the final strand woven into the tapestry of self-making: the development of a sense of the self as an artistic project to be presented to the outside world, as well as shaped from within. From an outside perspective, at least, how could anyone tell the authentic genius (the one God or nature chose) from the artificial one (the one who was just that good at public self-presentation)? Even at this early juncture, the figure of the successful, talented self-made man was dogged by its perpetual shadow: the canny self-presenter who managed to convince people he was who he wanted to be.

The Renaissance mythos of godlike nobility—that nature, or God, or fortune had adopted certain lucky figures as their own—went hand in hand with the more cynical promise that it was possible to just pretend that you were one of them. You might not be da Vinci—of whom Vasari breathlessly wrote that "whatever he turned his mind to, he made himself master of with ease"—but, by making things appear easy, you could give off that impression, at least for a while.[23]

*The Courtier* calls upon its would-be geniuses to pay active attention to the art of self-cultivation. Count Ludovico exhorts his listeners "to observe different men . . . [and] go about selecting this thing from one and that thing from another. And as the bee in the green meadows is ever wont to rob the flowers among the grass, so our Courtier must steal this grace from all who seem to possess it."[24] Sure, maybe genius itself cannot be learned or taught, but its outcome—earthly success—could, Castiglione suggests, be replicated through careful study, meticulous observation, and that most unfashionable of qualities: hard work.

CASTIGLIONE'S HANDBOOK WAS wildly popular, and not just among actual courtiers. By 1600, the book had been reissued a staggering fifty-nine times in Italy and had also been translated into German, Latin, Spanish, French, English, and Polish.[25] But it was not the only Renaissance handbook to suggest that dissembling—cultivating how others see you, regardless of the actual truth—might be necessary for success. In 1513, Florentine statesman Niccolò Machiavelli had published *The Prince*, a guidebook for rulers, inspired by his own experience of upheaval and division among the Medici family who had once been his patrons.

If *The Courtier* advocated the odd white lie—a concealment of effort here, a carefully calibrated gesture there—then *The Prince* espoused a code of straight-up mendacity. "One can make this generalization about men," Machiavelli scoffed. "They are ungrateful, fickle, liars, and deceivers, they shun danger and are greedy for profit; while you treat them well, they are yours . . . but when you are in danger they turn against you." A prince who wanted to remain in power had to be constantly presenting the right face to the world, inspiring alternatively awe, gratitude, and fear. His morality (or lack thereof) was irrelevant. What mattered was the part he was willing to play: sometimes a prince should "be a fox to discover the snares," at other times "a lion to terrify the wolves."[26]

We are a long way, here, from the vision of a cohesive and divinely arranged natural order as envisioned by Thomas Aquinas and other doctors of the medieval church. Nature, for Machiavelli, is brutal and meaningless. The prince's role is to choose at will from among the varying beasts of the forest to find a temporary model for his maneuvers. The ideal quality of a prince, for Machiavelli, is not genius as such but rather what he calls *virtù*—a word he uses not to mean virtue in the moral sense but rather manly effectiveness (the term also suggests "virility"). A prince should bend fortune to his will.

Other Renaissance authors used feminine imagery to conceive of nature or fortune as a mother, the protective parent of the chosen genius. But for Machiavelli, it was the role of the man of *virtù* to take fortune by force, an act he describes using the violent metaphorical language of rape. "Fortune is a woman," he insisted, "and if she is to be submissive it is necessary to beat and coerce her. Experience shows that she is more often subdued by men who do this than by those who act coldly. . . . Being a woman, she favors young men, because they are less circumspect and more ardent, and because they command her with greater audacity."[27]

Machiavelli's guidance, even more than Castiglione's, perhaps even more than Pico's, is a death knell for the worldview of divine order that our Renaissance thinkers sought to sustain. In the centuries to come, we will see a radical reimagining of the relationship between divine law, natural law, and the social order. No longer would the self-made man have to be fitted into an existing system. Instead, the system would be fitted to him.

# two

# "SHAKING OFF THE YOKE OF AUTHORITY"

T WAS THE LATE SIXTEENTH CENTURY AND MICHEL EYQUEM DE
Montaigne had one burning question: Why on earth did he have to wear
clothes? The French author was not particularly fond of covering himself up. Throughout the more than one hundred essays (a genre he basically
invented) Montaigne wrote in his lifetime, he alluded frequently to his desire
for both metaphorical and literal nakedness.

In the brief introduction to his *Essais*, written in 1580, Montaigne promises
his readers total honesty and disclosure of who he really is. Rather than trying
to impress them "with borrowed beauties" or pretty phrases, he promises that
"had I lived among those nations which (they say) still live under the sweet liberty of nature's primitive laws, I assure you I would easily have painted myself
quite fully and quite naked."[1] Nakedness, for the rhetorically flamboyant Montaigne, suggests honesty, trustworthiness, and, perhaps, a hint of transgression.

Among his gleefully freewheeling essays, on topics from the nature of
knowledge to the structure of politics, Montaigne frequently turns the subject
to both nudity and bodily functions. He remarks wryly, for instance, on the
emperor Maximilian, who "would never permit any of his bedchamber" to

see him on the toilet and would "steal aside to make water as religiously as a virgin."[2] Montaigne goes on to inform the reader that "I myself . . . [am] so naturally modest this way that unless at the importunity of necessity of pleasure, I scarcely ever communicate to the sight of any either those parts or actions that custom orders us to conceal."[3] In another essay, Montaigne meditates upon the "indocile liberty" of the male member.

But it was clothing—and the seemingly arbitrary way people wore it—that obsessed Montaigne most. In one essay, straightforwardly titled "On the Custom of Wearing Clothes," he invites his reader to wonder along with him "whether the fashion of going naked in these nations lately discovered"—by which he means what his contemporaries would have called the conquest of the New World—"is imposed upon them by the hot temperature of the air . . . or whether it be the original fashion of mankind?"[4] After all, he marvels, even in his native Europe, fashions for clothing differ. And other animals don't wear any clothing at all, regardless of the temperature.

His conclusion? That we have developed a kind of learned helplessness as a result of so-called civilization: "As those who by artificial light put out that of day," he writes, "so we by borrowed fashion have destroyed" our ability to walk about uncovered. Ultimately, Montaigne decides, it is not divine order, the laws of nature, or the dictates of reason but "custom only" that determines what people wear—or if they wear anything at all.[5]

The sheer arbitrariness of clothing is a theme Montaigne returns to again in another essay, one describing sumptuary laws: a series of legal codes, popular across Renaissance Europe, that sought to legislate what people wore according to their social position. These laws were largely though not exclusively designed to limit the opportunities of a burgeoning middle class to spend their newfound wealth on aristocratic fashions. In England, for example, only knights and lords could wear ermine or sable, furs traditionally associated with aristocratic heraldic symbols. In sixteenth-century Milan, artisans and other middle-class workers were forbidden to wear silk and could wear gold only in the form of a necklace worth under twenty-five scudi.[6] In Montaigne's own

France, he reports, "none but princes shall eat turbot, shall wear velvet or gold lace."[7] Theoretically, the role of the sumptuary laws was to preserve a kind of visual order to the social cosmos, the same vision of well-ordered universe we discussed in Chapter 1. In that vision, the aristocrats, the merchants, and the peasants were all easily distinguishable from one another. At a glance, you could tell who belonged where in the fabric of the universe. How you presented yourself, at least in theory, showed a fundamental truth about who you really were, a truth rooted in your social station and the class into which you had been born.

Montaigne found all of that ridiculous. "'Tis strange," he remarks, "how suddenly and with how much ease custom in these indifferent things establishes itself and becomes authority." Montaigne's issue wasn't just with the restriction of certain clothing to certain classes. Rather, it was with a concept that will become central to our understanding of the role of self-makers in an increasingly disenchanted world: custom.

For Montaigne, custom isn't just harmless tradition. Rather, it's what we're left with when we stop seeing the social world as inextricably connected to the natural one, or to the supernatural one. Custom suggests that the reason we do things—cut our hair, wear clothing, perform certain actions—is not because we ought to, or because so doing is part of what we were created to do by God. Rather, we do things simply because we always have, with no particularly good reason behind our actions. Our social lives, and the rules that govern them, are simply arbitrary.

Throughout his essays, Montaigne asks the same question over and over: "Where are we to distinguish the natural laws from those which have been imposed by man's invention?"[8] Over and over, he comes to the same conclusion. Most seeming truths or laws about the way things are, especially when they come to our social lives and identities, are not innate or God-given but mere accidents of history. Which means, Montaigne tantalizingly suggests, that we have the power to change them.

❧

THIS WIDER PHENOMENON, what I wish to term the disenchantment of custom, would come to define the entire social, philosophical, scientific, and intellectual movement—often considered under the umbrella term of the Enlightenment—that would shape the next few centuries of European thought. From Montaigne's time until the French Revolution in 1789, Western Europe—particularly, though not exclusively, France and Germany—would wrestle with an intellectual shift that would definitively dispense with a God-ordered view of the cosmos.

The Enlightenment, broad and varied though it was, would ultimately herald a variety of major revolutions, both ideological and quite literal, across the continent. It displaced the moral and political authority of the Catholic Church (already under threat across Europe by the success of the Protestant Reformation), as well as religious institutional power more broadly. It would usher in the development of new political concepts like natural rights, and with them a growing demand for political systems that could sustain them. And—most relevant to our story—it would mark a transformation in the cultural understanding of human beings and human destiny. Human beings, this new philosophy held, had not just the power but the right to shape their own lives.

A recurrent theme of the Enlightenment narrative is this: A human being (or, at least, one of certain kinds, classes, and gender) must untether himself from all those elements of custom—birth and blood, to be sure, but also religious superstition and unexamined social mores—that alienate him from his true, natural state. It is only in that state—a kind of metaphorical nakedness, if you will—that man could be truly himself and truly free.

Historians sometimes refer to the Enlightenment as an age of reason, defined by philosophers' obsession with the triumph of rationality over passions or feelings (often in contrast with their successors, the Romantics). Such an assessment—for a variety of reasons too long to get into here—is rather reductionist. But it's fair to say that the Enlightenment was an era where people understood themselves as triumphing over if not exactly passion, then at least superstition. It was an age where the mental capacities of the individual were understood as more powerful, more correct, and, well, just plain better than the unexamined and prejudicial assumptions of the social collective, be it king, community, or church.

The German philosopher Immanuel Kant, in his 1784 essay on what, exactly, enlightenment was supposed to be, famously defined it as "man's emergence from his self-imposed immaturity."[9] The unenlightened, by contrast, were depicted—like toddlers of the time would have been—as grasping at "leading strings" to guide them in their parents' direction. Denis Diderot and Jean Le Rond d'Alembert's *Encyclopedia*, likewise, celebrated the birth of what they saw as a new era "full of light," in which canny philosophers would at last "shake off the yoke of authority."[10] *Tradition, mores, custom, prejudice*—all these were dirty words for Enlightenment thinkers. Another philosopher, the Marquis de Condorcet, claimed that the goal of his (rather ambitious) *Sketch for a Historical Picture of the Progress of the Human Mind* was "to remove the true nature of all our prejudices."[11] The English philosopher John Locke marveled that "there is scarce that Principle of Morality to be named, or Rule of Vertue to be thought on . . . which is not, somewhere or other, slighted and condemned by the general fashion of whole Societies of Men, governed by practical Opinions and Rules of living quite opposite to others."[12]

The enlightened man, unlike his forebears, recognized that the social imaginary into which he had been born was merely a matter of chance. He could just as easily have been born into a different society, even a different country, with completely different customs and rules.

At its most extreme, the Enlightenment rejection of custom meant rejecting the idea of nationality altogether as something embarrassingly parochial. Eighteenth-century French philosopher Diderot, for example, wrote a letter to his Scottish contemporary David Hume, approvingly assuring him that "you belong to all nations, and you will never ask an unfortunate person for an extract from his baptismal register"—information, in other words, about his place of birth.[13] "I pride myself," Diderot went on, "on being, like you, a citizen of that great city: the world."[14] The enlightened man had to be, in other words, cosmopolitan: unrooted in any particular way of life. When, for example, the German-born French poet Georges-Louis de Bär celebrated "My Country" in a laudatory poem addressed to the same, the object of his affection was not a single nation but rather the whole world, broadly conceived. "I come without a choice, into this world perverse," he wrote. "There I am, thus I am, citizen of the universe / I'm a cosmopolitan, like [the philosopher] Diogenes / I embrace in my love all of humanity."[15]

Once we had been children, the argument went, content to live under the authority of custom, under the paternalistic power of a king, a church, a country, a God. Moral and intellectual adulthood, however, demands that we sever our leading strings altogether, to face the world naked, untethered, alone.

❧

YOU MIGHT BE wondering what I'm doing talking about nakedness and authenticity in a book that purports to be, at least in part, about fashionable dandies and artificial self-makers. What is authentic, after all, about Albrecht Dürer's meticulously rendered, product-heavy curls or the luxurious furs he wears in his portraits? What is authentic about the stiff suits of Beau Brummell, the green carnations of Oscar Wilde, or the preternaturally full lips of Kim Kardashian?

But it is precisely this Enlightenment obsession with clearing away custom in pursuit of our true, authentic, and naked selves that makes later concepts of self-creation possible. The idea that we can, and indeed should, shape our lives according to the destinies we want is intellectually plausible only if we think of the world not as an intricately woven tapestry—in which everything and everyone has its carefully chosen place—but rather as a blank canvas ripe for reinvention. The idea that our personal desires are the truest, deepest parts of ourselves and should dictate our lives and our fates is a direct successor to the Enlightenment's disenchantment of custom.

Of course, when it came to custom, few leading strings were as ripe to be sliced as the one tethering people to the Catholic Church. To be sure, the church had hardly done itself many favors, publicity-wise, in recent years. It was coming off centuries of ferocious religious violence, much of it fomented by the series of fractures within the church we today call the Protestant Reformation. There had been the tortures and executions carried out by the Inquisition, a papal agency formed in 1542 to neutralize the Protestant threat. Almost nowhere in Europe had been untouched by one of the brutal and bloody civil wars of religion—many between Catholic and Protestant factions—that had come to define the seventeenth century's geopolitical landscape. There had been the English Civil War (1642–1651), the Spanish-Dutch War (1568–1648), and the pan-German Thirty Years' War (1618–1648), whose death toll—5.75 million people slaughtered—exceeded as a percentage of the world's population the carnage of the First World War.[16]

These wars, like all wars, had political and territorial as well as ideological causes. But for those who had lived through their destruction or who had witnessed the desolation of their aftermath, religion—at least the hierarchical, institutional religion represented by the Catholic Church—was to blame. As the philosopher Voltaire wrote scathingly of his Christian brethren a century later: "This, then, was the reason why they dared to have God come to earth: to deliver Europe over to murder and brigandage for centuries!"[17]

This didn't necessarily mean that Enlightenment philosophers didn't believe in God at all. Many were at least outwardly Christian, even if their theology tended away from the dogmatic or doctrinal. Several were adherents of the then common religious tendency scholars now call Deism—the idea that an impersonal force of some kind had made the world and subsequently left it to run its own affairs, much as a clockmaker builds and winds up a clock. Some, however, like the French philosophers Julien Offray de La Mettrie and Paul-Henri Thiry, better known as Baron d'Holbach, were straight-out atheists. They espoused a purely material vision of the world, where God did not exist at all and where human beings had no obligations except, as Holbach put it, to "pursue their happiness by the most perfect freedom."[18]

Regardless of where exactly our Enlightenment authors came down on the question of whether there was some kind of supreme being out there, on one point nearly all of them could agree: the belief in a divinely sustained world—particularly a hierarchical one, where everyone and everything has its proper place, and where kings and popes could claim their divinely granted role at the top—was no longer sustainable. The post-Enlightenment world would hew closer to that of Machiavelli than that of Aquinas.

⸺ ⸙ ⸺

ANOTHER HISTORICAL FACTOR made the Enlightenment's disenchantment of custom all the more plausible. Encounters with non-European peoples—often through brutal acts of colonization—had made even plainer that "how we do things" was not a universal proposition. A whole genre of Enlightenment writing, from Montaigne onward, sprung up around the imagined purity and naturalness of the "primitive" inhabitants of non-European lands, those whose innate qualities had not been perverted by Western societal custom. In the 1721 "Persian Letters" of the philosopher and judge Charles-Louis de Secondat, more commonly known today as Montesquieu, two fictional Persian diplomats write letters home from France in which they marvel at the superstitions of their new country, astounded to discover the Europeans have "another magician . . . who has just as much power over the king's mind as the king does over his subjects." The diplomat was referring, of course, to the pope: a figure who "can make people believe that three are but one, that the bread one eats is not bread, and that the wine one drinks is not wine."[19] Similarly, in one of David Hume's dialogues, Hume has his speaker shock his friend with the bloodthirsty manners of the inhabitants of a fictional nation, only to reveal the practices he's describing were in fact perpetrated by the much revered founders of so-called Western civilization: the ancient Greeks. What one society called barbarous, these writers insisted, others called ordinary. What one society feared or repressed, another expressed with no compunctions whatsoever. And so, they implicitly asked, what was the good of repressing anything at all?

And, of course, there was the French philosopher Jean-Jacques Rousseau, who pioneered the bittersweet concept of the social contract: the means by which (he imagined) innocent, natural man gained such civilization-founding goods as property but in so doing lost the "natural liberty" he had experienced in his original state of nature. For Rousseau, the ills and ailments of humanity—"wants, avidity, oppression, desires, and pride"—could not be blamed on innate human nature or on Christian doctrines of original sin. Rather, they came from "ideas which were acquired in society," and society was to blame.[20] Rousseau advocated an inward turn, reminding the enlightened man that his own personal conscience was even more trustworthy than so-called reason. "Too often does reason deceive us," Rousseau writes. "But conscience never deceives us; she is the true guide of man. . . . He who obeys his conscience is following nature, and he need not fear that he will go astray."[21]

Rousseau's version of nature looks quite different from the version we saw in the last chapter. For Castiglione, Buonaccorso da Montemagno, or even Poggio Bracciolini, nature—along with her laws—was to be understood as something that created, formed, and bound the social order. When nature favored the genius with exceptional talent, for example, she was ordaining for him an equally exceptional place in society. In the Enlightenment, however, that vital link between nature and society was broken. Nature—the source of human authenticity, of human truth, of how humans really ought to live—began to be equated with a different authority: our feelings. What we experience, what we feel, what we want—all these are guides to the fundamental truth of who we really are. Naked, our leading strings severed, our customs overcome, our inner voice becomes our most useful guide. And what we ourselves desire, rather than what others desire for us, becomes a new source of authority.

And chief among human desires—on this point, Enlightenment authors tended to agree—was sex.

LET'S TURN TO another traveler's tale, this time by Diderot. Diderot's *Supplement to the Voyage of Bougainville* (1772) takes as its starting point the real-life story of Louis Antoine de Bougainville, who a year earlier had not only visited the island of Tahiti but had brought back with him a native Tahitian, Ahutoru, whose presence in Paris had made both men into celebrities. Seemingly uninterested in the actual experiences of the real-life Bougainville or Ahutoru, Diderot instead reimagined their encounter as a series of dialogues between a European priest and a fictional Tahitian he has renamed Orou.

Orou, we soon learn, is shocked by European mores: particularly what he perceives as European superstitious prudery regarding that "innocent pleasure to which Nature, the sovereign mistress of us all, invites everybody."[22] When the priest tells Orou that, in Europe, sex can take place only in marriage and that priests aren't allowed to have sex at all, Orou responds with shock: "Your laws seem to me to be contrary to the general order of things. For in truth is there anything so senseless as a precept that forbids us to heed the changing impulses that are inherent in our being, or commands that require a degree of constancy which is not possible."[23]

Sexual freedom was part of the wider gospel of authenticity, a motif that we can find from the Enlightenment all the way to the rise of punk. Once you free yourself from the shackles of societal authority, why wouldn't you give yourself over, guilt free, to your unbridled sexual urges? Yet the idea of sexual freedom, here, plays a double role, one that it will continue to play throughout the history of self-making. Sexual freedom is celebrated as an expression of unbridled, authentic desire. But it is also a winking political statement used to suggest that the writer (or performer) is somehow superior to, and distinct from, the bourgeois mores of the crowd, the thoughtless sheeple—to use a modern term—who hold on to traditional and outdated ideas of sexual morality. It is, in other words, both a celebration of the authentic and a kind of performance, a reminder that some people have the capacity to triumph over nature.

Throughout our history of self-making, we'll meet many self-makers who use sexual liberation, or the idea of nonnormative sexuality, as a political statement. Many of these figures are people we might today understand as queer: people whose gender identity and orientation do not fit the heterosexual, cisgender norm and whose personal and private lives reflect this fact. But many figures, too—both those we might now identify under the queer umbrella and those who might have understood themselves as straight—used the language, rhetoric, and imagery of nontraditional sexuality in their public personae to make a broader point about human beings and the world we live in. Human desire, the argument goes, is more complex, and more exciting, than the mode of living and reproducing that society and custom tells us is acceptable. From the studied, camp asexuality of Beau Brummell to the free-wheeling gender-bending of Jackie Curtis, from the aesthetic androgyny of the French fin de siècle dandies to the free-love communes of the 1960s, the story of self-making has also been a story about using sexuality—particularly outside of the heterosexual, monogamous, cisgender mainstream—as a way of indicating to the public that the self-maker is somehow above the norm or beyond the rules.

It's telling that alongside the Enlightenment's more theoretical philosophical tracts, the era also saw the flourishing of another kind of free-thinking—or, as it was known in French, *libertine*—literature: the anticlerical pornographic novel. These stories, in which discursive passages on the failures and hypocrisies of the Catholic Church alternated with graphic sexual fantasies, became something of a cottage industry in seventeenth- and eighteenth-century France. There were *L'Ecole des filles* (1660), *Vénus physique* (1740), and *Histoire de dom Bougre, portier de chartreux* (1741) to name just a few. The French government tried, unsuccessfully, to clamp down on the practice; between 1658 and 1789, France went from having four state censors to 178.[24] But the libertine novel was irrepressible. For the Enlightenment mind, the destruction of institutional authority and the celebration of personal liberation were inextricable from one another.

But something else was at stake here, something even more important—and maybe even more transgressive—than sex itself. The idea that our desires—for sex, for success, for fame, for creative self-expression, for money—are not just allowable or acceptable but actively constitutive of who we are as human beings. For the first time, in modern European history at least, the dominant intellectual culture was beginning to celebrate the idea that what we want might not be an occasion of sin or a distraction from a higher goal but actually the key to our purpose in the first place.

Few Enlightenment writers, though, grasped the connection between the disenchantment of custom, the divinization of the self, and the power of desire quite like the epoch's most controversial figure: the Marquis de Sade. Born into luxury as the aristocratic Donatien Alphonse François de Sade, the marquis soon became infamous for his transgressive—and often downright criminal—sexual behavior, including instances of rape, poisoning, and the abduction and systematic torture of prostitutes and servants alike, all in the service of the sexual hunger we now give his name: sadism. During the years Sade spent in prison for his various crimes, he authored a number of now-infamous pornographic novels. These lengthy and often unreadable fantasies describe not just various sexual trysts but rape, coprophilia, torture, and murder.

Like other libertine novels of the time, Sade's novels—including *Justine* (1791), *Juliette* (1797–1801), and the unfinished *120 Days of Sodom* (1785)—blend anticlerical and anti-institutional polemic with celebrations of sexual freedom. In this Sade is deeply influenced by the atheistic and anti-moral materialism of his contemporaries Julien Offray de La Mettrie and Baron d'Holbach, the latter of whose works Sade praised as "veritably and indubitably the basis of my philosophy."[25]

But Sade's libertine characters go further than Holbach or La Mettrie could have imagined. They rape, torture, and murder joyfully as a form of both sexual gratification and self-expression: the triumph of the powerful self over and against a meaningless world and its restrictions. They rejoice in sin for sin's sake. Evil, for them, is a rebuke to the pretensions of a God who no longer exists. "I am only sorry that no God really exists," one character in *Juliette* announces, because it means he is "deprived of the pleasures of insulting him more positively."[26] Another of Sade's characters helpfully explains that "it is not the object of libertine intentions which fires us, but the idea of evil, and . . . consequently it is thanks only to evil and only in the name of evil one stiffens."[27]

Evil, for Sade, is a gleeful repudiation of a nonexistent God and the idea that there is any divine order to human life at all. There is no meaning, Sade insists, to human existence. *Justine*—the story of a virtuous woman whose attempts to be good directly result in her undergoing a series of sexual humiliations and violent tortures—is a parody of the 1740 English novel *Pamela; or, Virtue Rewarded* by Samuel Richardson. In that story, the virginal heroine, after righteously fending off the illicit advances of her employer, eventually civilizes and then marries him. (*Justine*'s subtitle, *The Misfortunes of Virtue*, makes this parallel even more explicit.) Morality itself, for Sade, is meaningless; the only legitimate moral authority is our own innate desires, whatever they may be. "Our morals," he wrote in a 1777 letter from prison to his beleaguered wife Renée-Pelagie, are "determined by how we are put together," which is to say, an innate part of ourselves. "We can no more adopt a particular taste than we can become straight if we are born twisted, or make ourselves brunettes if we are redheads."[28]

While other Enlightenment authors see nature as a source of some kind of authority—to be contrasted with the illegitimate authority of custom—imbuing human beings with a meaningful sense of right and wrong, for Sade, nature is a fundamentally unstable category. The only thing natural, he suggests, is doing exactly what one wills—and doing away with morality altogether.

Today, Sade is more often than not remembered as an excitingly transgressive figure, the forefather of modern conceptions of freedom, and a patron saint of the writers, artists, and individualists who seek to thumb their noses at the oppressive and repressive state. The nineteenth-century poet Guillaume Apollinaire lauded the marquis as the "freest sprit who ever lived."[29]

The 1963 Peter Weiss play *Marat/Sade*—a dramatization of Sade's later life as a comfortable inmate performing his own plays at the insane asylum of Charenton, to which he was transferred from jail after a convenient diagnosis of "libertine dementia" (perhaps an Enlightenment-era precursor to "affluenza")—treats the marquis as a dangerous but alluring truth teller. Similarly, the 2000 Geoffrey Rush film *Quills* implies that Sade's imprisonment was due to his transgressive writing and that he played a major role in inciting the French Revolution. (In fact, only one of Sade's imprisonments, his last, was for his writing. The rest were for various convictions of sexual torture, rape, and assault. And while Sade himself claimed plenty of credit for inciting the Bastille riots from inside the prison—a claim to fame that bolstered his brief postrevolutionary self-reinvention as "Citoyen Sade," magistrate and democrat—the riot he actually started inside the prison stemmed from his objection to not getting special treatment from his jailers.)[30] In a 2015 interview, Gonzague Saint Bris, a biographer of Sade, marveled at the marquis's influence on the revolutionary French student movements of 1968. "I looked at all the placards, reading 'It Is Forbidden to Forbid' and 'Do Whatever You Desire,'" Saint Bris said. "I suddenly understood that our revolutionary phrases were actually from Sade."[31]

It would be an overstatement, despite Sade's recent rock-star rehabilitation, to credit him with the invention of the modern world, even as Sade, much like Dürer, would probably approve of such a genealogy. But it's nevertheless true that Sade, even more than his Enlightenment contemporaries, set the stage for the vision of man that would follow: a human being whose own desires, rather than those of an external authority, gave him the power to make himself the closest thing to a divinity in a godless world. Sade understood, too, that true freedom meant a process of self-definition. His libertines don't just do whatever they want. They explicitly see their doing what they want as a form of self-expression, the early modern equivalent of singer Ozzy Osbourne biting the head off a bat at a metal show. Their actions create their identities.

Yet in the works of Sade, we also find the encapsulation of another set of tensions that will inconveniently shadow our subsequent self-creators. If some people—whether by God's favor or personal effort or intellectual enlightenment or anything else—were capable of becoming self-makers, taking their destinies into their own hands, what did that mean for their relationship with all the other people in the world who couldn't, or wouldn't, do the same? From its genesis, self-creation by necessity demanded another category of human being: the lifeless, bovine public to witness the spectacle. Dürer needed an adoring audience. Sade needed victims.

The aristocracy of genius, after all, couldn't very well be open to everybody. Sade divides humankind into two kinds of people. The libertines are those cunning and clever enough to claim their place at the top of the evolutionary hierarchy. Their prey are the women, men, and sometimes children who suffer their depredations. In one telling vignette from 120 Days of Sodom, Sade's characters literally reduce their prisoners to objects, transforming human bodies into human chairs, tables, and chandeliers.

So what divides the libertines from their prey? For Sade, the answer lies in the willingness of the libertines to claim the crown through their acts of transgression. Perversity—the conscious calculation to shock in order to set themselves apart from the vulgar, mediocre crowd—is the mechanism by which they achieve originality.

Self-making, Sade reminds us, has liberatory potential. It has the power to help us transcend the often limiting or repressive circumstances into which we have been born. But he also reminds us of its shadow side. If we accept that some people have the natural ability or the determined willingness to change their circumstances, then how do we avoid coming to the very conclusion that self-making at its most idealistic tries to overthrow—that some people are simply better than others?

It's not just Sade. Throughout the history of self-making, transgression— our ability to present ourselves as superior to, and distinct from, the rules and customs of society, be they moral, aesthetic, or sexual—will become a way for self-makers to perform their identities and set themselves apart from the common herd. Think of the glam rock star David Bowie flirting with Nazi imagery in Berlin or of Andy Warhol making art out of photographs of a gory car crash.

~~~

SADE WASN'T THE only Enlightenment theorist to be fascinated by the relationship between human freedom, human creativity, and the human capacity for cruelty. Another less violent—though perhaps no less unsettling—example can be found in a short dialogue by our old friend Denis Diderot, entitled *Rameau's Nephew*. Written in the early 1760s, then revised a decade later, *Rameau's Nephew* takes the form of a fictional exchange between the unnamed narrator, known only as "I," and a fascinating, frighteningly amoral dandy: "Him," ostensibly the titular nephew of the famous musician Jean-Philippe Rameau.

The nephew is a less extreme libertine than Sade's. Certainly he doesn't rack up the same body count. But his view of the world is almost as chilling. A failed musical genius but a consummate actor, the nephew has mastered the necessary arts of hypocrisy and deceit, changing his persona at will to entertain, and manipulate, the wealthy aristocrats on whose largesse he depends. He is Castiglione's courtier with a Sadean flair. The nephew continually alters his outward appearance; we learn from the narrator that "nothing is more unlike him than himself."[32] The nephew does not dissemble virtue because "virtue makes itself admired," he tells the narrator, "and admiration is not amusing." Rather, he makes himself into something of a clown, a figure of fun, so that his wealthy patrons will keep inviting him to dinner. "And, if nature had not made me that way," he goes on, "the simplest thing would be to appear like that." The nephew is *artificial*; he is consciously putting on an act for the benefit of his audience. But importantly, he is simultaneously totally *authentic*, living his life not in accordance with any external moral principles but simply in harmony with his personal self-interest. He is "a happy thief among wealthy thieves."[33] After all, what's the harm of thieving, if everybody else is thieving, too? Considered one way, he is a liar and a con. Considered another way, he's simply living his best life.

The nephew, like his Renaissance forebears, is obsessed by the idea of genius. He envies his late uncle's musical talent, confessing that if he could get away with passing off the elder Rameau's work as his own, "I wouldn't have hesitated to remain myself and to be him as well."[34] But the nephew doesn't want to be a genius in order to produce great works or even, exactly, to rise through the ranks of society and achieve material success. Rather, the nephew, the narrator tells us, is "desperate to be anything but an ordinary person." He wants to belong to the aristocracy of genius for its own sake, to be the particular, special, and original kind of person who can set himself apart from other men, rather than belong to—horror of horrors—an *espèce*, a scientifically loaded French word meaning "type" or "species," which the nephew understands to "indicate mediocrity and the final degree of contempt."[35] Like Sade's libertines, the nephew sees the world as composed of two kinds of people: original, godlike geniuses and mere animals, *Homo sapiens* with no particular dignity of their own.

Like Sade's libertines, the nephew is fascinated by transgression against the established bounds of the moral order as a means of establishing his own originality. He approvingly recounts to the narrator the story of a famous renegade, apparently under investigation by the Spanish Inquisition, who befriends a wealthy Jewish man, another of the Inquisition's would-be victims. Convincing the wealthy man that they are both in danger, the renegade suggests they gather their possessions and flee the country together. In fact, the nephew tells the narrator, the renegade steals the wealthy man's possessions and sails away to safety, but not before denouncing the Jewish man to the Inquisition, leaving him to be presumably tortured and killed.

For the nephew, this story is not a morally abhorrent one but rather evidence of a true original: a man who has figured out how to manipulate the world in order to prove his superiority to it. "People spit on a petty cheat," the nephew muses, "but they can't hold back a certain respect for a grand criminal." What the nephew wants, he tells the narrator, is "to pull out of you the admission that I was at least *original* in my degradation."[36]

❦

THIS IDEA OF originality—the distinctive specialness of the man who cuts his leading strings and chooses his own destiny—will become central to the mythos of the self-made man, common to the narratives of both the capitalist entrepreneur and the self-fashioning artist.

The self-made man is no longer merely set apart by the will of God or nature. Rather, it is the fact that he has chosen his destiny, has actively shaped himself, has consciously turned his back on the mores of custom and circumstance that grants him this new, special status. His inner desires, rather than those of his society or his God, are the only laws he lives by. He is the master of his own universe. But that mastery, too, comes at a cost. The self-made man risks cutting himself off not just from the yoke of authority or from the leading strings of custom but from other people. The more he sees himself as special or distinct, his intelligence and creative power as setting him apart from bourgeois morality and custom, the less credence he gives to the experiences of those around him, particularly those whose viewpoints do not reflect his own.

Today's self-makers are unlikely to be as extreme as Sade or even Rameau's nephew. But what they share with their Enlightenment forebears is a willingness to celebrate human freedom in the abstract, while seeing the greatest threat to human liberty in other (presumably lesser) human beings themselves. Today's narrative of self-making, likewise, all too often divides the world into thrillingly free individuals and the boring, bovine herd. And the tantalizing allure of transgression—sexual, moral, aesthetic, or otherwise—remains one of the most profitable ways to tell the world which category you belong to.

## – three –

# "A SNEER FOR THE WORLD"

ONDON'S MOST TALKED-ABOUT PARTY WAS KICKING INTO
high gear. The date? July 1813. The setting? One of the city's most
prestigious venues: the Argyll Street Rooms in Mayfair, so exclusive
that, in the words of one amused French traveler, "the wives and daughters of
your most respectable country gentlemen no sooner arrive in London than,
forgetting all high feelings of conscious virtue and hereditary pride, they seem
anxious to purchase, at any price, the honor of belonging."[1]

The partygoers belonged to London's most compelling clique. They were
the young, aristocratic, and highly fashionable set known as the ton, who gathered at insular fortresses like the Argyll, Almack's, or White's to drink, dance,
gossip, and—most important—secure a mate of equal status. Access to such
gatherings was ferociously policed. A subscription to the Argyll, for example,
cost ten guineas (about $500 in today's money) for a gentleman, twelve for a
married lady, and sixteen for a de facto family membership for perhaps the ton's
most desperate of would-be members, a mother and her unmarried daughter.[2]
Like today's aspiring members of posh private clubs like Soho House or Zero

Bond, a prospective subscriber also had to be carefully scrutinized by a host committee: one that would assess not only the supplicant's birth, blood, and bank account but also something much more mysterious: the ineffable quality of bon ton itself.

Literally translated as "etiquette," bon ton—in Regency England at least—had a far more complicated meaning. Something between elegance, grace, class, and charm, the magic of bon ton signified, as sprezzatura had once done in Renaissance Italy, that its possessor belonged to a special, elite class of persons. They were members not only of a literal, hereditary aristocracy but, perhaps even more importantly, of an aristocracy of *style*. Having bon ton in the Regency era, like having "it" in early Hollywood, meant that you had a personal power that transcended any of the facts about where you came from or what you actually did. It did not come from God, from your family, from your country, or even from your private club. Rather, it came from you and your ability to present yourself to the world.

The hosts of this July party had bon ton in spades. Four of the coterie's most illustrious members—Lord Alvanley, Henry Pierrepont, Henry Mildmay, and George Brummell—had become infamous about town for their fine dress and even finer manners. After winning a fair bit of money at cards, they'd collectively decided to use the proceeds to finance a particularly spectacular occasion to entertain—and impress—their circle.

The party had gotten off to a promising start. The rooms were, predictably, stunning; one contemporary guidebook refers to the Argyll as "at once the most splendid and commodious place of amusement in the metropolis."[3] The hosts, likewise, were impeccably arrayed. Although, by 1813, men's evening fashion tended away from the baroque and bewigged toward the simple and well tailored—a shift the ton themselves had implemented—on that particular night, the style choice was ironic. The hosts wore elaborate historical costumes of two centuries prior, depicting themselves as seventeenth-century footmen, each carrying a heavy, multipronged candelabra.[4]

Then, a somewhat unwelcome guest turned up.

Prinny, as his friends knew him, hadn't been on the ball's original guest list. He'd had one too many fallings-out with his former best friend Brummell, perhaps the most notorious of the hosts. Prinny had made it clear, however, that he wanted to attend, and under some duress an invitation had grudgingly been procured for him.

Prinny made his way toward the hosts. A stout, awkward man and prone to overdress to what his contemporaries scathingly called a "tawdry degree," Prinny was rarely the most fashionable or best liked man in the room.[5] Undeterred by the lukewarm reaction to his presence, he headed first to Lord Alvanley, bowing to him in accordance with proper etiquette. Next he greeted the two Henrys, shaking each one's hand. Then, finally, he came to Brummell. "Seemingly," one contemporary recounts the scene, "as if [Prinny] did not know who he was or why he was there . . . without bestowing upon him the slightest symptom of recognition passed on."[6]

But Brummell was not to take the snub lightly. "Alvanley," he loudly asked, in the cool drawl that had already become a hallmark of his public personality, "who's your fat friend?"

The cut silenced the room.

It was already unthinkable that anyone would speak like that to Prinny, who was more formally known as Prince George Augustus Frederick, the prince regent of Wales and—due to the illness of his father, George III—the de facto ruler of the entire British Empire. (At the elder George's death in 1820, Prinny would become King George IV.) But it was doubly unthinkable that the person launching the insult to the most socially important person in the room was not a royal himself, nor even an aristocrat, but a mere commoner.

George Bryan Brummell—better known by his somewhat hagiographic nickname, Beau—was the son of an ordinary civil servant. Worse still, he was the grandson of the proprietor of a boardinghouse that may have doubled as a house of ill repute. Sure, Brummell had a bit of money inherited from his upwardly mobile father, but the amount—the equivalent of about £2.5 million in today's money—was hardly staggering, especially by the standards of London's burgeoning new-money elite. His social position was, by then, decent enough. After a brief stint courting scandal at the posh boarding school Eton and then at Oriel College, Oxford, Brummell had—with the help of the prince, whom he'd likely met and impressed when the royal visited Eton—found his way into a hard-drinking but well-heeled cavalry regiment that in practice doubled as Prinny's fashionable entourage. But it wasn't birth or money that had propelled Brummell to the very heights of London society. Wealth and status hadn't brought him to his former intimate friendship with the prince of Wales, whose best man he had been, or to his position as—in the words of one contemporary—the ton's "supreme dictator," a man who lay "down the law" when it came to what and who were in or out. Brummell "fomented the excesses" of London's social scene; he made "ridiculous [its] scruples, patronized its novices," and, most importantly, "exercised paramount dominion over all."[7]

What Brummell had, and what Prinny decidedly didn't, was bon ton. And although Brummell wouldn't exactly come out of that ill-fated night a success—the final withdrawal of Prinny's favor and a necessary financial corrective to Brummell's lifelong propensity for gambling and spending too much money on clothes ultimately doomed him to a life spent in de facto economic exile in France—in some ways, Prinny would come out far worse. He would, to be sure, ultimately become King George IV, but Prinny would never experience the kind of adulation he hoped the crown would bring him. A new kind of aristocracy, that of the ton, had been born before his eyes. And the kind of celebrity that Beau Brummell had pioneered in London drawing rooms and private clubs—grounded not in birth or blood or even skill, but in the sheer magnetic force of personality—would come not just to threaten but indeed to supplant Prinny's primacy.

"I care nothing for the mob," Prinny was known to sigh, "but I care for the dandies."[8] The dandies, for their part, were perfectly happy to mock their princes.

In 1812, the year before the prince regent and Brummell's final falling out, a satirical poem composed in Prinny's voice by another ton member, the Irish writer Thomas Moore, shows just how powerful Brummell's celebrity was held to be. Moore's Prinny protests that he never gets angry:

> *Nor wish there should come ill*
> *to mortal—except (now I think on't) Beau* BR-MM-LL
> *who threaten'd last year, in a superfine passion*
> *to cut* ME, *and bring the old king into fashion.*[9]

Satire aside, Beau Brummell had little interest in, or actual capacity for, effecting political change. But he understood and profited from the seismic shift taking place in the society of Regency England and, more broadly, in industrialized cities all over Europe: the rise of a burgeoning, self-made middle class and with it new ways of thinking about aristocracy, power, and the potential to fashion one's own life.

And Brummell, like Castiglione and Machiavelli and Rameau's notorious nephew before him, understood that perception—especially the perception of the right people at the right time—was at the heart of this new avenue toward power. Perception was something that the clever and intrepid could learn how to shape. Brummell understood, too, the strange sprezzatura-sprung paradox at the heart of self-creation: that the artificial had to at least appear authentic. You had to try hard and also make it look like you were one of the elect who didn't have to. In other words, fake it until you make it.

Central to Brummell's public persona, as we shall soon see, was his tendency toward haughty indifference. He had a bored nonchalance that implied that even a snub from the prince of Wales himself could not penetrate his emotional armor. A godlike disengagement—a freedom from and superiority to other people, even princes—was necessary for the person who wanted to truly create himself anew.

Beau Brummell has been called many things. The Romantic poet Lord Byron—not a man prone to understatement—allegedly once called Brummell the greatest man of the nineteenth century.[10] (Napoleon came second. Byron himself came third.) Novelist and illustrator Max Beerbohm called him "the Father of Modern Costume."[11] A more recent biographer, Ian Kelly, called him the first "truly modern celebrity."[12] Certainly, Brummell was among the first to recognize that his public persona could be monetized in the manner we now refer to as sponsorship, using his exalted status as arbiter of good taste to enrich himself. Tailors extended to Brummell near limitless credit, sometimes giving him free items in the knowledge that Brummell wearing them would be the best advertisement possible. Indeed, Brummell might well be said to have been not just an early celebrity but in fact one of the world's first influencers. His public persona was so well known, and his taste was so fervently emulated, that his personal likes and dislikes became London fashion. Brummell was famous for being himself—and he could sell products to other people who wanted to be Brummell.

All Brummell had to do was be seen wearing something; the next day, it would be sold out all over London. When he took to wearing beaver hats, for example, the beaver population in North America plummeted all but overnight.[13] Stories abound about the fashionable public's fascination with every aspect of Brummell's life, particularly what he wore. Admirers thronged to Brummell's house in Chesterfield Street to watch him bathe, shave, and dress over the course of several painstaking hours. His own "private" morning routine was of particular interest to Brummell's fans, who ached to learn how, exactly, Beau Brummell became Beau Brummell and to apply his aesthetic insights to their own lives. There was exfoliation with a coarse-hair brush, followed by a bath of milk, followed by a process of spitting in a silver bowl chosen specially for the purpose. Someone as stylish as Brummell, after all, would never stoop to spit into common clay. Then, the pièce de résistance: Brummell's meticulous tying of his necktie, with the help of his erstwhile valet. The valet would go out of his way to pass visitors on his way downstairs to ensure that guests saw his armfuls of so-called failures: improperly tied ties that, no longer freshly starched, would have to be discarded.

At the peak of Brummell's fame, even wellborn London aristocrats relied on his good favor to get them into top clubs like Argyll or White's and lived in terror of his witticisms, which would inevitably spread like pox through London society. (The duke of Bedford never quite lived down the day when he, asking Brummell what the latter thought of his new coat, received the withering answer, "You call this thing a coat?")[14]

~~~

YET BRUMMELL—LIKE DÜRER or Sade—was less original than he might at first glance appear. Rather, Brummell's talent lay in his ability to channel and manipulate the tensions of his time, to gain a monopoly, as it were, on this burgeoning concept of bon ton.

Just as genius had been the buzzword in Renaissance conceptions of self-made men as divine bastards, so, too, did bon ton help delineate a special category of human being, the kind who could snub a prince and get away with it. It was all very well and good to be an aristocrat of the blood. But someone with bon ton was an aristocrat of something all the more mysterious: style.

The difference between Regency bon ton and Renaissance genius is that the latter could be, at least nominally, defined. It involved being skilled at something—artistic talent or intellectual ingenuity—in the service of creating a work that could be seen or used or appreciated by other people. Bon ton, by contrast, was entirely self-referential, the Jane Austen–era equivalent of being famous for being famous. You couldn't acquire it simply by being wellborn. But, vitally, you also couldn't acquire it by having a lot of money, inherited or earned. "Into this sanctum sanctorum," one contemporary wrote of exclusive club Almack's, "the sons of commerce never think of entering. . . . Three fourths of nobility knock in vain."[15] The duke of Wellington himself was once turned away from a ball on the grounds that he was eight minutes late. One member of the captain of the guard was so offended at having been denied an

Almack's subscription that he challenged the husband of one of the admission committee's patronesses to a duel.[16] Meanwhile, the impecunious poet Moore, author of the satirical poem about Prinny's "superfine passion," was inducted into the ton despite his low and Irish birth on account of his fine wit.

The possessors of bon ton are described by contemporaries in language that blends the imagery of royalty with that of gods: they are "that most Distinguished and Despotic CONCLAVE . . . the Rulers of Fashion, the Arbiters of Taste, the Leaders of Ton, and the Makers of Manners, whose sovereign sway over 'the world' of London has long been established on the firmest basis, whose decrees are Laws and from whose judgment there is no appeal."[17]

To understand bon ton and the curious role that it played in Regency life, we have to understand the social upheavals that characterized Regency London and post–Industrial Revolution Europe more broadly. Regency London was defined by its cultural and economic change, in particular by the money flooding in from new sources: the twin modern pillars of colonialism and capitalism. If the intellectual developments of the Enlightenment had challenged the hierarchical vision of the divine cosmos in theory, then the Industrial Revolution destabilized it in practice.

New forms of wealth, bolstered by industry and international commerce alike, arose to threaten the primacy of the old agrarian-aristocratic system. Trade, in particular the import and export of luxury goods, had become London's lifeblood. Between 1700 and 1795, the number of ships entering London's port grew from 6,900 to 14,800; meanwhile, the total value of goods passing through the city more than tripled.[18] Trading companies like the East India Company, first founded in 1600, advertised a potential path to outrageous fortune for enterprising merchants or sailors—or, at the very least, to those willing to turn a blind eye to the less salubrious dealings in the colonies. In 1710, the East India Company made around a dozen voyages annually. By 1793, that number had more than quadrupled to fifty-three.[19]

The wealth produced by the import and export of luxury goods, furthermore, created a burgeoning class of potential buyers for this influx of products.

From high-end clothing to exotic spices, items once considered the exclusive prerogative of the aristocratic class could be obtained simply by strolling into a high-end shop—provided, that is, that you had the guineas to pay for them.

It is a peculiar irony of the period, of course, that these products, which heralded the fantasy of social mobility in England, were generally obtained through colonial depredations or, in the case of sugar (for example), the labor of the enslaved. From the myopic perspective of the average Londoner, however, this boon in trade spelled untold potential for social advancement. You could start out, as one Fenchurch Street local named Abram Newman did, as a solidly middle-class wholesale grocer, buy into a risky partnership in a re-export firm specializing in coffee, chocolate, and tea, and wind up one of London's richest men. By the time of Newman's death in 1799, he had amassed a fortune of £600,000, about twenty times Brummell's inheritance.[20]

Capital—another mysterious animating force pulsing through London society—did not care about where or how you were born. In this regard, at least, it made men nominally equal. "Enter into the Royal [Stock] Exchange of London," the Enlightenment philosopher Voltaire marveled, and you'll see "deputies from all nations assemble for the advantage of mankind. There the Jew, the [Muslim], and the Christian bargain with one another as if they were of the same religion, and bestow the name of infidel on bankrupts only."[21]

LONDON'S STATUS AS a capital of trade in luxury goods made two important things possible. To a hitherto unprecedented extent, you could now leapfrog the social hierarchy. And, no less important, you could advertise that social change by what you drank (coffee), what you put into it (sugar), and, above all things, what you wore.

Just a few centuries earlier, sartorial expression had been the privilege of a very specialized few. To create one's self-image through fashion was something almost exclusively done by royalty, those elite and God-ordained figures whose bodies doubled as expressions of divine will, and whose faces could be marshaled in the service of political propaganda. Elizabeth I, for example, was adept at creating and disseminating images of herself as the Virgin Queen, whose providentially appointed status as ruler allowed her to transcend the perceived limitations of her sex. So, too, Dürer's patron, the Holy Roman emperor Maximilian I of the House of Habsburg, very consciously presented himself to his public as a chivalrous medieval knight. He commissioned so many elaborate and expensive suits of armor that he had to purchase a separate residence just to store them.[22] And, of course, there was France's Louis XIV, the Sun King, whose sartorial splendor was calculated to make him appear, as one astonished contemporary put it, "like the men whom the poets represent to us as transformed into gods."[23] King Louis not only dressed himself splendidly; he used fashion as a means of controlling his entire court. He correctly surmised that courtiers who spent all of their time (and money) scrambling to keep up with the latest fashions would hardly be in a position to think about political rebellion. Male and female courtiers alike were mandated by virtue of their station to purchase and wear highly specific garments, each one corresponding with their precise place in the Versailles pecking order.

Clothing, in other words, had for centuries been a means of expressing a particular kind of power, rooted in a particular vision of the cosmos, with the king (or queen) at its center. Divine power and divine authority flowed through royalty. To them was granted the right of appearing as a demigod.

But central, too, to this vision of the cosmos was the idea that everyone, of every station, had clothing that was appropriate for them to wear. To speak about "authenticity" or "self-expression" would have been unthinkable; the most authentic thing one could possibly express, through clothing or otherwise, was one's place in the social imaginary. To dress differently from one's station was seen as a form of dishonesty, punished by social opprobrium or—in the case of those eras that had formal sumptuary laws—monetary fines. Society, after all, rested on a fundamental compact: the outer, visible world reflected its inner, fundamental truths. The Elizabethan-era playwright Robert Greene, for example, criticizing vanity more broadly, condemns "not the weed [i.e., clothing] but the vice, not the apparel when 'tis worthily worn but the unworthy person that wears it."[24]

Those who destabilized this hierarchical connection between inner and outer were deemed unnatural in other ways, particularly those to do with gender and sexuality—an association we've seen already in the writings of Sade. Men who dressed above their station, in particular, were often understood as effeminate, potentially even homosexual. One Renaissance advice giver, using a Classical reference associated with homosexual relationships, cautions courtiers that "your garments should not be extremely fancy or extremely ornate, so that no one can say you are wearing Ganymede's hose."[25]

By the time we reach Brummell's England, however, this understanding of the world has already collapsed. The intellectual movements of the Enlightenment have hollowed out conceptions of such an orderly cosmos. Clothing choices, like everything else, are instead recognized as mere unhappy accidents of custom. (Remember that Montaigne wished he didn't have to wear clothes at all.) Gone is the certainty that there is any reality—in the sense of being God-given or created for a particular purpose—to where and how we find ourselves born. After all, in an increasingly socially fluid world, the rank and station of our birth have less and less relevance to where we may end up.

And so reality—as Brummell and so many of his dandy contemporaries realized—must be something we compose and express for ourselves. And Brummell realized, too, that clothing, rather than being an external expression of an internal truth, had become an opportunity to perform that new reality. You could say that his artifice was in fact evidence of a new kind of authenticity. Brummell made his outward self fit the godlike image he had in his head.

Almost overnight, Brummell's signature style—not elaborately bedecked or ornately colorful but rather sleek and even minimalist—had become the reigning fashion in London. It was preferable even to the clumsier clothing choices of the king himself. One baronet was apparently fond of recounting a trip to the prestigious London tailor Schweitzer and Davidson, during which he asked the tailor which fabric was most in style at the moment. At first, the tailor wavered. "The prince wears superfine, and Mr. Brummell the Bath coating." Then, he made his recommendation clear. "Mr. Brummell has a trifle the preference."[26] Prinny may have been the future king of England, but Brummell was the "king of the dandies," as one contemporary put it, and that was what counted.[27]

But it wasn't just Brummell who had learned the power of fashion to create and express individual personality rather than social station. Regency England more broadly was a place where what you wore and how you wore it could express your political identity as well.

Consider the 1795 powder tax, a sartorial controversy that divided London. That year, Prime Minister William Pitt (the Younger) had sought to raise government funds to help support the Napoleonic Wars. To do so, he levied a new tax on hair powder, a necessary accessory for the wealthy and upwardly mobile middle class alike, who at the time still wore powdered wigs. Pitt legitimized this tax on the grounds that the powder, which was derived from cornstarch, risked wastefully misusing a valuable food product in a time of agricultural and political instability. While powder itself was already being taxed, Pitt's additional tax on the right to powder one's hair amounted to an annual sum of one guinea: about two weeks' salary for the average London laborer.[28]

Sure, such a tax wasn't likely to overburden London's wealthiest, the sorts of people who could afford to powder every day. But for the aspirational middle class—those artisans, laborers, and traders used to powdering on Sundays and holidays, who were under particular pressure to keep up appearances— the tax proved burdensome indeed.

Almost overnight, hair powder—and whether you did or didn't use it— became a statement not just about how much money you had but where you fell on the political spectrum and how you felt about the Napoleonic Wars. Members of the conservative Tory Party, who by and large supported foreign wars (and who tended to belong to more aristocratic backgrounds to begin with), carried on powdering. Reformist Whigs, whether or not they could afford the tax, stopped powdering altogether, on the grounds that their wigs would be powdered with "human blood."[29] (As it happened, wig powder was normally made from inedible parts of the corn plant, but this fact rarely made it into public discourse.) Soon, London streets were filled with regular altercations between the "powdered" and "unpowdered." People's stances were worn, quite literally, on their heads.

The press, predictably, went wild. One satirical poem rewrote Hamlet's famous soliloquy for the times, determining that "to wear a wig / or not to wear a wig" was the great question of the day. A comic print, *The Rival Pigs*, depicts the clash between the "guinea pigs"—pretty fashion victims—and the "pigs without a guinea," who could not pay.[30]

Enter the ton with a solution. Richard Barry, the dissolute and fashionable seventh earl of Barrymore, along with his two brothers, showed up in public one day with short-cropped hair. The sort of hair, in other words, that didn't take any powder at all. All of a sudden, the question of whether you powdered or not—to say nothing of what political stance you took on the Napoleonic Wars—was entirely moot. The dandies had spoken louder than any government or newspaper could. Short hair was the fashion now.

THIS SENSE OF placid disengagement, a superiority to the scrabble of political life, was an integral part of the philosophy of the ton, from Barry to Brummell. It was an important part, too, of the somewhat paradoxical conception of bon ton itself, which never managed to be either fully democratic or fully reactionary in nature. To be sure, bon ton was in some senses a social leveler, an opportunity for a penniless wit like the Prinny-paraphrasing poet Thomas Moore, or a middle-class upstart like Beau Brummell to gain access to otherwise impenetrable corridors of power. But it was also, at the same time, a social closing of the ranks. It created a social scene even more regimented, more exclusive, than the actual aristocracy. By conceiving of bon ton as an inexplicable, if not literally supernatural, force, one that you either had or you didn't, members of the clique could legitimize and embrace certain self-makers while conveniently keeping others—the gaudier "sons of commerce," say—outside Almack's gates. The world of bon ton, while it welcomed self-makers up to a point, was an oligarchy, not a democracy. The dandies ruled by fiat.

But the fantasy of control that bon ton offered wasn't just about keeping other, lesser people out. It was also about a certain kind of mastery over oneself—or, to be more precise, about cutting off certain parts of one's humanity in the service of becoming a hallowed demigod.

Bon ton, like sprezzatura and Rameau's nephew's vision of originality before it, was characterized by a posture of not caring too much. The ideal possessor of bon ton had to cut himself off not only from the leading strings of custom but from the chains of sentimental attachment, regarding the rest of the world from a vantage point of superiority. Brummell was famous, after all, for being— or at least appearing to be—constantly bored. In his 1845 biography of Brummell, published five years after Brummell's death, the French writer (and fellow dandy) Jules Barbey d'Aurevilly praised Brummell for escaping the "slavery" of amorous attachment. (We to this day know very little about Brummell's sexuality or personal life. Aside from a few flirtations—one of which appeared to have given him the syphilis that ultimately killed him—Brummell seems to have formed no romantic or sexual bonds with anyone of any gender. Contemporary biographers uniformly remark on his perceived coldness and disinterest in sex.) "To love . . . is to always be . . . the slave of one's desire," Barbey d'Aurevilly mused. "The arms which clasp you the most tenderly are still a chain." By contrast, Brummell's "triumphs had all the insolence of indifference."[31]

Central to the fashion of the ton was its subtlety, the fact that it could only truly be appreciated by an elite few who were able to recognize the superior craftsmanship of seemingly minor details. "If John Bull [i.e., every-man] turns around to look at you," Brummell was fond of saying, "you are not well-dressed."[32] Brummell's style—and that of the whole Regency ton— was characterized by its lofty and geometric simplicity. It, like the quality of bon ton itself, evoked a sense of being removed from the whole world. While Brummell's nonchalance lacked the outright fascination with evil that we find in, say, Sade's libertines or even Rameau's nephew, the dandy of the Brummell mode shares with his Enlightenment forebears a sense that self-creation demands a clear division between self-creators and those unfortunates who are either incapable or unwilling to make themselves with equal creativity. Originality demands separation from the herd. Self-definition had to come, at least in part, from closing oneself off from undue influence.

This paradox—the push-pull between innate superiority and social fluidity, between aristocracy and democracy—would come to define self-making in the centuries to come. And it would come, too, to foster the development of two distinct narratives of self-making: the aristocratic, largely centered in Europe, and the democratic, which, as we shall see, came to be centered in the United States. These models would ultimately converge in the twentieth and twenty-first centuries, and they were not entirely as disparate as they might at first glance appear.

The difference, however, was a question of emphasis. Was the mysterious quality that set self-makers apart from non-self-makers something with which you were born (as in genius or bon ton), regardless of the actual circumstances of your birth? Or was it something you could choose to have, something you could adopt with a sufficient amount of hard work and effort?

The aristocratic model, by and large, conceived of self-creation as an innate phenomenon, something that resisted mere reduction to, say, self-made economic success, even as the shadow of capitalism could be found everywhere. (Beau Brummell, though perhaps the paradigmatic self-creator of the aristocratic type, was only in a position to meet and impress Prinny in the first place because his upwardly mobile father had been able to send him to an exclusive boarding school like Eton. Long before tailors were giving Brummell clothing on credit, he had to use his reasonably substantial inheritance to afford at least his first few outfits.) Self-creators of this type often understood themselves—or at least claimed to understand themselves—as working *against* the increased social mobility and fluidity of the modern world, trying instead to recover a "true" or "spiritual" (if not blood-based) aristocracy that linked all

chosen self-creators in a single, superior legacy of the dandy, a word that comes
into common usage during that time.

If there is an early nineteenth-century manifesto for this type of self-creator,
we can find it in French author Honoré de Balzac's 1830 handbook-cum-
novella *Treatise on Elegant Living*. Written ten years before Brummell's death
(but well after his downfall), Balzac fictionalizes a visit by a group of French
dandies to an elderly, exiled Brummell. (Balzac, in contrast to a number of
other contemporary writers on this issue, including Barbey d'Aurevilly, uses
"dandy" derogatorily, to mean someone who tries too hard to be elegant. However, the way he describes his ideal "elegant man" is very similar to how, say,
Barbey d'Aurevilly describes the dandies.)

These young members of France's ton equivalent hope that Brummell
will help them create a set of laws—a kind of aesthetic Napoleonic Code—for
aspirant bon-ton-havers back home. But Balzac's Brummell refuses. Elegance,
he tells them, can never be codified, precisely because real style is never democratic. "Not all legs are called upon to wear a boot or a pair of pants in the
same way," Brummell insists. "Will there not always be those that limp, those
deformed, or ignoble?"[33] The dandies, the "People of elegant living," are the
"natural aristocracy" of any country.[34]

Balzac mournfully harkens back to the God-centered, hierarchical, medieval view of the cosmos he believes the modern world has lost. "The moment
that two books of parchment [i.e., the Bible] no longer stand for everything,
when the natural son of a millionaire bath attendant and a man of talent
have the same rights as the son of a count, we can no longer be distinguished
by anything but our intrinsic value."[35] Balzac—and Balzac's Brummell in
particular—sees the figure of the elegant man as the culmination of the natural human need to find some sort of organizing principle, to identify the special among them. The aristocracy of style is a means of reasserting hierarchy
in an increasingly democratic world.

The "elegant man" in Balzac's telling isn't just a fashionable man. Rather,
he is someone who restores to the world a sense of that old cosmos defended so

vociferously by sumptuary laws. He is someone whose exterior sartorial expression accurately reveals something true and innate about himself and what is lacking in others. Speaking approvingly of elegant self-expression, Balzac tells us that "the exterior life is a sort of organized system that represents a man as accurately as a snail's colors recur on its shell."[36] After all, Balzac asks, "why would clothing always be the most eloquent of styles if it were not really the whole man, man with his political opinions, man with the text of his existence, man made into a hieroglyph?"[37] Here, too, we see a tension between authenticity and artifice. By curating his clothing in a stylized way, the dandy is authentically expressing something fundamental about himself: his grace and superiority.

By creating his life as a public form of expression, by choosing carefully his clothing, his speech, and his physical manners, this man creates a vision of elegance that restores a sense of hierarchy, order, and divinity to a world that, Balzac implies, heavily needs it. But, at the same time, the organized system doesn't come from God or from a sanctified social order but simply from the elegant man's own desires. We're living in a divinely ordered world, in other words, but God is not out there in the heavens. Rather, he is within the self-creator.

Balzac's treatment of the elegant man points to some of the contradictions bound up in the European vision of the aristocratic self-maker. He resists the socially fluid world of commerce and moneymaking, although, chances are, he has benefitted from them, as Brummell and indeed "de" Balzac had (Balzac's father, born a poor artisan, had changed his name from Balssa to the better-sounding Balzac. Honoré himself had added the nobiliary particle). The elegant man's aristocratic manner is innate and inalienable but nevertheless could—sort of, maybe—also be learned. In the novella, despite the character Brummell's obstreperous snobbery, Balzac's dandies do ultimately produce a handbook full of useful maxims.

THROUGHOUT REGENCY ENGLAND, we find plenty of hints that aristocratic dandyism might well also be learned, or at least feigned, by those clever enough to ascertain its rules. Members of both the ton and the wider, less august, literate middle class became obsessed with the fashionable genre known as the dandy novel. These stories featured Brummell-like dandy characters alongside thinly disguised versions of other notable ton members. The novels were nearly all produced by one enterprising publisher, Henry Colburn, who had hit upon a near-perfect business model. Colburn would hire cash-poor members, or purported members, of the ton to write the books under cover of anonymity, then hire other authors on his roster to write positive reviews of these novels in various ton-approved gazettes and journals he owned. Nearly all of these novels featured a dandy whose elegant maxims could be studied and memorized by attentive readers. There was Robert Plumer Ward's *Tremaine: Or, the Man of Refinement*. There was Mrs. Gore's *Cecil: Or, the Adventures of a Coxcomb*, whose dandy protagonist, Jack Harris, is lovingly described as possessed of "impertinence," which allows him an aristocratic "wit for the putting down."[38] And there was *Pelham*, by Edward Bulwer Lytton, which features an extensive code by which a would-be dandy might live. "Do not require your dress so much to fit as to adorn you," we learn. "Nature is not to be copied, but to be exalted by art."[39] Pelham is not above a little Machiavellian dissembling either. "A man must be a profound calculator to be a consummate dresser," we learn from Pelham. "One must not dress the same, whether one goes to a minister or a mistress; an avaricious uncle."[40] Fashion is not just about expressing some fundamental truth about the self—be it one's social station or, as Balzac suggests, one's innate superiority—but also about cannily transforming the self into who one wants to be.

But few dandy novels capture the calculations involved in aristocratic self-creation quite like one of Henry Colburn's most controversial publications, *Vivian Grey*, published in 1826 and written by an anonymous "man of high fashion" who, Colburn assured readers, "keeps the first society."[41] The novel was a successful one, at least at first, greeted with all the fanfare

Colburn's novels customarily received, both from the smart set and from the middle-class readers who liked to fantasize that they, too, could one day be part of it. The ton journals lauded it. The *Star Chamber* provided a speculative "key" to its characters, helping readers figure out who might be based on whom. And all of London started speculating on who, exactly, its illustrious author could be.

Vivian Grey himself, for his part, wasn't just a nonchalant or a disengaged dandy. Rather, he was an actively, gleefully amoral one. Equal parts Beau Brummell and Rameau's nephew, Grey knows the true secret of dandyism: that "personal distinction is the only passport to the society of the great."[42] In today's society, Grey concludes, "a man must either have blood, a million, or be a genius."[43]

Such genius, however, isn't simply a knack for painting or for learning Latin or Greek. Rather, it's a talent for self-invention, along with a willingness to maneuver—ethically or otherwise—in a society that cares only for appearances. The sole question on Grey's mind is, "Who is to be my enemy tomorrow?"[44] In Grey, the dandyist posture of disdain reaches its fullest expression. We learn that the motto by which he lives is, "A smile for a friend, and a sneer for the world, is the way to govern mankind."[45] Grey goes into politics, embarks upon various schemes and machinations, and—although he ultimately fails in his efforts—does so compellingly enough to enthrall London's literati.

At least until his author was revealed. Days after the novel's publication, the ton was shocked to learn that the writer of *Vivian Grey* was not one of their own number but rather a middle-class Jew—an "obscure person," as a scandalized writer for *Blackwood's* reported, "for whom nobody cares a straw"— who had gotten into the novel-writing business in order to pay off his debts. At once, London clamored to condemn the author who had gotten one over on them. He was a schemer, they insisted, and must have wormed his way into superior social circles in order to steal gossip, or even people's private papers, from his newfound acquaintances. One representatively anti-Semitic reviewer suggested that London's next big literary hit would be called *The Complete*

*Picklock: Or, How to Gain Access to the Private Diaries of Your Friends,* by Solomon Prig, Ishmaelite.[46]

The author, Benjamin Disraeli, defended his work. "In *Vivian Grey*," he later wrote, "I have portrayed my active and real ambition." Sure, there were some minor differences. Vivian Grey had decided against attending Eton on the grounds that his superior interest took him elsewhere; in real life, Disraeli had been denied admission because of his Jewish blood. But Disraeli's passion for self-invention—through clothing and personal machination alike—would come to be a mirror of Grey's own. "I wish," Disraeli once wrote, "to act what I write."[47]

Shortly after *Vivian Grey's* publication, Disraeli was blackballed from almost every one of London's major clubs. He would never be admitted to White's—one of Brummell's favorite haunts—an honor Disraeli had once likened to receiving the royal Order of the Garter. And he would give up novel writing altogether, deciding instead to go into politics.

In 1874, he would become prime minister.

The Prinnies of the world were on their way out. And, as the nineteenth century wore on, even the snobbish ton itself would lose some of its social power. The future belonged, increasingly, to men like Disraeli, if not Vivian Grey himself, who were willing and able to use their self-presentation for profit. Bon ton, they knew, was not born, but made.

– four –

# "WORK! WORK!! WORK!!!"

IT WAS A TUESDAY EVENING IN OCTOBER 1859, AND ONE OF
America's most famous orators was about to deliver one of the signature
lectures of his fifty-plus-year career.

The venue, the National Market Hall of Philadelphia, was almost certainly
packed. The speaker, Frederick Douglass, was a fixture on nineteenth-century
America's burgeoning lecture circuit, which was among the era's most popular forms of entertainment. People from all over the Eastern Seaboard had
already thronged to town halls and church basements to hear Douglass speak.
He often told the enthralling story of his own life. His first autobiography, one
of three he would publish, had sold over thirty thousand copies in its first five
years in print and had been lauded by reviewers as "the most thrilling work
which the American press has ever issued."[1] In other speeches, he declaimed,
in theatrically bombastic style, on questions of contemporary politics and
morality.

Tonight's lecture was of the latter kind, on a subject dear to Douglass's
heart: "Self-Made Men." Such men—and Douglass counted himself as one—
had come from humble beginnings, "without the ordinary help of favoring

circumstance," but had nevertheless "attained knowledge, usefulness, power, and position," and had, most important, "buil[t] up worthy character."[2]

"If they have travelled far," Douglass told his rapt listeners, "they have made the road on which they had travelled. If they had ascended high, they have built their own ladder."[3] These were the people for whom the United States—not even, at this point, a century old—had been designed, the rightful beneficiaries of the Declaration of Independence's dream of human equality and life, liberty, and the pursuit of happiness. They were the people who doubled as proof that the American experiment had succeeded.

Back in old Europe, Douglass went on, men were judged by the wealth and station of their fathers. Not so in new America. Here, he declaimed, "society very properly saves itself the trouble of looking up a man's kinfolks in order to determine his grade in life and the measure of respect due him."[4] Even the scions of the great and the good, in this promised land, had to earn their paternity, at least metaphorically speaking. Such wellborn sons, Douglass told his audience, citing some of the country's best-known last names, "must prove themselves real Clays, Websters, and Lincolns," at least if they wanted "the cordial respect and admiration generally awarded to their brilliant fathers."[5]

Douglass denied that these self-makers had any particular innate qualities that made them well-placed to succeed, despite their origins. Genius, Douglass insisted, was a red herring. After all, "what is called genius is often found by the wayside, a miserable wreck, the more deplorable and shocking because of the height from which it has fallen."[6] Nor could the success of certain men be explained away by luck, by simply having been at the right place at the right time. To hold such a view, Douglass scoffed, was to "divorce a man from his own achievements . . . [leaving] him without will, motive, ambition and aspiration."[7]

For Douglass, a single word summed up what separated self-made men from the rest of humanity. "And that word"—he repeated it several times for emphasis—"is WORK! WORK!! WORK!!! WORK!!!!"[8] Work—the active, careful, willful cultivation of the self—was what made possible the stellar rise of

America's self-made men, "of whatever variety of race or color." It was, he heavily hinted, key to his own success.

Douglass's story was, in his telling, a robust narrative of such quintessential American self-making. Born into chattel slavery on a Maryland plantation in 1818, Douglass never knew his father. (He speculated that he was the biological offspring of his legal master, Aaron Anthony, part of the long-standing antebellum practice of plantation rape.) His early life, like that of so many enslaved Black Americans, had been brutal. One of Douglass's signature rhetorical devices was to bare to his audience the whipping scars upon his back, what he called his "diploma" from that "peculiar institution" that had so educated him in American racial injustice.[9] He had, however, secretly taught himself to read and write, with the help of the *Columbian Orator*, a popular manual of elocution that encouraged would-be speakers to model themselves on Classical greats like Cicero.

But it was 1833—a date enshrined in both Douglass's autobiographies and his lectures—that Douglass saw as a turning point in his own life. It was the day that "rekindled in [his] breast the smouldering embers of liberty."[10] The man who was at the time considered his legal master, Thomas Auld, had hired a young Douglass out to Edward Covey, a notoriously violent "breaker" of enslaved people. Covey had treated Douglass as he treated all the men under his supervision, whipping and beating him regularly. But one day, Douglass fought back and won. "I was a changed being after that fight," he wrote. "I was nothing before I WAS A MAN NOW. It . . . inspired me with a renewed determination to be a FREEMAN." After all, Douglass went on, "a man, without force, is without the essential dignity of humanity. Human nature . . . cannot honor a helpless man."[11]

Douglass's newfound conviction of his own internal dignity sparked him to pursue a life free from bondage. In September 1838, Douglass disguised himself as a free Black sailor, hopped on a steamboat, and escaped north. He chose for himself a new surname—Douglass was a character in Sir Walter Scott's epic poem *The Lady of the Lake*—to replace the one he had been given on the plantation. He worked first as a day laborer in Bedford, Massachusetts, proud at last to join the ranks of men paid for their work, before being "discovered" by acolytes of the abolitionist William Lloyd Garrison at a New Bedford anti-slavery meeting. Before long, Garrison had hired him, on a respectable annual salary of $450, to tell the story of his journey from bondage to freedom to abolitionist audiences all over New England.

His lecture "Self-Made Men," like Douglass's writing more broadly, was simultaneously a clarion call to abolish chattel slavery in the United States and an expression of full-throated optimism about the country that had tolerated it for so long. His work proclaimed that America was, or at least could one day soon be, a place where any man, "whether Caucasian or Indian, whether Anglo-Saxon or Anglo-African," could become a "self-made man."[12]

We do not know how "Self-Made Men" was received that particular October night, although we do know that Douglass was a consummate and impressive orator. The suffragette Elizabeth Cady Stanton, who saw Douglass speak in Boston in 1842, later recalled how he had "stood there like an African Prince, conscious of his dignity and power, grand in his physical proportions, majestic in his wrath."[13]

But he likely had other things on his mind that night. While Douglass was in Philadelphia praising America's promise of equality, another former friend and colleague, the white abolitionist John Brown, had given up on the American dream altogether. Convinced that America had been indelibly corrupted by slavery, Brown hoped to establish a new, slavery-free nation in the Appalachian Mountains and was willing to die—and indeed kill—to achieve it. Two nights earlier, Brown and twenty-one allies, many of whom had escaped enslavement, had led a raid on the US arsenal in Harpers Ferry, Virginia, prompting a two-day siege. That morning, Brown and his six remaining conspirators (five had fled, and the rest had been killed) had been taken into custody by a company of US Marines. By the end of the year, all would be executed for treason.

Just two weeks before the raid, Douglass had met with Brown, who had asked him to join his cause. But Douglass had refused. He had been born into slavery and seen firsthand its horrors, and he had seen, too, the collective apathy with which so many white, ostensibly liberal Americans treated their Black brethren, publicly advocating for human equality while condoning slavery or even holding slaves themselves. Nevertheless, Douglass still believed that it was through America, rather than in spite of it, that men like him could achieve true equality and true freedom. He had maintained a steadfast faith in the American promise, often breaking with other colleagues to do so. By this time, Douglass had already become estranged from Garrison, in part because of Garrison's unwillingness to try to legislate abolition within, rather than around, the existing political system.

However, Douglass's meeting with Brown was enough to put him under suspicion, at least for a time. A warrant had gone out for his arrest. Immediately after delivering his speech, Douglass fled home to Rochester, New York, then crossed the border into Canada. He spent the better part of the next year and a half abroad, lecturing around the United Kingdom. It was only in spring of 1860, following the death of his daughter Annie, that Douglass would return, once the political furor over Harpers Ferry had died down.

For the rest of his life, Douglass would continue to express his faith in an America that—though he often roundly criticized its hypocrisy—he saw as perhaps the only place on earth where self-made men had a chance to shake loose the shackles of their birth. He would go on to present "Self-Made Men" countless times over the next thirty years. He would last deliver it in 1893, two years before his death and thirty years after the Emancipation Proclamation had announced that all people born, like Douglass, into slavery would at last be considered free.

⁓⁓

IF BEAU BRUMMELL represented the apex of the aristocratic, European model of self-making, then Frederick Douglass personified in his life and work its democratic, American alternative. Douglass did not originate the term "self-made men"—the phrase was first popularized, if not exactly invented, by the politician Henry Clay, who had used it in an 1832 speech to the US Senate—but he would ultimately become synonymous with it.

Self-making, for Douglass, was not simply a privilege afforded to those imbued with an innate gift, as the thinkers of the Renaissance believed. Rather, Douglass insisted, self-making was an act anyone could participate in, so long as they were willing to work hard. The self was an open field to be tilled; the self-maker had to learn to carefully cultivate it, through mental and physical toil alike, if he wanted to be able to shape his own destiny.

True nobility was to be found exclusively in the will to work. Indeed, in one of his editions of "Self-Made Men," Douglass directly quotes a Robert Nicoll poem (helpfully titled "True Nobility") that both echoes and builds upon Montemagno's and Bracciolini's Renaissance dialogues of the same name.

> *If manliness be in his heart*
> *He noble birth may claim.*
> *We ask not from what land he came,*
> *Nor where his youth was nursed;*
> *If pure the stream, it matters not*
> *The spot from whence it burst.*[14]

For Douglass, and in the American democratic tradition more broadly, self-making had a profound moral element. It was not simply something someone could choose to do in the service of personal self-betterment. Rather, it was a political and ethical necessity, the condition that legitimized human freedom in the first place. As Douglass had said, the Clays and Websters and Lincolns of the world had to earn their sonship, proving that they deserved to be the children of such illustrious fathers. So, too, were all Americans, Black and white alike, called to cultivate their own selves in order to prove their worthiness to participate in this new and dangerous phenomenon: democracy.

"We have as a people," Douglass told his listeners, "no past and very little present, but a boundless and glorious future. . . . Our moral atmosphere is full of the inspiration of hope and courage. Every man has his chance. If he cannot be President he can, at least, be prosperous. In this respect, America is not only the exception to the general rule, but the social wonder of the world."[15]

Douglass scoffs at what he sees as the traditional European model of social hierarchy, one characterized by "divine-right governments and . . . [Roman Catholic] doctrines; with her sharply defined and firmly fixed classes."[16] But there is something of a religious sense, nevertheless, in his portrait of the workings of the world. God may not have predetermined the social order, in Douglass's account, but he has nevertheless arranged for some kind of connection between hard work and positive outcome. Douglass's world, deep down, is a fundamentally fair one, an orderly one, running on right moral principles. The wise man, Douglass insists, "knows that the laws of God are perfect and unchangeable. He knows that health is maintained by right living; that disease is cured by the right use of remedies; that bread is produced by tilling the soil; that knowledge is obtained by study; that wealth is secured by saving and that battles are won by fighting. To him, the lazy man is the unlucky man and the man of luck is the man of work."[17] Custom, circumstance, birth—these may lack divine weight. But the moral character of hard work remains, for Douglass, thoroughly enchanted.

⁓⁓

BUT DOUGLASS'S VISION of self-making—one that blends a moral call to self-cultivation, a faith in the fairness of the universe, and a vision of hard work as the animating principle—was not unique. Rather, Douglass was consciously working within and expanding upon the post-Enlightenment liberal political tradition. American thought had been in dialogue with this tradition since the republic's founding nearly a century before.

The political history of liberalism is, of course, too long and complex to encapsulate here. Nevertheless, for our purposes, when we talk about liberalism, what we are talking about is a discourse, largely but not exclusively centered around English and Scottish philosophers of the Enlightenment period, that focused its intellectual efforts on the promotion of human freedom as a necessity for human flourishing. It is out of this tradition that we find, for example, the concept of human rights, those inalienable qualities by which all men have the right to (in the words of the English political theorist John Locke) life, liberty, and property. All human beings (or, at least, all men) should be understood not merely as members of a class or clan but as autonomous individuals, each with the same fundamental worth as any other. A virtuous political system had to account for and reflect that truth, preserving and sustaining these inalienable rights. The founders of the American project understood their Constitution as an attempt at enshrining such a virtuous system in law. Life, liberty, and property may have made its way into the Declaration of Independence as life, liberty, and the pursuit of happiness, but the fundamentals were there. "We hold these truths to be self-evident, that all men are created equal, that they are endowed by their Creator with certain unalienable Rights."[18]

Central to the liberal narrative of America was the quintessentially Enlightenment idea that mankind had, in a sense, outgrown its childhood. Paternalistic authority might have been all well and good for the men of another era, but, having cut their leading strings, men were now fit to govern themselves. America's founding fathers were highly conscious of themselves as participants in an experiment, one whose success would prove right their faith in human equality. In 1787, for example, Alexander Hamilton opened the *Federalist Papers*—among the most influential of the United States' early political documents—by marveling that "it seems to have been reserved to the people of this country . . . to decide the important question, whether societies of men are really capable or not of establishing good government from reflection and choice, or whether they are forever destined to depend for their political constitutions on accident and force."[19] The eyes of the whole world, Hamilton knew, were on America. Old Europe would be watching to see whether the new republic succeeded or failed.

That same year, the politician James Wilson attempted to persuade the Pennsylvania convention to adopt what we now think of as the US Constitution by celebrating the uniqueness of the "scene, hitherto unparalleled, which America now exhibits to the world—a gentle, a peaceful, a voluntary, and a deliberate transition . . . only as progressive steps in improving the knowledge of government and increasing the happiness of society and mankind."[20]

The story of history, in other words, was a story where human beings were growing in maturity. At last come of age, they were finally in a position to reject dependency—on a church, on a crown—in favor of this promised self-governance.

But self-governance by a nation required self-governance by individuals. A political order that granted power to the people could only sustain itself if the people in question were capable of showing themselves to be responsible. Indeed, the logic went, freedom required certain kinds of self-control. To be unable to control oneself was to exist in a kind of moral slavery, an image that recurs in much of liberal thought. There was, of course, political slavery, to be subject to the tyranny of an external force. In the 1770s, for example, New York loyalists to the British crown, wary of brewing revolutionary fervor, cautioned one another against the dangers of "becom[ing] enslaved by Tyrants within."[21] But there was also slavery to one's own passions, the self in bondage to its baser instincts. It is this kind of slavery—rather than, say, the chattel slavery of American plantations—that then congressman Abraham Lincoln condemns in his 1842 Temperance Address, more than twenty years before his Emancipation Proclamation. For Lincoln, abolishing alcoholism—a scourge on human free will—would signify "a stronger bondage broken; a viler slavery, manumitted; a greater tyrant deposed."[22] Only through a strict program of national temperance, Lincoln told audiences, would "the victory . . . be complete—when there shall be neither a slave nor a drunkard on the earth."[23]

Such language might seem remarkably tone-deaf against the backdrop of widespread American chattel slavery. But, perhaps surprisingly, it forms a major part of Douglass's own political understanding. Chattel slavery, for Douglass, was an unmitigated moral evil, but moral evils came about, in part, because slaveholders were in bondage to the worst part of their own natures. They, no less than the men they enslaved, were obligated to practice self-cultivation in the service of virtue. In his 1845 address "Intemperance and Slavery," Douglass posited that "if we could but make the world sober, we would have no [chattel] slavery."[24] American acceptance of slavery as an institution, he insisted, was a form of drunkenness, one that careful self-mastery could overcome. "If the slaveholder would be sober for a moment . . . we could get a public opinion sufficiently strong to break the relation of master and slave."[25]

Douglass's optimism here is rooted in one fundamental assumption: that human beings, deep down, are perfectible. The moral work they do in self-examination, as well as the intellectual and physical labor they perform, will gradually make them better. This self-cultivation, in turn, will lead to the creation of a freer and more equal society, in which slavery has been abolished altogether. One form of slavery, he is convinced, begets another.

⁓

YET HOW COULD so many good, committed liberals—philosophers and statesmen who were otherwise so dedicated to the ideals of human freedom and self-governance—allow chattel slavery to flourish in America? Indeed, although much of Europe practiced slavery throughout the seventeenth and eighteenth centuries, the two countries by far most guilty of the practice were Great Britain and the United States. The irony of such a contradiction was not lost on people at the time. The Scottish philosopher John Millar remarked in 1779 that "it affords a curious spectacle to observe that the same people who talk in a high strain of political liberty . . . make no scruple of reducing a great proportion of their fellow-creatures into circumstances by which they are not only deprived of property but almost of every species of right."[26] The English essayist Samuel Johnson put it even more succinctly: "How is it that we hear the loudest yelp for liberty from the drivers of negroes?"[27]

The answer to that question can tell us something not only about slavery in America but also about the shadow side of the American vision of self-making as a whole, an insidious undercurrent that will continue to run throughout the narrative of American self-creation. The first part of the answer is intellectual. Human freedom was envisaged as morally earned and, furthermore, attained by certain actions and attitudes more associated with colonizers than with those colonized. Central to the liberal tradition is the double image of cultivation. Human dignity is inextricably linked to the claiming and transformation of land (and subsequently of the self, the interior landscape). What separates mankind in his intellectual, enlightened adulthood from those seeming savages we find in the accounts of, among others, Rousseau, Montaigne, and Diderot, was his ability to exercise control over nature.

In John Locke's 1690 *Second Treatise of Government*—one of the foundational texts of the liberal political tradition—he argues that private property is legitimized through human ingenuity. Locke invites the reader to ask what the difference is between private property and that which belongs to nature itself. His answer: human effort. "He that is nourished by the acorns he picked up under an oak," Locke writes, "or the apples he gathered from the trees in the wood, has certainly appropriated them to himself. . . . That labor put a distinction between them and common: that added something to them more than nature, the common mother of all, had done, and so they became his private right."[28]

The cultivation of land and, more broadly, the exercise of human will and creativity over nature became the primary mechanisms for thinking about the human condition. The landowner tilling his fields became the paradigm for what it meant to be a civilized human being in the first place. He was inevitably contrasted with uncivilized or savage peoples, who were seen as incapable of exercising such control, supposedly living freely off the bounty of nature. Locke also had a hand in drafting the 1669 *Fundamental Constitutions of Carolina*, which enshrined in law every freeman's "absolute power and authority over his negro slaves."[29] Liberal language about human rights was in this regard often contradictory—insisting on equality and yet locating human dignity in highly specific conceptions of what (some) people were capable of doing. Those who did not fit the paradigm of what human beings should be, conversely, were understood as moral children, still needing the authoritative guidance of those civilizations that had already come of age. Thus, for example, does the English philosopher and statesman John Stuart Mill, a major proponent of the ideal of personal liberty who was nevertheless employed by the colonial East India Company, insist in 1874 that so-called barbarians are too intellectually immature to observe a social contract. "They cannot be depended on for observing any rules," he announced, and therefore "nations which are still barbarous have not got beyond the period during which it is likely to be for their benefit that they should be conquered and held in subjection by foreigners."[30]

Even Douglass himself draws such a parallel between the stereotypes of hardworking, self-cultivating America and the indolent, naturally bountiful Africa in "Self-Made Men." "Under the palm tree of Africa," Douglass argues, "man finds, without effort, food, raiment and shelter. For him, there, Nature has done all and he has done nothing. The result is that the glory of Africa is in her palms—and not in her men."[31]

The democratic narrative of self-making, in other words, relied heavily on the tensions between the universal moral imperative to self-create—heavily bound up with ideas of colonial conquest and the mastery of nature—and the implicit rejection of those who either would not or could not do so. After all, self-creation was, at least theoretically, open to everybody willing to work hard and claim property, particularly land, for themselves. Therefore, those who failed to do so must in some way deserve their socially inferior positions. The democratic promise of self-making came with a troubling corollary that would prove foundational to modern self-creation narratives: you could blame the people that didn't make themselves. Like the aristocratic tradition of Sade and Brummell, the seemingly more democratic narrative of self-creation also neatly divided the world into robust self-makers and barbarous children. Whereas the aristocratic tradition assigned little ethical weight to this distinction—people were either special or they weren't—the democratic tradition loaded self-making with morality. You were *supposed* to shape your own fate, so if you didn't, it meant that you had failed.

〜✥〜

WHILE THE LIBERAL intellectual tradition often relied heavily on these images of cultivation and the civilizer-savage binary, such a binary is hardly solely responsible for the founding fathers' tolerance of chattel slavery. Very few liberal thinkers outright defended the practice. Even Locke, who helped assure its legality, only ever advocates for one form of what he sees as just slavery, that of the prisoner of war defeated in a fair battle.

Rather, many philosophers and politicians supported slavery for a far less intellectually ambitious reason: it was financially convenient. Slavery in England had allowed for the importation of luxury goods like chocolate and sugar from the colonies. Slavery in the United States was a major economic engine of the young republic, one that helped ensure, among other apparent luxuries, a steady supply of cheap cotton. In England, aspirant members of the ton had achieved self-expression by purchasing the clothing and other external accoutrements of upwardly mobile life without worrying too much about the slave labor behind it. In America, too, a middle-class lifestyle was far easier to achieve if you had ready access to affordable luxury goods and unpaid human labor to tend your home and lands. Thus, for example, did founding father Patrick Henry publicly decry slavery as "repugnant to humanity . . . inconsistent with the Bible, and destructive to liberty" before turning around and admitting that he in fact owned slaves. His defense? "The general inconvenience of living here without them."[32] Across the pond in England—where about a million people lived in slavery—a satirical 1788 poem mocked slaveholders' hypocrisy and greed:

> I own I am shocked at the purchase of slaves . . .
> I pity them greatly, but I must be mum
> For how could we do without sugar and rum?
> Especially sugar, so needful we see
> What, give up our dessert, our coffee and tea?[33]

The aristocratic vision of self-making had often explicitly mandated an underclass: those who were not so fortunately chosen. These were the people Sade's libertines could rape and murder with impunity. On a less extreme level, they were the John Bulls, the bourgeois everyman, against whom Beau Brummell defined his highly subtle style.

But all too often, the democratic vision of self-making—the one where every hard worker could achieve a middle-class lifestyle—also had its implicit underclass: the enslaved peoples, conveniently left out of many liberal narratives (though not, of course, Douglass's), whose labor made the trappings of luxury affordable to the bourgeoisie.

Self-cultivation in the first century of the United States thus came to take on a double meaning, two narratives that had already begun to intertwine. The first was the idea of moral self-cultivation: the virtuous citizen who had to learn to control himself and, particularly, his impulses in order to participate in this new political experiment. The second was the ideal of self-making as a means of joining the comfortable bourgeoisie, of working hard in order to obtain certain creature comforts and display outward signifiers associated with the middle class. The American promise, after all, was that a lowborn man could, with enough effort, become a gentleman. Now, he had to learn to act like one. Once you pulled yourself up by your bootstraps, as the age-old idiom went, you had to play the part.

⚬⚬⚬

THE EARLY YEARS of American publishing were dominated by the cottage industry of what we might call self-improvement books: manifestos that would help readers navigate their journey into gentility. These books were, in essence, *The Courtier* for a world without princes, *Vivian Grey* for a world without aristocrats. They explained how to live virtuously and how, no less importantly, to demonstrate that virtue to other people.

An American reader anxious to become a self-made man had many options at his disposal. He could peruse the more genteel "courtesy books"—like 1715's

*The School of Good Manners*—designed to help American readers, particularly children, mimic the social codes of their upper-class English counterparts. Some of the advice given by these books involved exterior signifiers, for example, how to act at a dinner party. ("Gnaw not thy bones at the table but clean them with thy knife.")[34] Other maxims were moral, designed to foster the appropriate virtuous attitude toward work. ("Let thy Recreation be Lawful, Brief, and Seldom," *The School of Good Manners* solemnly advised children, encouraging them, too, to "Let thy Meditations be of Death, Judgment, and Eternity.")[35] A young George Washington even put out his own such book: *Rules of Civility and Decent Behavior in Company and Conversation*, an adaptation of a Renaissance-era French text exhorting self-control, both aesthetic ("Bedew no mans face with your Spittle, by approaching too near him when you Speak") and moral ("Labor to keep alive in your breast that little spark of celestial fire called conscience").[36]

An American aspirant could read, too, secular hagiographies depicting the lives of industrious and virtuous self-made men in a manner once reserved for Christian saints, designed to inspire the reader to live a similarly self-controlled life. There was *Representative Men*, written by the transcendentalist philosopher Ralph Waldo Emerson in 1850 and featuring biographical sketches of Plato, Montaigne, and Napoleon, among others. Writer Charles Seymour's 1858 *Self-Made Men* featured sixty-two such sketches, with a more explicitly American focus. Representative self-made men included former president Andrew Jackson and statesman Daniel Webster. These sketches tended to follow a predictable pattern: a lowborn man works hard, studies, exercises sobriety in all aspects of his life, and ultimately succeeds in achieving a respectable station.

Even the abolitionist author of *Uncle Tom's Cabin*, Harriet Beecher Stowe, published two hagiographic volumes, *Men of Our Times* (1868) and *The Lives and Deeds of Our Self-Made Men* (1872). The latter featured flattering life stories of both Frederick Douglass and Abraham Lincoln. Lincoln's life story had already passed into the wider American mythos; he had been born in poverty in a Kentucky log cabin, only to "work all day as long as any of us, and study by fire-light in the log house half the night."[37] Importantly, while many of the men profiled achieved a degree of economic success, very few of them were entrepreneurs or became wildly, disproportionately wealthy, at least not by the standards of the robber barons and other self-made millionaires who would come to the forefront in the next century's Gilded Age. The self-made man of antebellum America was resolutely middle-class. He received a proportionate, but by no means excessive, reward for his sobriety and virtue. He exemplified not greed but, in Stowe's words, "frugality, strict temperance, self-reliance, and indomitable industry." His goals were only ever "to know and do THE RIGHT."[38] Wealth was never to be pursued for its own sake but rather was understood as a moral reward for virtue in an orderly world, one in which the idea of work took on a quasi-sacred significance. It was through virtuous labor that a would-be self-made man could simultaneously lift himself up out of poverty or anonymity and, far more important, achieve his full humanity and fulfill his God-ordained purpose. After all, wasn't the act of cultivation—of land and of the self alike—what separated civilized, mature humanity from its barbarous and savage counterpart?

This understanding of cultivation took on not only a moral but a spiritual cast. Self-cultivation wasn't something that you should do only to be a good citizen but also to be in harmony with your divine purpose. God—a less doctrinally conceived god, to be sure, than the God of historic Christianity, but a god all the same—wanted you, as we might put it in contemporary terms, to be your best self.

We can see this understanding of self-cultivation as a spiritual imperative in "Self-Culture," an 1838 lecture by the Harvard-trained minister William Ellery Channing. Channing was a Unitarian, a member of a Christian but somewhat unorthodox religious tradition that grew out of the Protestant Reformation and that had become particularly prominent in England and America. For Unitarians like Channing, traditional Christian understandings of original sin—and the human depravity that went with it—were deeply wrongheaded. Human beings, Channing believed, could reach perfection in this life; indeed, it was their divine purpose to do so. "Self-culture is possible because we can enter into and search ourselves," Channing insisted. "We have a still nobler power, that of acting on, determining, and forming ourselves. . . . We can fix our eyes on perfection and make almost every thing speed toward it."[39] Like Giovanni Pico della Mirandola before him, Channing saw self-cultivation as the very thing that made us human. "Of all the discoveries which men need to make," he argued, "the most important . . . is that of the self-forming power treasured up in themselves. . . . There is more of divinity in it than in the force which impels the outward universe."[40]

Here, too, the language of self-making and the language of divinity are inextricable from one another. Whatever is divine, whatever is supernatural, whatever is spiritual in the world we live in, it is to be found by looking inward: into the power and potential of our own selves.

❧

THESE BOOKS AND texts were part of the development of the democratic strain of American self-making. For starters, they helped establish the narrative of the virtuous self-made man in the American consciousness. But they had another purpose as well. They helped codify self-making as a fundamentally private endeavor, one that each individual, by reading and internalizing these self-help books and guides, had to do alone. Central to the narrative of the American self-made man was an assumption of fatherlessness, whether literal (as in the case of Douglass) or metaphorical. In America, men were their own fathers. By directly inspiring readers to civic virtue, without an intermediate authority—be it a religious figure or a familial one—these books made the case to American readers that self-creation was a fundamentally private proposition, to be attained without social influence. In Emerson's *Representative Men*, for example, we learn that "the boy believes there is a teacher who can sell him wisdom . . . [but] the aid we have from others is mechanical compared with the discovery of nature in us."[41] Likewise, Channing reminds his listeners that self-cultivation often involves rejecting or turning away from the noxious influence of other people. "Another important means of self-culture," he insists, "is to free ourselves from the power of human opinion and example, except as far as this is sanctioned by our own deliberate judgment."[42] Only our interior conscience is seen as authoritative. What we feel, what we want, these are the authentic elements of who we are. Human opinion—no less than in the writings of the Enlightenment philosophers—can be consigned to the dustbin of custom.

Self-cultivation, these authors suggest, is also a form of self-expression. By cultivating our interior landscapes, we are showing the world who we really are, liberated both from the so-called slavery of our baser instincts and from the bondage of other men's opinions. As Emerson put it, "There are in each of us all the elements of moral and intellectual excellence; that is to say, if you act out yourself, you will attain and exhibit a perfect character."[43] The self-made man didn't so much create himself from scratch as he learned to support what was already there all along by weeding his vices and tending to his virtues.

BUT FEW AMERICAN handbooks of self-making come close to the optimistic intensity of another of America's paradigmatic self-creators: writer, philosopher, and founding father Benjamin Franklin, for whom moral self-culture and bourgeois industry were always inextricable from one another. For Franklin, the whole project of life, as he recounts in his 1791 autobiography, was "the bold and arduous project of arriving at moral perfection."[44] In both his *Autobiography* and his more practical books, like the regularly updated *Poor Richard's Almanack*, Franklin expresses the importance of control over the self for both moral and economic benefit. We learn, for example, that he meticulously structures his time, labeling each of his waking hours with a particular purpose in the hopes of making the most out of his day. He describes in detail his method, how he "made a little book, in which I allotted a page for each of the virtues."[45] For Franklin, these virtues were Temperance, Silence, Order,

Resolution, Frugality, Industry, Sincerity, Justice, Moderation, Cleanliness, Tranquility, Chastity, and Humility.

Franklin goes on: "I rul'd each page with red ink, so to have seven columns, one for each day of the week. . . . I cross'd these columns with thirteen red lines, marking the beginning of each line with the first letter of one of the virtues, on which line, and in its proper column, I might mark, by a little black spot, every fault I found upon examination to have been committed respecting that virtue upon the day."[46] Virtue, for Franklin, is not just inextricable from the industriousness of economic success. It is literally to be measured in the same way, with a profit-loss ledger. And the kinds of virtues Franklin was interested in—sobriety, simple living ("Early to bed and early to rise / makes a man healthy, wealthy, and wise," one his most famous maxims goes), financial frugality—were tailor-made to help readers secure a comfortable middle-class existence. Virtue was an easily intelligible system, something akin to the modern-day life hack. Arrange your life the right way, squeeze every moment of productivity out of your time like so, and suddenly you can be not only virtuous morally but also successful in business, the trappings of your exterior life reflecting the worthiness cultivated within. "To acquire those [virtues] which are wanting," Franklin once wrote a friend, "is the subject of an art. . . . If a man would become a painter . . . he must be taught the principles of the art, be shown all the methods of working, and how to acquire the habits of using properly all the instruments. . . . My art of virtue also has its instruments, and teaches the manner of using them."[47]

Franklin was not a Christian. While he included among his goals the desire to "imitate Jesus and Socrates," he, like Channing, was suspicious of some of Christianity's more esoteric doctrinal requirements. Rather, he, like many of the Enlightenment philosophers, was a Deist, believing in a vague, impersonal creator-God who had made the world then left it to its own devices. It fell to human beings, particularly those human beings who knew how to exercise their power, to remake the world. And what was most divine in them—Franklin, like so many of his contemporaries, believed—was their ability to exercise that creative power. That such internal virtue coincided with material wealth was a convenient bonus. Our ability to shape our lives had become the foundation of both a new political philosophy and a new theology, one governed by the notion that our self-cultivation would help us become the creatures we were always supposed to be. Self-making was simultaneously a creative act and an expressive one. It was a chance to show the world who we really are and to achieve the success that is our due. In this way, the democratic vision of self-making resembles what we might today call self-actualization: the idea that becoming our truest, best, and most successful selves is not only desirable but in fact the fulfillment of our purpose on this planet.

The groundwork had already been laid for a new way of thinking about self-making, one that linked moral worth with productive industry and financial success. Certain kinds of people who were willing to work hard and pull themselves up by their bootstraps were not only capable of changing their circumstances but positively deserved their success in life. The democratic model of self-making was, in this way, both a promise of liberation and a new kind of prison. The life of a middle-class gentleman was, theoretically, available to any (free, male) person willing to practice the art of self-cultivation. But this also meant the birth of a new narrative about those who failed to make themselves: the idea that they were simply too lazy, too feckless, or too foolish to succeed. After all, if Frederick Douglass's promise of the self-made man was open to everybody, then anyone unable to self-make must have failed to take advantage of the promise of the American dream.

By the next century, this moralizing of success would become even more extreme. The Gilded Age would transform the dream of democratic self-making into a cult of the capitalist entrepreneur. The fig leaf of virtue would largely be forgotten. And wealth itself would become divine.

# five

# "LIGHT CAME IN AS A FLOOD"

I N THE AUTUMN OF 1878, THOMAS ALVA EDISON HAD A PROBLEM. He hadn't invented the light bulb—yet. Or, to put it more precisely, he *had* invented a light bulb, but he couldn't keep it lit for more than a few minutes at a time. He still had not figured out how to regulate the temperature of the light bulb's internal filament, meaning that the incandescent bulb would immediately overheat, and the filament would promptly melt down.

Unfortunately, Edison was running out of time. All over North America and Europe, inventors like him were working on, and patenting, their own electric projects. Sooner or later, electricity would wind up harnessed by somebody. The English chemist Joseph Swan, Edison knew, was hard at work on a rival light bulb. Two Canadians, Henry Woodward and Mathew Evans, had already patented an inefficient design five years before.

But, that fall, Edison had an even more pressing deadline to face: the journalists were coming. Back in September, he'd assured the popular press that his latest invention, the incandescent light bulb, was complete. "I have it now," he assured the *New York Sun*'s Amos Cummings, boasting that "everybody will wonder why they have never thought of it—it is so simple."[1] He'd already made his sales pitch: "When the brilliancy and cheapness of the lights are made known to the public," (which would be, he assured Cummings, in just "a few weeks") America would undergo another scientific revolution. "Illumination by carbureted hydrogen gas"—the inefficient, expensive, and often dangerous gas lamps common on American streets and in American homes— would be "discarded." In its place, electricity.

Electricity, to the Gilded Age mind, wasn't just a technology. Rather, it was a mysterious, thrilling, invisible, quasi-magical force that had become synonymous with scientific discovery and with the whole arc of human progress. It was, as one guidebook put it, that "subtle and vivifying current," the source, not just of light, but of life itself. "Comply with electricity's conditions," another writer marveled, "then but turn a key, and the servant of all life will be present in life and power."[2]

If electricity was magic, then Edison was its chief magician, at least according to the press. He was the "Wizard of Menlo Park," a reference to his New Jersey laboratory, as well as the "Napoleon of Science," the "Genius of Menlo Park," and the "Jersey Columbus." He was almost certainly America's greatest inventor. But he was also one of the country's canniest self-promoters, forging close personal relationships with those journalists who could be trusted to write adoring, if not always strictly accurate, copy.

Just one year prior, Edison had invented the phonograph to great fanfare. Restless, he'd at once promised reporters that he would produce "something at least as good as the phonograph every year."[3] The papers—their circulation boosted by the scores of fans clamoring to find out what their favorite wizard would be up to next—had bolstered that narrative.

The time for the promised demonstration drew closer. Already, rumors of the impending revelation had caused something of a financial crisis in London, as gas shares plummeted in anticipation of Edison's latest success. One of the inventor's associates urged him to form a British-based electricity company as soon as possible, the better to capitalize upon the "universal free advertising" the *Sun*, the *New York Herald*, and other papers had given him, "such as cannot be bought for money under any circumstances."[4]

Edison's invention may not have been ready yet, but Edison certainly was. The inventor, as ever, had a plan. He informed journalists that they would each receive a brief, private demonstration of the new light bulb's capacities in his Menlo Park laboratory. They could marvel at what Edison had achieved before he swiftly ushered them away, ensuring they'd be out of the room long before the bulb burned out. Edison's reputation as a cunning genius would remain intact.

The plan worked. The press, credulous as ever, rhapsodized about the "light: clear, cold, and beautiful." In contrast to the famously harsh electric arc lights, the most common available electric light at the time, "there was nothing irritating to the eye." Instead, they marveled, "you could trace the veins in your hands and the spots and lines upon your finger nails by its brightness," pronouncing the invention "perfect."[5] Edison, for his part, kept the charade up nicely, telling another visiting journalist that the bulb on display would burn "forever. Almost."[6]

In the end, of course, Edison worked out the kinks of what would become one of the nineteenth century's most emblematic inventions. On New Year's Eve of 1879—a little over a year after the press demonstration—Edison would host another, larger public display, this time with a bulb that didn't burn out. (The secret? Carbon filaments, as Edison had discovered in October of that year.) By then, Edison's displays and his claims of ever more awe-inspiring intellectual glory had become regular fixtures of the news cycle. As one exasperated newspaperman groaned, "There is no reason why [Edison] should not for the next 20 years completely solve the problem of the electric light twice a year without any way interfering with its interest of novelty."[7] Edison's gamble, blending genuine technological innovation with a couple of white lies and a cozy relationship with the press, had paid off. He may have harnessed electricity, but he had also harnessed another invisible power: celebrity.

Edison understood that success in the Gilded Age was a matter of exertion and carefully managing public expectations. Sure, he had come up with the phonograph, but when asked by some guests which historical figure he'd most like to hear on his new invention, he'd shocked them by naming onetime French political upstart Napoleon. "You know," he explained to his audience, who had apparently expected him to name Jesus Christ, "I like a hustler."[8]

THE STORY OF American self-making in the antebellum era had been the story of the American dream: work hard, pull yourself up by your bootstraps, and free yourself from the bondage of the outmoded (and European) world of custom, convention, and class.

This narrative, as we have already seen, involved not just an implicit morality but a whole metaphysical worldview. Human beings were supposed to self-make, fulfilling their fundamental purpose. And, no less important, the fulfillment of that purpose would somehow be rewarded in this life with material success.

By the late nineteenth century, the self-made man would no longer be understood merely as a virtuous, frugal citizen but rather a successful capitalist entrepreneur, someone who had figured out how to harness money and bend it to his will. He was, increasingly, a mogul or an entrepreneur. He might be a captain of industry like Andrew Carnegie (the steel magnate who was born in poverty in rural Scotland) or John D. Rockefeller (the billionaire oilman born to a New York lumberman). Or else he might have made his fortune—as did Rowland H. Macy, Alexander T. Stewart, and John Wanamaker—hawking luxury goods to the newly rich through increasingly popular department and dry-goods stores.

Money came to be understood as the natural goal of the self-maker, rather than a fortuitous side benefit of a more broadly virtuous life. Meanwhile, poverty came increasingly to be seen as the natural consequence of being a failed self-maker, a just punishment for a moral failing. Those who could not or would not achieve riches in this dizzying new economy were now understood as being responsible for their own sad fate. As one representative sermon from the era, preached by the New York pastor Henry Ward Beecher, put it, "No man in this land suffers from poverty unless it be more than his fault—unless it be his sin."[9]

This linking of work and morality ultimately gave rise to another phenomenon: the reimagining of the wealth gap as a metaphysical reality, based on an eclectic mix of scientific and spiritual principles. Equal parts quack science and vague spirituality, a number of movements—the craze for social Darwinism, the birth of the self-help phenomenon known as New Thought—attempted to explain the era's wealth inequality by understanding it as a natural consequence of the laws of nature, which were, at least in part, divinely ordained.

If the Enlightenment saw a disenchantment of custom—there was no metaphysical or divine reality to the traditional social order—then the American Gilded Age saw a version of custom's rebirth, albeit in slightly modified form. The way your life turned out did, in fact, say something about your relationship with God, or providence, or nature, or whatever the source was of that mysterious and potentially magical energy that governed and animated human existence.

A capitalistic mirror image of the medieval worldview, the mythos of the Gilded Age self-made man held that the wealthy were, if not exactly chosen by God, then nevertheless more deserving of divine favor by virtue of their willingness to work hard and think positively. This spiritual power was increasingly understood not as a personal phenomenon—God picking certain geniuses as his chosen "bastards"—but rather as a resource to be mined. The power of self-making came to be portrayed as a kind of mysterious, unseen energy coursing through the world, which a clever and enterprising young man could learn how to harness and control.

An energy, in other words, that looked and sounded a lot like electricity itself.

WHEN IT CAME to the public imagination, at least, the line between scientific discovery and spiritual truth was easily blurred. Electricity—poorly understood, at least by average newspaper readers—was a source of both aesthetic and moral fascination. It was a pulsating power that had always flowed, invisibly, through human existence. In this triumphant era of technological discovery, men—clever, enterprising men like Thomas Edison—had now learned to use it for their own ends. "By means of electricity," Nathaniel Hawthorne wrote in his 1858 novella *The House of the Seven Gables*, "the world of matter has become a great nerve: vibrating thousands of miles in a breathless point of time."[10] The memoirist Henry Adams, likewise, recalled in 1910 his youthful experience of encountering the electric dynamo, an experience he casts as a discomfiting religious awakening. He felt the dynamo, he tells us, "as a moral force, much as the early Christians felt the cross." Adams goes on: "The planet itself seemed less impressive, in its old-fashioned . . . daily revolution, than this huge wheel, revolving within arm's length. . . . Before the end, one began to pray to it; inherited instinct taught the natural expression of man before silent and infinite force."[11] The electric dynamo was a literalization of human potential: ingenuity rendered into pulsating possibility. It was, for Adams, at once a "Mysterious Power!" and a "Gentle Friend," a "Despotic Master!" and a "Tireless Force!"[12]

All across America, electricity began to be understood, metaphorically or literally, as synonymous with the fundamental energy underpinning human technological progress. When, for example, the Businessman's Club of Evanston, Illinois, switched over to electric lighting in 1890, the organization staged a mammoth "pageant of progress," a celebration of the power of the human spirit to harness nature. The event culminated in a dirge played for the old world (represented by the gas lamps that were gradually dimmed and then put out), followed by a buoyant march as the three hundred electric bulbs were switched on for the first time.[13] Meanwhile, in New York City, one Broadway show, *Excelsior*, celebrated the Great White Way's adoption of electric lighting by dramatizing the battle between darkness and light, that "strife betwixt knowledge and ignorance which has constantly attended the advance of civilization."[14] Similarly, at the 1901 Pan-American Exposition, organizers staged a "Rainbow City" to celebrate the previous century's technological progress. Attendees were encouraged to walk past the "Bridge of Triumph" and the "Fountain of Abundance" before arriving at the exhibition's centerpiece: an enormous "Electric Tower," topped by a gold statue of the "Goddess of Light," a vision of electricity rendered literally divine.

This vision of human progress had, however, a shadow side. Almost invariably, celebrations of electricity featured ironic glimpses of those peoples the organizers felt lacked ingenuity. Non-white, non-Western peoples were used as props to signify the old, vanishing world order. The world, these celebrations insisted, was divided into two kinds of people: successful self-makers who had managed to achieve the liberal dream of technological mastery over nature, and those who remained in a childlike state of dependence. Self-cultivation, and cultivation of nature more broadly, were integral parts of becoming an enlightened human being.

This division was often portrayed in starkly racial terms. Just down the road from the Goddess of Light, the Rainbow City featured staged mockeries of Black Americans as well as non-white peoples more broadly. A troupe of 150 "Southern Darkies" performed "plantation song and dance," while a "Moorish Palace" offered attendees the chance to glimpse scantily clad women gyrating to ostensibly "oriental" music. Even more explicit was the 1893 Chicago World's Fair, where the "Court of Honor"—filled with buildings dedicated to electricity, agriculture, manufacture, and other examples of human power—was surrounded by exhibitions devoted to poking fun at perceived human savagery and the allegedly primitive cultures of Africans, Arabs, and Native Americans. "What an opportunity was here afforded to the scientific mind to descend the spiral of evolution," crowed the *Chicago Tribune* with wonder, "tracing humanity in its highest phrases down to its almost animalistic origins."[15] The implication was clear. Learn to harness electricity, marshal technology, and be one of history's doers or be left behind as a vestige of a savage past.

Meanwhile, scientifically dubious self-help books had started to use the language of science—including electricity and a related term, "magnetism"—to hawk products and methods they claimed could cure disease. Gershom Huff's 1853 *Electro-Physiology*, for example, insisted that most illness derived from the fact that many Americans had lost their natural ruggedness and instead become "servile imitators" of European decadence.[16] The cure, Huff insisted, was to properly balance the "electric fluid"—a mysterious "controlling force which imparts vigor to vitality"—in the body.[17] Likewise, John Bovee Dods's 1850 *The Philosophy of Electrical Psychology* argued that electricity was a kind of unifying force linking the spiritual and physical body. Dods posited an "electro-psychological state" in which men could be hypnotized by those who knew how to harness it.[18]

That's not to say that most Gilded Age Americans literally thought of electricity as divine or magical per se. But electricity, among other technological and scientific developments, became part of a wider vocabulary for a worldview that linked civilizational progress, personal self-reliance—particularly when it came to wealth and poverty—and a nebulous sense of divine justice. The world just worked a certain way, ensuring that some people, deserving people, would always come out on top. The worldview of Gilded Age America was coherent: those who worked hardest would always succeed.

This wasn't just a moral view. Rather, it was a scientific one. Or, to be even more precise, it was a view that blended science (and sometimes pseudoscience) and spirituality using vague but authoritative-sounding language about energy, magnetism, and life force to suggest that human life—and, indeed, the natural world more broadly—was governed by nebulous external forces that the mind could not just understand but harness. Looking within yourself and achieving success *out there* became even more closely intertwined.

The success of this new, hybrid worldview was strengthened by the fact that, increasingly, America was moving away from traditional, Christian accounts of the world, God, and how the two worked together. While most Americans were still happy to call themselves Christian and even attend church, their worldview was as influenced, if not more so, by the latest scientific developments as by what they heard from the pulpit. And the message there, too, was changing. Throughout the nineteenth century, many Christian churches, particularly Protestant ones, were actively seeking to reconcile themselves to what they saw as modern scientific discovery. In Europe, academics like David Strauss and Albert Schweitzer were trying to uncover the "historical Jesus," the presumably ordinary mortal man underneath layers of superstitious myth. In America, movements like Unitarianism actively sought to hold on to the perceived moral core of Christianity while doing away with its most discomfiting supernatural claims. Pastors like William Ellery Channing—of the previous chapter's "Self-Culture" lectures—and Henry Ward Beecher used their sermons to argue for a synthesis of traditional Christianity and new, progressive ideas about the human spirit.

~~~

As HENRY ADAMS recalled in his memoirs, what "puzzled" him most seriously about the Gilded Age was the "disappearance of religion."[19] During the late nineteenth century, Adams recalled, "the religious instinct had vanished, and could not be revived. . . . [That] the most intelligent society, led by the most intelligent clergy, in the most moral conditions . . . should have solved all the problems of the universe so thoroughly as to have quite ceased making itself anxious about past or future seemed . . . the most curious social phenomenon."[20]

But, as Adams himself recalled, that didn't mean that Gilded Age Americans weren't interested in the questions of religious life: What was it all for? What did it mean? What might be out there or, rather, in here, the energies coursing through human society as well as through the natural world? New scientific discoveries, often reshaped through spiritualized language, became mechanisms for thinking and talking about the inchoate forces governing human life.

Among the most prominent of these new discoveries were the theories of animal evolution promulgated by Charles Darwin. Published in England in 1859, Darwin's book *On the Origin of Species* had not just heralded a revolution in the scientific understanding of how certain species came to evolve into other species. It had also, against Darwin's own wishes, heralded a revolution in how the human experience itself was understood: as a constant, triumphant march toward progress and perfection that inevitably left unworthy inferiors in the dust. "The survival of the fittest"—a phrase absent from the original *On the Origin of Species* (although Darwin himself would ultimately come to use it)—became the lens through which to understand all human life.

For English philosopher and biologist Herbert Spencer, the man who coined the phrase, the survival of the fittest wasn't just a scientific fact about animal evolution. It was also, more pressingly, an immutable law about human societies. Spencer was the father of the set of theories known as social Darwinism, a rather simplistic understanding of Darwinian evolution that held, essentially, that all of human life was in competition for scarce resources. Those more capable of amassing wealth—and defeating their fellow man in the process—would live to pass on their genes to their ever more successful children. This was ultimately part of a wider arc of history that would end in humans evolving into their optimal selves. "Evolution," Spencer insisted, "can end only in the establishment of the greatest perfection and the most complete happiness."[21]

That "happiness" Spencer envisioned, however, wasn't for everybody. He had nothing but contempt for those he saw as unfit: nature's rejects, who were either too sick or too stupid or too lazy to attain the success he saw as the powerful man's due. Ultimately, Spencer predicted, the poor would die out—whether of illness or malnutrition or crime, he didn't much care—clearing the way for their genetically superior successors. "The whole effort of nature," Spencer wrote, was to "get rid of" the poor, "to clear the world of them and make room for better."[22] Some social progressives of the Victorian era, conscious of the wealth gap that marked nineteenth-century London, advocated for social reform to ameliorate the wretched conditions of the poor. But Spencer rejected such calls as not only unnecessary but actively wicked, an attempt to stem the tide of natural law itself. To keep the poor or sick alive, Spencer insisted, was to keep humanity in an artificial state of inferiority. Rather, "if they are sufficiently complete to live . . . it is well that they should live. If they are not sufficiently complete to live, they die, and it is best they should die."[23]

Spencer's view of the world was both scientific (or at least pseudoscientific) and spiritual. His understanding of the divine—he referred to it by the elliptical phrase "the Unknowable"—was certainly not orthodox, but it nevertheless gave a kind of moral valence to the natural order whose principles he so vigorously upheld. If the laws of nature declared survival of the fittest to be the fundamental human condition, then it was morally wrong to interfere. Whatever morality or rightness there existed in the world had to rest in allowing the plan of nature, or the Unknowable, to unfold. This plan, in Spencer's understanding, would culminate in humanity reaching its fullest potential. There was no contrast between "nature" and "civilization," such as we find in, say, the Enlightenment accounts of Locke or Rousseau. Rather, nature and civilization were one and the same. Human social life derived directly from natural law.

Here we find a somewhat curious reimagining of the medieval view of the role of custom in the social hierarchy. Our Enlightenment authors had rejected custom entirely, and with it the idea that there was anything natural or fixed about one's social position. But the social Darwinists, and the prophets of Gilded Age capitalism more broadly, renewed the link between the law of nature (a concept that occupied an uneasy middle ground between the explicitly theological "natural law" of Thomas Aquinas and scientific descriptivism) and human social outcomes. There was something running through human life that ensured that the deserving and hardworking achieved economic success and the lazy and indolent remained in poverty. That something, furthermore, had a moral and eschatological purpose: a progressive vision of human life in which each individual was just a link in a much longer chain. Spencer likens civilization to "the development of an embryo or the unfolding of the flower." It is, in other words, something that has a purpose.

Spencer's theories were already popular in England. Between the 1860s and the early twentieth century, his books would sell nearly four hundred thousand copies.[24] "Probably no other philosopher," one contemporary remarked, "ever had such a vogue as Spencer had from about 1870 to 1890."[25] Even Darwin himself was astonished—and more than a little horrified—by the public reaction to Spencer's interpretation of his work. Darwin ironically remarked on how he'd seen in one Manchester newspaper an article "showing that I have proved 'might is right' and therefore that Napoleon is right and every cheating tradesman is also right."[26]

American writers soon took up the drumbeat of social Darwinism, seeing in it a handy way of explaining away Gilded Age social inequality. Among the most influential of these advocates was William Graham Sumner, a Yale political scientist whose 1881 essay "Sociology" used the idea of social Darwinism in support of unfettered, dog-eat-dog capitalism. Economic competition—no less than the competition for food or water or territory among nonhuman creatures—was one of the ways that nature selected for the fittest. The only moral law, Sumner went on to say, was the law of harnessing nature itself, pursuing evolutionary self-interest to its natural conclusion. He rejected the idea that nature demanded any moral quality from human beings other than hard work. Instead, Sumner insisted—in language that echoed Machiavelli's sexually charged account more than three hundred years earlier—"nature is entirely neutral. She submits to him who most energetically and resolutely assails her. Nature could be harnessed and was malleable. She grants her rewards to the fittest, therefore, without regard to other considerations of any kind."[27]

Those rewards? Cold, hard cash. Money, for Sumner, was the divine energy of the universe converted into clearly quantifiable capital. "Millionaires," Sumner elsewhere insisted, "are a product of natural selection." Any kind of aid to the poor, conversely, was an unnatural "survival of the unfittest."[28]

Not only was it ethical to seek personal enrichment, Sumner argued, but it was necessary. Amassing money was how you knew you were in sync with natural law in the first place. "It would not be amiss," Sumner reflected, for children to hear "a sermon once in a while to reassure them, setting forth that it is not wicked to be rich, nay even, that it is not wicked to be richer than your neighbor."[29]

Sumner was not the only figure to meld religious doctrine and a new fascination with the magic of wealth. Henry Ward Beecher, a devotee of Spencer, preached social Darwinism from his Sunday pulpit, insisting that, in essence, God wanted people to be rich. Not that Beecher was that concerned with the exact dictates of God or the Bible. He saw himself, as many preachers did, as a liberalizing, modernizing force, someone for whom, as he told his congregation at Brooklyn's Plymouth Congregational Church, "the cords are not so tight" as they once were.[30] His Christianity was not the staid, backward-looking, conservative Christianity of an outmoded era, which he, like his Enlightenment forebears, derided as mere "superstition." Rather, "intelligent religion" could, he argued, accommodate this new theory of evolution, and with it this new vision of human perfectibility: the slow arc of history from "matter organic and animal," to matter "moral, intellectual, and civic," and finally "to communion with and unity with God himself."[31] All of creation was tending toward its final fulfillment. Darwinism, of the animal and social variety alike, was surely the work of a "benevolent intelligence . . . drawing up from the crude towards the ripe, from the rough towards the smooth, from bad to good, and from good through better to best."[32] Humankind was only getting better, so long as you didn't worry too much about those human beings progress had left behind.

Beecher also made literal an often implicit element of this new scientific-spiritual language of hard work and individual prosperity. The world's divine energy—the current of intellectual electricity, the powerful law of nature—was accessed not by looking outward to a God in the heavens, but inward into the self. Knowledge of God or the divine was not to be found in scripture, or by listening to a pastor, or by following a set of external rules. These were, after all, easily dispensable forms of custom. Rather, divine truth could be found by examining the self. Echoing earlier theorists like Ralph Waldo Emerson, Beecher insisted that "we cannot understand God by mere enunciation," simply repeating knowledge that comes to us from outside. Instead, "the elemental qualities of the divine disposition must be evolved in us first, and the application to the divine nature is gradually unfolded to us afterwards."[33]

It is impossible to overstate the role of this inward turn in the story of self-making. Not only the *truest* parts of the self but also the most *divine* could be accessed by looking inside oneself, rather than relying upon the customs or dictates of the outside world. The same law of nature that demanded the survival of the fittest could be harnessed by following one's own deepest instincts, especially those toward personal fulfillment and self-enrichment. The pursuit of money in the capitalist system was a kind of holy act, a form of self-expression by which those who hoped to claim the title of nature's fittest could most completely express their humanity. What it meant to be human, in other words, was to hustle. Our hustling instinct, furthermore, was the evidence of divine energy in us.

The moral element of democratic self-making—evident already in the civic virtue called for by Douglass and Channing—here reached its apotheosis: you are morally required to enrich yourself, at any cost.

━━◦━━

FOR THEIR PART, millionaires were happy to take this new religion of prosperity as, well, gospel. Plenty of the Gilded Age's robber barons spoke glowingly of this modern revelation. John D. Rockefeller, at one time the country's richest man, was also a regular churchgoer and Sunday school teacher at the Erie Street Baptist Mission Church, where he frequently sought to justify his own wealth on religious grounds. In one Sunday school address, Rockefeller summarily informed his young and impressionable listeners that "the growth of a large business is merely the survival of the fittest" and thus a fully appropriate subject to discuss before church. The Christian squeamishness about the less fortunate had to be squashed. After all, he insisted, "the American Beauty rose can be produced in the splendor and fragrance which bring cheer to its beholder only by sacrificing the early buds which grow up around it." This wasn't, he hastened to add, an "evil tendency" but rather "the working out of a law of Nature and a law of God."[34]

Likewise, another of the Gilded Age's most successful self-made men, Andrew Carnegie, understood his dizzying wealth as the justified reward of following natural law. In his autobiography, Carnegie describes the first time he read Herbert Spencer on social Darwinism in language that sounds uncannily like a religious conversion. "Light came in as a flood," Carnegie recalled, "and all was clear. Not only had I got rid of theology and the supernatural, but I have found the truth of evolution." That truth was that human beings like Carnegie were supposed to be rich. "Man was not created with an instinct for his own degradation," Carnegie rhapsodized, "nor is there any conceivable end to his march to perfection. His face is turned towards the light."[35]

But it wasn't just the lucky millionaires who saw their success as something they'd earned by following these inchoate laws of nature. From the 1860s onward, a whole cottage industry of self-help books and lectures sprung up claiming to help eager, ordinary readers connect with their inner divine power in order to achieve health and, more importantly, wealth. Influenced by transcendentalists like Ralph Waldo Emerson, the ideology known as New Thought (it was also sometimes called the "mind cure") first flourished in 1860s New England, when a clockmaker called Phineas Quimby decided to try his hand at faith healing.

By the 1860s, there were plenty of would-be healers across the Eastern Seaboard. They were all anxious to harness different kinds of spiritual-scientific energy—remember the claims of *Electro-Physiology*—to achieve tangible results. Quimby was, initially, a disciple of the eighteenth-century German physician Franz Mesmer, whose practice of mesmerism was grounded in the belief that all human beings had an "animal magnetism" that could be channeled and manipulated. But Quimby was frustrated by a major issue: not all of his patients got better. Some, in fact, remained just as sick as when he'd started. His conclusion? That some patients simply didn't want to get better.

Quimby soon became obsessed with the idea that positive thinking could yield practical results. His technique, New Thought, emphasized tapping into the "Christ within" in order to unlock internal divine power, which patients could use to heal themselves. Human beings didn't have to become gods, in other words. They already were gods; they just had to recognize it. It is the same logic we find in many of today's spiritual self-help books dealing with the "law of attraction" or "manifestation." It is the idea that our internal desires help us connect to the energy of the universe, and in turn that energy can be harnessed to help us achieve our goals in this life.

For the first few decades of its life, New Thought was primarily used as a health cure. Quimby's early followers—including Mary Baker Eddy, who was inspired by Quimby to start a New Thought–Christian hybrid religion, the Church of Christ, Scientist—used their techniques to heal the body. But by the late nineteenth century, New Thought had fused with the religion of capitalism to apply the techniques of the mind cure to the wallet.

From the late nineteenth century onward, hundreds of New Thought books were published, each with the same central claim: you can think your way to wealth. By learning to look inward and harness their divine potential through positive thinking, young would-be Carnegies and Rockefellers could attract wealth, proving that they, too, were nature's fittest. Human beings were responsible for their own financial destinies; all they had to do was tap into the energy within.

Bolstered in part by the growth of the publishing industry in the late nineteenth century, these books—like John Fiske's *Outlines of Cosmic Philosophy* (1874) and *The Destiny of Man* (1884), Henry Drummond's *Natural Law in the Spiritual World* (1883) and *The Ascent of Man* (1894), Lyman Abbott's *The Theology of an Evolutionist* (1897), and William Walker Atkinson's *Thought-Force in Business and Everyday Life* (1900), to name only a very small selection—all promoted the same narrative: You can "hack" social Darwinism, to use a modern term. All you needed to do was focus.

"A person is limited only by the thoughts that he chooses," James Allen insisted in 1903 in *As a Man Thinketh*, assuring readers that "the outer conditions of a person's life will always be found to be harmoniously related to his inner state."[36] If someone was sick, if someone was poor, it wasn't because of worker exploitation or wage theft or the horrific conditions of early twentieth-century tenement housing or any other form of social inequality rampant in Gilded Age America. Rather, it was simply because he didn't want to get better or improve his condition. Just as the social Darwinists believed in the survival of the fittest, so, too, did the New Thought proponents insist that those who suffered under economic inequality deserved their fate. "If we lack anything," New Thought writer Charles Fillmore explained, "it is because we have not used our mind in making the right contact with the supermind."[37] Like Sumner and Spencer, these writers dismissed the efforts of social reformers, whom they accused of encouraging indolence and stymying self-reliance. Charles Benjamin Newcomb, for example, author of the quixotically titled *All's Right with the World*, condemned the "despotism of mistaken kindness" and "foolish anxieties concerning the welfare of others."[38] After all, he wrote, "no one alive can become a 'victim' to another else God does not govern absolutely."[39]

By and large, these books blended the language of science and spirituality, framing the link between the inner self and the outer world as the result of mysterious "personal magnetism," an "attracting force" as William Walker Atkinson put it, "radiating from man."[40] For Atkinson, and for the New Thought gurus more broadly, this magnetism was something between literal electricity and metaphorical charisma, "the subtle current of thought-waves . . . projected from the human mind" into the world. These thoughts, Atkinson told readers, went out from their thinker in a "subtle current, which tables along like a ray" and would inevitably "go on its errand charged with a mighty power, and will often bear down the instinctive resistance of the minds of others to outside impressions."[41]

Reading between the lines here, we can see the secret to New Thought's "magic." Its power lay in its promise to help those who wanted to become self-made create an effective persona capable of influencing and shaping the minds of others. The democratic narrative of self-making, no less than the aristocratic model pioneered by Beau Brummell, had a slick corollary: you can achieve success by convincing people of things. After all, hadn't Thomas Edison managed to propel himself to the status of "Wizard of Menlo Park" not just by inventing the light bulb but by convincing the press that he'd done it ahead of schedule? It was Edison's relationship with journalists, as much as his work at the laboratory, that had allowed him to defeat his rivals in the popular imagination.

Few self-made men of the Gilded Age, however, were quite as good at convincing people of things as Phineas Taylor Barnum, the flamboyant show-man, frequent hoaxer, and sometime politician most famous today for having cocreated the Barnum & Bailey Circus. Born an innkeeper's son in Connecti-cut, Barnum started out his career in newspaper publishing, where he quickly learned that what people thought of you mattered almost as much to your suc-cess as what you actually did. But Barnum's claim to fame would not come until, in 1835, at the age of twenty-five, he changed careers. He reinvented himself as a showman who would exhibit fantastical "freaks" and scientific marvels at expositions and fairs. These were the same places where techno-logical and social progress and thrillingly primitive "savagery" were often on display side by side. His first subject? An enslaved elderly Black woman, Joyce Heth—whether Barnum legally "rented" or "bought" her remains a subject of dispute—whom Barnum insisted was in fact the 161-year-old former nurse of George Washington and the world's oldest living woman. Barnum invited audiences to gawk at Heth, whom he declared a medical marvel. Further-more, he drummed up extra interest in her by planting a notice in a newspa-per calling his whole act a hoax: Heth was "not a human being" but rather a "curiously constructed automaton, made up of whalebone, India-rubber, and numberless springs."[42] The plan worked. Heth became a sensation—at least until her health failed and she died. Undeterred, Barnum invited the public to view, and pay for, a public autopsy to determine her age, at which point he nonchalantly "discovered" that she'd been a fraud this whole time.

Barnum's whole career proceeded in much the same way. He'd "discover" a marvel (his next big project was the diminutive "General Tom Thumb," in reality a child with dwarfism), usher them around the globe, and collect the vast majority of the profits. He cannily knew how to exploit the media's hunger for sensationalism. In 1851, in one of his most famous gambits, he separately promised three newspapers exclusive photographs of his next exhibition. What he claimed were beautiful, tantalizingly primitive "Feejee Mermaids" were, in fact, likely half of a monkey sewed to half of a fish. All three papers happily published their identical "exclusives" on the same Sunday morning.

Barnum would ultimately go on to become wildly wealthy and equally famous. According to one apocryphal story, when he met Ulysses S. Grant in the 1880s, shortly after the former president's return from a trip to Europe, Grant acknowledged that Barnum was by far the bigger celebrity. "Wherever I went," Grant sighed, "the constant inquiry was 'Do you know Barnum?'"[43] And while he would later express regret for his ownership of slaves, Barnum defended as harmless "humbug" his practice of manipulating the press and the public in service of financial gain. After all, what was a little massaging of the truth? He was simply manipulating public perception in an indication that he was willing to tap into his inner potential in order to transform reality around him.

In his 1880 self-help book, *The Art of Money Getting*, Barnum echoed his contemporaries' faith in self-reliance. "Those who really desire to attain" wealth, he insisted, "have only to set their minds upon it, and adopt the proper means, as they do in regard to any other object which they wish to accomplish."[44] And sometimes that meant inventing the truth, rather than simply telling it. In one chapter, Barnum admiringly tells the story of a hatmaker, Mr. Genin, and his use of one of the world's first viral marketing gimmicks.

Genin famously spent far beyond his means at an auction for the first ticket to see Jenny Lind, an opera singer and one of Barnum's charges. Nobody, Barnum tells us, knew who Mr. Genin was, at least not until this mysterious "Genin, the hatter" paid an outrageous $250 for the ticket. Soon the question "Who is 'Genin, the hatter'?" was on every gossip's lips, and everybody who was anybody claimed that they owned an original Genin hat. Genin's "novel advertisement" more than made back his expenditure. Over the next six years, Barnum tells us, he sold an extra ten thousand hats, bolstered by his newfound fame.

Likewise, in his 1866 *The Humbugs of the World*—a rollicking guide to those men who, like him, were more concerned with managing impressions than with hard work—Barnum insists that humbug is not only necessary to success but part of the human condition. After all, "in what business is there not humbug?"[45] Boot makers, grocers, butchers, stockbrokers—all of them cheat a little bit (he might well have added to that list the authors of New Thought self-help books).[46] Besides, Barnum added, people enjoy being cheated. It's a form of entertainment.

Frederick Douglass may have seen "WORK! WORK!! WORK!!!" as the fundamental basis of human dignity, the means through which men could lift themselves into their fullest humanity. But for Barnum, and for those who would come after him, self-making—and the money that came with it—would come from another source: that magical, electrical ability to convince other people that you were one of the fittest after all.

# six

# "THE DANDY OF THE UNEXPECTED"

I N LONDON IN 1892, EVERYBODY—OR, AT LEAST, EVERYBODY who was anybody—was talking about one thing: green carnations. Nobody was sure, exactly, what wearing a green carnation meant, or why it had suddenly become such a deliciously scandalous, dazzlingly fashionable sartorial statement. All anybody knew was that one day, at a London theater, someone important (stories differed as to who exactly it was) wore a green carnation, or maybe it had been a blue one (stories differed about that, too). Green carnations may have had something to do with sexual deviance. They may also have had something to do with the worship of art. And the whole thing somehow had to do with Oscar Wilde, the flamboyant playwright, novelist, and fame-courting dandy who—as he never tired of telling the press—put his talent into his work but put his genius into his life. Wilde lived his life as a work of art (or let people think he did). The affair of the green carnation gives us a little glimpse into how.

One story about what exactly happened comes from the painter Cecil Robertson, who recounts his version in his memoirs. According to Robertson, Wilde was keen to drum up publicity for his latest play, *Lady Windermere's*

*Fan*. A character in the play, Cecil Graham—an elegant and witty dandy figure who rather resembled Wilde himself—was ostensibly going to wear a carnation onstage as part of his costume. And Wilde wanted life to resemble art. "I want a good many men to wear them tomorrow," Wilde allegedly told Robertson.[1] "People will stare . . . and wonder. Then they will look round the house [theater] and see every here and there more and more little specks of mystic green"—a new and inexplicable fashion statement. And then, Wilde gleefully insisted, they would start to ask themselves that most vital of questions: "What on earth can it mean?"

Robertson evidently ventured to ask Wilde what, exactly, the green carnation did mean.

Wilde's response? "Nothing whatsoever. But that is just what nobody will guess."[2]

It's unclear how much of Robertson's story is true. If any large group—including the actor playing Cecil Graham—wore green carnations at the *Lady Windermere's Fan* premiere on February 20, nobody in the press commented upon it. That said, the author Henry James, who was in the audience that night, remembers Wilde himself—the "unspeakable one," he called him—striding out for his curtain call wearing a carnation in "metallic blue."[3]

Within days, carnations were everywhere. Just two weeks later, a newspaper covering the premiere of another play, this one by Théodore de Banville, reported a bizarre phenomenon: Wilde in the audience, surrounded by a "suite of young gentlemen all wearing the vivid dyed carnation which has superseded the lily and the sunflower," two flowers that had previously been associated with Wilde and with fashionable, flamboyant, and sexually ambiguous young men more generally.[4] A little over a week after that, a London periodical published another piece on this mysterious carnation. It is a dialogue between Isabel, a young woman, and Billy, an even younger dandy—heavily implied to be gay—about the flower, which Billy has received as a *gage d'amour* (the French is tactfully untranslated) from a much older man. Billy shows off his flower to the curious Isabel with the attitude of studied nonchalance: "Oh, haven't you seen them? . . . Newest thing out. They water them with arsenic, you know, and it turns them green."[5] The green carnation is something desperately exciting, understood not by ordinary society women but by Brummell-style dandies, shimmering with hauteur. It's deliciously dangerous, perhaps even a tad wicked; the carnations are colored with poison, after all. It's also, in every sense of the word, a little bit queer.

The green carnation's appeal as a symbol of something esoteric persisted. Two years after the premiere of *Lady Windermere's Fan*, an anonymous author—later revealed to be the London music critic Robert Hichens—published *The Green Carnation*, a novel that appears to be very obviously based on Oscar Wilde's real-life homosexual relationship with the much younger Lord Alfred "Bosie" Douglas. That relationship would prove to be Wilde's downfall. In 1895, Wilde would be arrested on charges of "gross indecency" at the behest of Bosie's influential father and spend two years imprisoned at Reading Gaol. Wilde would emerge penniless and psychologically shaken, and he died in effective exile in Paris a few years later. Indeed, *The Green Carnation*, despite being a work of fiction that Wilde didn't even write, would be presented at his trial as evidence of his moral and sexual degradation. The press, meanwhile, took Wilde's own propensity for carnations "artificially colored green" as another admission of guilt. By then, it was allegedly common knowledge that such a flower was worn by "homosexuals in Paris."[6]

In *The Green Carnation* (the novel, that is) we see Oscar Wilde reimagined as the playwright Esmé Amarinth, the "high priest" of what we learn is the "cult of the green carnation."[7] Amarinth and his followers are all dandies. Their religion is a passionate worship of the artistic and the artificial, which they believe is superior to the meaningless, empty, and brutal world of nature. Like Rameau's nephew before them, they are fascinated with originality and the way in which a soupçon of carefully chosen transgression can help them ascend the dull, natural plane and reach a higher, more divine form of existence.

Placing a green carnation into his buttonhole, one of Amarinth's devotees, Reggie, muses how "the white flower of a blameless life was much too inartistic to have any attraction for him." Rather, we learn, Reggie "worshipped the abnormal with all the passion of his impure and subtle youth."[8] Meanwhile, Amarinth predicts that the artificially green carnation will soon be replicated by nature. Just as Wilde's seemingly arbitrary decision to promote the green carnation had, within years, transformed the flower into a gay fashion symbol whose origins nobody could seem to remember, so, too—in Amarinth's telling, at least—would reality change to fit the fantasy. "Nature will soon begin to imitate them," Amarinth is fond of saying, "as she always imitates everything, being naturally uninventive."[9]

*The Green Carnation* is not a very good novel. Oscar Wilde, who was briefly accused of being its anonymous author, declared angrily that he most certainly had not written that "middle-class and mediocre book."[10] He had, of course, invented that "Magnificent Flower"—the arsenic-green carnation— but with the trash that "usurps its strangely beautiful name," Wilde had "little to do." "The Flower," he concluded, is "a work of Art. The book is not."[11]

Be that as it may, *The Green Carnation*, though it is certainly a satirical exaggeration, can tell us much about this strange, new class of young men cropping up not only in London but also in Paris, Copenhagen, and so many other European capitals during the nineteenth century: the dandy. Inheritors of the mantle of Beau Brummell but far more flamboyant in their affect—John Bull would *certainly* have turned around to look at them in the street—these modern dandies didn't just live their lives artistically. Rather, as Hichens's novel suggests, they had discovered in their obsession with beauty and self-fashioning a new kind of religion, a worship of the unnatural and the artificial as a means of escaping from both the meaningless void of "nature" and the equally meaningless abyss that was modern life.

These dandies believed—or at least made out that they believed—that the highest calling a person could have was a careful cultivation of the self: of clothing, sure, and of hairstyle, but also of gesture, of personality. And behind that belief lay a kind of bitter nihilism, as poisonous as arsenic itself. Nothing meant anything, unless you decided it did. A green carnation could signify homosexual desire, or aesthetic dandyism, or "nothing whatsoever," depending on your mood and what you felt like conveying to the world that morning.

Self-creation was possible, even desirable, even godlike, precisely because there was no meaning in the world without it. The world was nothing but raw, formless material for the clever and the enterprising to shape to their will. Truth was not objective, something out there in the ether. Rather, it was something for human beings to determine for themselves by shaping the impressions and responses of other people. "Reggie was considered very clever by his friends," we learn from Hichens, "but more clever by himself. He knew that he was great, and he said so often in Society. And Society smiled and murmured that it was a pose. Everything is a pose nowadays, especially genius."[12]

Vivian Grey's "sneer for the world" had become something every dandy needed to possess.

⁕

ACROSS THE ATLANTIC, as we have seen in the past two chapters, the democratic model of self-creation in the eighteenth and nineteenth centuries had been elevated to a kind of intuitionalist religion, one in which the hardworking and enterprising could tap into the latent electrical energies of the immanent world in order to gain health, wealth, and recognition. The mantra of work had transitioned from a call to virtuous citizenship into a moral imperative to make money, to make oneself a success.

But during that same period, a complementary narrative of self-creation had proliferated across European cities. It was particularly popular among artists and writers like Wilde who held that artistic creation, rather than grubby moneymaking, was the key to human superiority, and that artistic creation of oneself was the highest calling of all. Largely based in and around Paris—with a few, like Wilde, centered in London—these dandy authors carefully cultivated their public personae for reasons both mercenary and spiritual. Many of these writers practiced something of a double life. They were dandies themselves but also wrote about (often autobiographical) dandies in their fiction, just as Benjamin Disraeli had done with Vivian Grey. Honoré de Balzac, for example, created the popular character of Eugène de Rastignac, Jean Lorrain created Monsieur de Phocas and Monsieur de Bougrelon, and Oscar Wilde created Dorian Gray.[13]

This aristocratic model of self-creation practiced by the dandies still stressed genius or bon ton—which is to say, the special quality of a chosen few—as the basis of setting apart self-creators from other men, but it understood that this bon ton was, as Hichens says, a "pose." If Beau Brummell had possessed something rather vaguely defined—a je ne sais quoi that rendered him effortlessly elegant—then the dandies of the fin de siècle had filled in the blanks of that definition. It was successful artifice.

Unlike the American entrepreneur, the European dandy was emphatically not a democratic figure. He belonged to an elite and unapproachable class of persons, evincing a genteel horror at the idea of any form of labor. Nevertheless, like his analogues across the pond, he understood that the aristocracy he inhabited was not entirely innate, let alone (horror of horrors) natural.

Rather, his superiority came from a careful exertion of the will, as well as an excising from the self of any dangerous attachments or social obligations that might pull him down into the mire of custom. As onetime Brummell biographer Jules Barbey d'Aurevilly put it in his 1845 manifesto on dandyism, the dandy exemplifies "glacial indifference without contempt." He is a "man who bears within him something superior to the visible world."[14]

That's not to say, of course, that there were no American dandies, nor that there were no European entrepreneurs—far from it. The eighteenth and nineteenth centuries in Europe, like in America, had given rise to an ever more powerful middle class of economically self-made men. At the same time, certain Victorian social trends—like the English obsession with "muscular Christianity," a quasi-religious, colonial obsession with male physical fitness—echoed the American fixation with hard work and self-control. Meanwhile, America had its share of fops, such as the New York socialite Evander Berry Wall, christened "the king of the dudes" (a word once synonymous with dandyism), who was allegedly the first person to wear a dinner (tuxedo) jacket instead of tails to a formal ball, pioneering the sartorial phenomenon known as black tie. (Wall, for what it's worth, eventually moved to Paris.)

But as cultural mythologies, the image of the Carnegie-style magnate never quite had the same cachet in Europe as it did in the United States, and the image of the dandy likewise was never quite as loaded in a country that lacked the memory of old aristocracy toward which dandyism gestured. A telling counterexample proves the rule: an 1819 American play *False Appearances*. The play, a comedy, follows the story of two lowborn men working as apprentices who decide to run away from their employers in order to pose as gentlemen, only to discover that the effort involved in keeping up a dandyish affect (they have to take turns wearing a single suit) is far more difficult, and less rewarding, than good old-fashioned hard work.

THE ENTREPRENEURS AND dandies, importantly, understood themselves to be total opposites. The entrepreneurs dismissed the dandies as indolent and insufficiently masculine. The dandies, for their part, despised not just entrepreneurship but the false promises of the whole changing democratic world, which seemed to collapse the (in their view necessary) hierarchical distinctions between people. For example, the French poet Anatole Baju was one of the founders of the French literary movement known today as Decadent, which counted many dandies among its ranks. Baju wrote in his manifesto that the Decadents defined themselves against "your Social Darwinism, your Laws, your Morality, and your false Aesthetics."[15]

Meanwhile, America's social Darwinists struck back at Oscar Wilde. One satirical *Harper's Weekly* cartoon from 1882 depicts the Wildean dandy as a Darwinian monkey, a symbol of societal and scientific regression whose influence would turn "our young men into drawling asses and our maidens into pulling idiots."[16]

In pushing against the social Darwinists, however, the aristocratic self-makers understood themselves as fighting something even more insidious: the democratic modern world itself. The social mobility that made certain kinds of economic self-making possible (including, often, the dandies' own) had, in their telling, transformed the world for the worse, creating a confused morass in which nobody knew his proper place. We have seen this sentiment already back in Chapter 3, in Balzac's *Treatise on Elegant Living*, which cast elegance as a means of establishing social hierarchy in a postrevolutionary world. Likewise, in an 1863 manifesto on dandyism, the French poet Charles Baudelaire referred to dandies as members of a "new aristocracy . . . based upon heavenly gifts conferred by neither work nor money," one that he feared he would live to see "drowned" by the "rising tide of democracy."[17]

Not that these dandies were necessarily aristocrats themselves, at least in the sense of blood or birth. Indeed, most were from what we'd think of today as the upper middle class, the very same social rank they so despised. Barbey d'Aurevilly, like so many of our dandy theorists, was a member of the middle class. He had trained as a lawyer before becoming a writer, adopting the noble-sounding "d'Aurevilly" in later life from a childless uncle. Baudelaire's father was a civil servant. Wilde's father was a doctor. Dandyist author Jean Lorrain was the child of a ship owner (he changed his name from Paul Alexandre Duval). The French writer Joris-Karl Huysmans, author of *Against Nature*, was not only the child of a middle-class schoolmaster but in fact spent most of his life funding his novel-writing career working as an ordinary, bourgeois civil servant.

Yet, by and large, the dandies of the nineteenth century practiced a kind of reactionary aesthetic posturing. Most flirted with hard-right politics and traditionalist Catholicism in between liaisons with occultism and satanism. They derided democracy and spoke warmly and nostalgically of a hierarchical past where everybody from peasant to king knew their place in the social order. At the same time, however, it remains an open question whether our dandies would have actually wanted to live in the world they longed for. Traditionalist

Catholicism, for example, might have stern views about the open homosexuality that was part of many dandies' lives.

~~~

THE SEEMING CONTRADICTION of the self-made man who despised other self-made men lay at the heart of the dandy mythos, and it can help us to understand why aristocratic and democratic self-making are not so different as they first appear.

We can only understand the dandyist obsession with being self-made, being original, being irreplaceable against a wider set of cultural anxieties. These anxieties had also been thrown into relief by the technological and social changes that defined America's Gilded Age.

Everything, it must have seemed in the nineteenth century, was changing. The French Revolution had dispensed, seemingly once and for all, with the hierarchies of the ancien régime, though not exactly for long. The military commander Napoleon Bonaparte—a self-made man if there ever was one—promptly installed himself as emperor. After his defeat, France would spend the next century careening from republic to monarchy to empire (under Napoleon's nephew, Napoleon III) and back again. New inventions—Edison's phonograph and electric light bulb, the typewriter, the telephone, the camera, the automobile—were changing how people moved through space and communicated with one another.

Even the physical landscape of people's lives was changing, as cities—already crowded in the eighteenth century—became ever more chaotic. In 1801, for example, Paris had half a million inhabitants. By 1890 that number had skyrocketed to 2.5 million.[18] London, likewise, had one million residents in 1801; by the start of the First World War, its population would reach seven million.[19] New York, too, would see its population grow from sixty thousand at the dawn of the nineteenth century to nearly 3.5 million at its close.[20] These cities, furthermore, looked different from the cities of the past. Their streets were newly illuminated—first by gas lamps, then by electric light—and filled with new department stores and shopping centers where newly middle-class people could, for the first time, buy newly mass-produced wares at prices that suited a new middle-class salary. In his 1883 novel *The Ladies' Paradise*, French author Émile Zola describes one of these department stores—the "paradise" in question—as a dizzying temple to consumer consumption, a "new religion" to supplant people's "wavering faith" in the church.[21]

There were new boulevards and new cafés with outdoor terrasse seating designed to overlook the newly wealthy people promenading in the newest fashions. Or one could read one of the many newspapers, cheaper and more plentiful than ever, thanks to the relaxation of stamp duties (in England) and the softening of censorship laws (in France). In 1851, for example, there were seventeen daily newspapers in England. By 1864, there were ninety-six, with eighteen dailies in London alone.[22]

And there were advertisements everywhere—both in newspapers and plastered all over the city streets—reminding Parisians and Londoners and other urban Europeans of all the thrilling possibilities of this rapidly changing world. The growth of the railway industry in Europe had led to an explosion in the advertising industry, as companies scrabbled to reach their ever growing customer bases. One British magazine lamented that you couldn't walk through London's streets without being assailed with exhortations to buy, buy, buy: "If a house . . . becomes tenantless on a given day," the reporter sighed, "the next shall see it covered to the very chimney top with posting-bills."[23] Another writer, using a slang term for love letters, complained, "Half our billet-doux end with an eloquent appeal to run to some cheap grocer's and buy a pound of his best Hyson."[24] Personal fashion items were at the vanguard of this advertising revolution. By 1880, British soap company Pears was spending £100,000 a year on advertising.[25] Suddenly, anybody—or at least anybody with even the slightest disposable income—could look and smell like a gentleman or a lady. And the newspapers were keen to demonstrate exactly how.

It was enough to overwhelm anybody. "Old Paris is no more," Baudelaire lamented in one of his poems, sighing that "the form of a city changes more quickly, alas, than the human heart." Paris was a city of "new palaces, scaf-folding, blocks of stone."[26] Across the channel, the English poet Alfred Austin bemoaned how "huge" London had become, "huger day by day / oe'r six fair counties spread[ing] its hideous sway."[27]

For the fin de siècle dandies, in particular, such transformations were especially galling. After all, how could you consider yourself special and distinct when everybody around you considered themselves special and distinct, too? As early as 1830, just forty-one years after the French Revolution, Balzac lamented how this new century of democracy had made it difficult for people to distinguish themselves from one another. "In the year of grace 1805," Balzac says—referring to the first years of Napoleon's postrevolutionary reign—"it [was] infinitely pleasant for a man or woman to say to themselves when look-ing at their fellow citizens: 'I am above them, I dazzle them, I protect them, I govern them, and everyone of them can clearly see [this], for I am a man who speaks, eats, walks, drinks, sleeps, coughs, dresses, differently than those daz-zled, protected, and governed.'"[28]

We have seen already how the myth of the special self-maker—be he a dazzlingly wealthy entrepreneur or a dazzlingly dressed dandy—requires an analogous figure: the audience member, or the person we might today think of as merely "basic." By the late nineteenth century, this class of normal people began to be described in two distinct ways: as a single, shapeless mass and as mere inanimate machines, rhetorical tropes that we see reflected throughout the wide swath of dandyist literature.

The first of these tropes is *la foule*: the crowd, the rabble, or the mob. Dandy authors were obsessed with *la foule*, that teeming mass of ordinary peo-ple against whom they struggled to define themselves. A central motif of the dandyist novel is a desire to escape the mob entirely. In Joris-Karl Huysmans's 1884 novel *Against Nature* (also translated as *Against the Grain*)—a major influence on Wilde's work—the protagonist Des Esseintes is a neurasthenic aristocrat who wishes to escape the travails of the modern world by shutting himself up in a country house full of beautiful art: a "refined . . . hermitage equipped with all modern conveniences, a snugly heated ark on dry land in which he might take refuge from the incessant deluge of human stupidity."[29] Des Esseintes fills his retreat with beautiful, lifeless objets d'art—most famously a jewel-encrusted tortoise—in the hopes of creating an unreal atmosphere of totally controlled beauty, free from the folly of human life. (His attempts at entering the real world go poorly; on one trip to London, he becomes so over-whelmed with horror that the people he meets are not as interesting as Charles Dickens characters that he has to cut the journey short.)

The most important thing for a dandy is to prove that he is not part of *la foule*, by whatever means necessary. And the swiftest route to such proof, the dandies almost uniformly agree, is that same quality Rameau's nephew dreamed of: originality. In his 1845 manifesto on dandyism, Barbey d'Aurevilly lists originality as the sine qua non of dandyism. "Always produce the unex-pected," he writes, "that which could not logically be anticipated by those accustomed to the yoke of rules."[30] To be a dandy, he insists, is to cut oneself off from other people—their rules, their customs—and show exactly how unlike other people one can be. Dandies established themselves, like Sade's libertines, through transgression. They showed the rules and customs of a given society for the poses that they were. They played with gender norms. They sighed at bourgeois morality and life, and indeed at life itself. In the French symbolist Auguste Villiers de l'Isle-Adam's play *Axël*, the lead characters commit suicide because they realize that life will never live up to their aesthetic fantasies. "Liv-ing?" they scoff at the play's close. "Our servants will do that for us."[31]

In the 1876 short story "Deshoulières," by Jean Richepin, the titular char-acter takes this maxim of originality to an extreme. Deshoulières dreams of becoming the "dandy of the unexpected," a dream that soon becomes an obsession. Brilliant and bored, Deshoulières lives in terror of being catego-rized by others. He applies false hair and makeup to confuse and confound the people around him, constantly changing up his appearance. Unable to commit to anything—he would then become *expected*—Deshoulières finally figures out the only unexpected thing he can possibly do: brutally murder his mistress, with no provocation, simply because she does not expect it. Arrested and condemned to death, Deshoulières even insists on going to his execution originally; he leans back so that the guillotine will not slice his neck but instead go clean through the head.

Yet (imagined) murder was not the only way that the dandies enjoyed original transgression. Among the most prevalent signifiers of dandyist originality was sex—or, rather, "unnatural" sex, which is to say sex that fell outside the paradigm of traditional heterosexuality. Many dandies were what we would now consider gay or bisexual, although they would not have had access to those terms. Throughout much of the late nineteenth century, the predominant way of conceiving queerness was through the category of the "invert," a term mainly used to describe feminine and/or homosexual men. In 1867, the German lawyer Karl Ulrichs made history by speaking publicly about a certain "class of persons"—he counted himself as one—who were attracted to the same sex. His conception of the *Urning*, as he called it, was of a woman's soul in a man's body (lesbians, less often discussed, were male souls in female bodies). Regardless of their private, specific orientation, however, dandies tended to understand and talk about their sexuality in language that celebrated and highlighted, rather than minimized or justified, their so-called unnaturalness. Their expression of their sexual and gender identity separated them from a "nature" they saw as dull and deficient, and which they had fortunately transcended. Male dandies dressed in ways that were traditionally coded as feminine. One American paper referred to Wilde as "manne or woman or child/either/and neither" and "half of men and half of women."[32] The rare female dandy—like Rachilde, born Marguerite Eymery— often adopted male drag.

The dandy's cruelest insults were often reserved for the cisgender, female-presenting woman, particularly those women whose attempts at self-creation through makeup or fashion uncomfortably paralleled the dandies' own. "Natural" women were treated with the same contempt with which the dandies greeted nature more generally. They were fleshy, smelly, ordinary, subject to disease and decay. In Baudelaire's 1847 novel *La Fanfarlo*, the narrator falls in love with a beautiful dancer, only to find that the reality of Fanfarlo doesn't live up to the fantasy once she removes her makeup and lives a normal life, daring to bear children and gain weight. (His feelings for her, unsurprisingly, don't last.) The same thing happens in Wilde's *The Picture of Dorian Gray*, where Dorian falls in love with the actress Sibyl Vane, only to find that once she is out of character she is no longer of interest to him. ("Mourn for Ophelia, if you like," snorts Dorian's mentor, Lord Henry, once Sibyl has killed herself in despair. "Put ashes on your head because Cordelia was strangled. . . . But don't waste your tears over Sibyl Vane. She was less real than they are.")[33] These women—painfully ordinary, trying and failing to use the tools of technology and artifice to lift themselves above mundane, bourgeois reality—were a source of fascination, contempt, and terror for the dandies. They exemplified the frightening fluidity of a modern world in which anybody could transform into someone else.

But *la foule* was only one of the rhetorical tropes through which the dandies expressed their obsession with, and fear of, the way technology and social change had democratized elements of the self-creation they held so dear. Another theme that came to the forefront of the literature of this period was the speculative figure of the robot or android: a humanoid, human-seeming (and, more often than not, female-presenting) figure that turns out to be nothing but mere machinery. Sade's pornographic novels had posited two classes of people: free libertines and, essentially, fuckable furniture. In the same way, this next wave of dandyist literature used the burgeoning genre of science fiction to posit the difference between the "real" person (usually male, usually an artist) and the "fake," mass-produced individuals—the literalization of those whom modern Twitter parlance might mockingly call "NPCs," like the non-playable characters encountered in video games.

It would not be a stretch to say that the dandies were obsessed with robots. They were obsessed, too, with what robots represented: the idea that some people were real and valuable, and others merely mass-produced products of modernity. It's telling that the dandy robot story often consigned certain people—women, people of color, members of inferior social classes—to the rank of android. Recall, for example, how P. T. Barnum drummed up conspiracy theories that the enslaved woman he displayed for profit was in fact a lifeless automaton. In Huysmans's *Against Nature*, Des Esseintes derisively refers to women as "automata, all locked up at the same time with the same key."[34]

Likewise, in a newspaper column, the notable dandy author Jean Lorrain profiles a courtesan named "La Belle Madame G," whom he heavily implies is not a woman at all but a robot (made, tellingly, in America, home of technological industry). Possessing the "immobility of a ghostly doll," Madame G is operated by a "spring mechanism hidden in the silk of her bodice," conveniently one that her "Monsieur . . . knows how to work."[35] Meanwhile, the Goncourt brothers—two Parisian writers and men-about-town—recount in 1858 a visit to a local brothel, where they learn of the doubtless apocryphal existence of another brothel, one where all the women are in fact "imitation women," robots complete in "every detail" and indistinguishable from human prostitutes.[36]

The robot woman, in these stories, represents the dandies' dark mirror image. She is artificial, as they are. Her reality is a carefully cultivated presentation. But far from being a self-maker—someone with the capacity to determine her own destiny and presentation to the world—she is simply a product, formed by the ingenuity of another (usually male) genius. There is an inherent inequality lurking in the idea of self-making. Self-creation is what makes us actualized as human beings, but not all people can achieve it to that extent. In the figure of the automaton, this idea reaches in metaphor its chilling conclusion: some people are more human than others.

By far the most extreme example of this trope can be found in the 1884 novel *Tomorrow's Eve*, by *Axël* author Auguste Villiers de l'Isle-Adam. *Tomorrow's Eve*—as in, the Eve of the future—tells the fictionalized story of Thomas Edison. But Villiers's Edison, unlike the real man, is no entrepreneurial inventor, nor is he a celebrity. Rather, Villiers reimagines him as a dandy artist whose supreme creation is an automaton: an "Imitation Human Being" whose "operation will be a little more dependent on electricity for her model, but that is all."[37]

In Villiers's telling, Edison is simultaneously a technological wizard and a more literal one. The android (Villiers pioneered the term) ultimately develops a real human soul through a convoluted spiritual process Villiers never quite explains. Edison is not just playing God; rather, he is a kind of god, using his artistic powers to harness creation to his will. "I AM GOING TO STEAL HER OWN EXISTENCE AWAY FROM HER," Edison declares of the mediocre actress who is doomed to serve as the android's model (the capitalization is Villiers's), and "capture the grace of her gesture, the fullness of her body, the fragrance of her flesh . . . her complete identity, in a word. I shall be the murderer of her foolishness, the assassin of her triumphant animal nature . . . and then, in place of this soul . . . I shall infuse another sort of soul."[38] Villiers contrasts Edison's masterful artistic creation with the mediocre and failed attempts at self-creation of two of the novel's few women: Alicia, the model for the android, and a dancer, Evelyn Habal, whom Edison (in an extremely convoluted manner too long, and frankly too ridiculous, to get into here) has also unwittingly involved in creating the android. In one scene, Edison shows his friend Lord Ewald a (then novel) film reel of Evelyn, who seduced a friend of his away from his broken-hearted wife. We originally see Evelyn dancing alluringly, "in a sequined costume . . . as lively and sharp as life itself." Then Edison shows Ewald a picture of the real Evelyn, without makeup: a horrific monster, "a little bloodless creature, vaguely female of gender, with dwarfish limbs, hollow cheeks . . . and almost bald skull."[39] Edison reveals her tricks—wigs, makeup, false teeth, stockings—one by one, in a chapter unsubtly called "exhumation." Self-creation was something, Villiers suggests, that was acceptable for artistic, dandy men, less so for ordinary, middle-class women.

It is tempting to dismiss the broader strokes of the dandyist treatment of women—failed actresses and failed robots alike—as nothing but garden-variety misogyny. Certainly, some of the more chauvinistic passages of these works are uncomfortable to read today. But the dandies' conflation of women, automata, and *la foule*, taken together, can tell us something profound about their wider cultural concerns. They feared a destabilized world in which both nature and industrial capitalism seem to have failed to provide a sense of meaning. Self-making had become more accessible by virtue of technological and social change. But at the same time, it had to be conceived of—as in the case of the snobbish ton—as *less* accessible, a means of self-assertion in an ever more anonymous urban landscape. If everybody could be special, after all, how could the would-be self-maker hold on to his own distinct specialness, and therefore his superiority to other people?

The literary trope of the robot became a way for dandy authors to express their anxieties and fears about being human in an era where everything, even people, seemed replicable. Central to the dandyist aesthetic was a bleak nihilism, a sense that the world, both of nature and of civilization, was fundamentally meaningless, an endless series of poses and coincidences. The democratic narrative of self-making in America had wedded itself to spiritualized self-help movements like New Thought, fostering a cultural mythology where the self could tap into some primordial energy or mystic, electric force within. However, the aristocratic self-makers of Europe lacked such optimistic faith. There was nothing sacred, they suggested, as Sade had before them, except what they themselves could create. They were living, they felt, in an era where the brutal, empty truth of nature had been exposed and where there was no choice but to build up something else in its stead.

"Nature has had her day," scoffs Des Esseintes in *Against Nature*, comparing her to a "petty shopkeeper selling one article of goods to the exclusion of all others." Indeed, Des Esseintes goes on, there is "not one of her inventions which the ingenuity of mankind cannot create; no Forest of Fontainebleau, no fairest moonlight landscape but can be reproduced by stage scenery illuminated by the electric light; no waterfall but can be imitated by the proper application of hydraulics, till there is no distinguishing the copy from the original."[40] The technological inventions of the nineteenth century, the dandies felt, had disenchanted the world once and for all, a truth they saw as tragic rather than hopeful.

Against such a backdrop, the ideal of self-making took—in a slightly different manner than it had in America—a newly religious cast. Self-making became an act not just of managing one's public image but of exercising the closest thing to godliness the world contained. After all, if there was no God and no reason or purpose or order to nature, then the human will—the ability to fashion oneself, as Giovanni Pico della Mirandola had once suggested—was the next best thing. Dandies were, as Barbey d'Aurevilly described them, "miniature gods."

Few dandies, though, took this religious call to self-creation quite as seriously as Joséphin Péladan, a French novelist, playwright, and mystical occultist. He was partial to going around Paris in ceremonial robes, a lace ruff, and an astrakhan hat, and he adopted the title "sar," ostensibly (and implausibly) the title of ancient Akkadian kings.[41] He wrote a series of manifestos, equal parts self-help and spiritual exhortation, including *How to Become a Mage* (for men), *How to Become a Fairy* (for women), and *Kaloprosopia* ("beautiful personality"). Péladan encouraged readers to tap into their innermost selves in order to create themselves as works of art and thus become divine.

The artistic equivalent of New Thought's get-rich-quick schemes, Péladan's guides urged readers to "create your own magic, not because your efforts are motivated by vanity, but because you are seeking in yourself the originality of a work of art."[42] That magic demanded, as in America, an inward turn. "Seek no other measure of magical power," Péladan writes, "than that of your internal power: do not judge another being except by the light they emit. To perfect yourself by becoming luminous, and like the sun, to warm the latent ideal life around you, there is the whole mystery of the highest initiation."[43] As in the United States, self-making had become linked with the idea that there was something spiritual, maybe even magical, about turning inward. In a world without a clear sense of God, meaning, or order, our own desires—to become who we wanted to be—had become paramount to understanding the very point of existence.

Not all dandies were quite so explicit about the magical underpinnings of their ideology. But regardless of the specifics of their religious beliefs or professions, the dandies saw the self as the only standard—moral or metaphysical—by which the rest of the world could be measured. The self that severed itself from *la foule*, that created its own laws, could become a kind of god. As Oscar Wilde put it, in the mouth of *Dorian Gray*'s Lord Henry: "To be good is to be in harmony with one's self. . . . Discord is to be forced to be in harmony with others. One's own life—that is the important thing. As for the lives of one's neighbours . . . they are not one's concern. Besides, Individualism has really the higher aim. Modern morality consists in accepting the standard of one's age. I consider that for any man of culture to accept the standard of his age is a form of the grossest immorality."[44]

The aristocratic and the democratic narratives of self-making had different emphases and different aesthetics, but in this they agreed. The man who cut himself off from the limitations of the society around him and listened instead to his own desires and longings was not just superior to the common rabble. He was also, fundamentally, more human: higher on the evolutionary food chain, more in touch with the mysterious energies at work in the universe, and more in tune with the very purpose for which he had been put (or put himself) on earth.

THESE TWO NARRATIVES of self-making were likewise more intertwined than either the dandies or the entrepreneurs would have liked to admit.

Although the dandies framed themselves and their ideology in opposition to the modern world they claimed to despise, the truth was more complicated. The very technological and social changes they rejected—the growth of the literate middle class and of the popular press—were the precise things that kept the dandy novelist selling books. Oscar Wilde's green carnation, after all, had started out as a publicity stunt to assure that everybody in London's literary and theatrical circles would be talking about *Lady Windermere's Fan*. Writers of dandyist books—Jean Lorrain, Rachilde, Villiers, or even Huysmans—knew that popular interest in their scandalous, or at least picturesque, private lives would drum up buyers. People who were fascinated by the dandies' lives, or who wanted to learn to replicate them, were, after all, their most loyal customers.

Barbey d'Aurevilly may have decried *la foule* in his writings, but that didn't stop him from showing up to an interview with journalist Octave Uzanne in an elaborate costume of "silks, satins, lace, green and purple velvet, cuffs of extravagant guipure lace . . . trousers with a gold band" and referring to his elegantly carved walking stick as "my wife"—all the better to make sure the public knew exactly how much of a dandy he was.[45] Huysmans, likewise, was fond of spilling to the press all about his interest and scandalous involvement in the occult, a surefire way to convince the public to buy his 1891 novel *Là-bas*, set in the Parisian satanist underworld.

The line between artistic creation and commercial branding was never entirely clear. When the novelist and reporter Rachilde needed to apply for a permit, then required, to wear men's clothing, she cited in her request letter her editors' hope that her cross-dressing would garner some much needed publicity for her literary career. "Don't refuse me," she begged the prefecture, "the means of being original."[46]

Even Oscar Wilde, perhaps the greatest of all dandies, was not above a little crass commercialism. One of the highlights of his career was his wildly successful 1882 American lecture tour, during which he crossed the country giving talks on dandyism and art for art's sake. In fact, the tour was funded by a theater promoter, Richard d'Oyly Carte, who hoped that Wilde's public persona would gin up interest in an upcoming operetta by Gilbert and Sullivan, *Patience*, which featured a dandy character modeled on Wilde himself.

Wilde's job, as he crossed America, was to perform "Oscar Wilde" the character and to spread the gospel of dandyism beyond Europe. Soon, Wilde's
image—or that of cartoon dandies based on him—would be ubiquitous, found
on dandy-branded circus tickets and dandy-branded soaps.

The walking work of art had also made himself into a walking
advertisement.

# seven

# "I SHALL BE RULING THE WORLD FROM NOW ON"

**T**HE SUN WAS SETTING OVER THE ADRIATIC IN SEPTEMBER 1919, and Italy's most popular military leader was about to come out onto the balcony to make a speech to the city he had just conquered.

That city had a few different names, depending on whom you asked. The Italians called it Fiume. The Slovenes called it Reka; the Croatians, Rijeka. In each case, the city's name meant "river," a reference to the Rječina (or, if you were Italian, the Eneo, or if German, the Flaum), which flowed from the region's hilly hinterlands through the center of the city to meet the Adriatic Sea. For centuries, that river had doubled as a border between competing territories. It had, for a time, separated Hungarian from Austrian territory under the broader Austro-Hungarian Empire. On this day, it would mark the border between the newly formed Kingdom of Serbs, Croats, and Slovenes and the territory the military commander had come to form: the Italian Regency of Carnaro.

According to the Treaty of Versailles—ratified just a few months earlier—all of Fiume was supposed to belong to the new Balkan kingdom, one of the many tricky territories the Allied powers had attempted to reassign in the wake of the Austro-Hungarian Empire's spectacular collapse. But, emboldened by the chaos of the postwar global order, Gabriele D'Annunzio had other ideas.

Short, slight, and almost grotesquely unhandsome, D'Annunzio hardly looked like a military commander. But that had not stopped him from leading 2,500 Italian soldiers—largely drawn from the ranks of the brave, if often reckless, shock troops known as the *arditi*—into the city earlier that day, claiming Fiume for Italy.

"Italy" was itself a new concept. The Kingdom of Italy—a unified nation, rather than a loosely affiliated collection of city-states and minor kingdoms—was not quite fifty years old. But the dream of Italy, a nation that would double as the rebirth of the once-great Roman Empire, was on everybody's mind. And central to that dream were the *irredenti*, those "unredeemed places" where (at least some of) the population spoke Italian and that one day might be united under this new kingdom's banner. Fiume had long been such a place. And, with the geopolitical order in turmoil, now seemed to D'Annunzio the perfect time to make that dream a reality.

If there was anything D'Annunzio was good at, it was peddling dreams. The whole day thus far had seemed like something out of a fairy tale, or else a farce. Contemporary accounts recall D'Annunzio's arrival as something between a military assault and a cocktail party, with Italian women in full evening dress carrying guns onto the main square. D'Annunzio himself had turned up in the city in a bright red Fiat car so overflowing with flowers that observers initially mistook it for a hearse.[1]

Yet, even by D'Annunzio's standards, his first appearance as Fiume's new ruler was a masterpiece of stagecraft. Striding out onto the balcony of the Hotel Europa, D'Annunzio bellowed out the cosmic significance of his conquest to the adoring populace below. "In the mad and cowardly world," he intoned, "Fiume is the symbol of liberty. In the mad and cowardly world, there is a single pure element: Fiume. There is a single truth and it is Fiume. There is a single love: and this is Fiume. Fiume is like a blazing searchlight that radiates in the midst of an ocean of abjection."[2] Fiume, D'Annunzio insisted, wasn't just a military victory for the Italian people. Rather, it was a spiritual victory, the triumph of human potential over the decay and decadence of a brutal modern world that had lost sight of any possibility of transcendence. It was a victory of beauty over ugliness, of strength over weakness, of magic over matter. It was a sign that the vanished glory of powerful empires like old Rome might, at last, be returning to a world that sorely needed it. Italy, D'Annunzio promised his listeners, would bring that glory back.

There was only one problem. Italy had nothing to do with D'Annunzio's military campaign. The Italian government not only hadn't sanctioned the operation, but it was currently scrambling to do damage control before "the Regency of Carnaro," as D'Annunzio termed his new government (Carnaro was the Italian name for the whole region), turned into a diplomatic catastrophe. D'Annunzio had somehow managed to galvanize a little under two hundred Italian *arditi* from outside Trieste and convince them that it was a good idea to march on Fiume, about a hundred kilometers away. The other 2,300 soldiers had joined up en route.

D'Annunzio was not even a trained military commander. Although he frequently regaled anyone who would listen with stories of his heroism during the First World War, when he'd technically enlisted as a fighter pilot at the age of fifty-two, most of D'Annunzio's actual work during the war consisted not of flying planes but of disseminating propaganda. The military raids of which he boasted involved D'Annunzio helping to air-drop nationalist pamphlets he'd written over cities like Vienna and Trieste.

Words, not bombs, had been D'Annunzio's weapon of choice for most of his career. By the start of the First World War in 1914, D'Annunzio had already made a name for himself as one of Italy's most illustrious—to say nothing of most scandalous—novelists and poets. Flamboyant, charismatic, egotistical to the point of sociopathy, D'Annunzio had been infamous for decades not just for his writing but also for his outré public persona. A consummate dandy in the mode of Oscar Wilde, Jules Barbey d'Aurevilly, or Joséphin Péladan,

D'Annunzio was never far from the newspaper's headlines. The society rags breathlessly tracked his constantly changing litany of famous lovers ("A woman who had not slept with him made herself ridiculed," commented one contemporary).[3] All of Italy marveled over his profligate spending. D'Annunzio borrowed thousands of lira (often from his mistresses) to acquire jewels, horses, and priceless objets d'art he had no intention of actually paying for. He was renowned for his fastidiousness, even obsession, regarding his personal appearance. Among his many extravagant purchases was a custom-made perfume that he insisted, with absolutely no factual basis, was based upon a secret formula he'd discovered in an ancient manuscript.[4] Sometimes the tabloid headlines were ones D'Annunzio had placed himself. He'd gotten his start as a society reporter and was not above using Barnum-esque humbug to sell his own work. D'Annunzio had managed to attract attention for his first book of poems, for example, by spreading the rumor that its author had died tragically young in a horseback-riding accident.[5]

D'Annunzio was lauded by his many admirers as *il vate*: the prophet. A recurring theme of his written work—and the one that connected best with his audience—was the restoration of Italy's past glory and the primordial strength and spirit he associated with soldiers and heroes of that lost era. Writing paeans to "the splendor of blood" and "the strength and power of the people," D'Annunzio urged Italy to military action. He was an early supporter of Italian intervention in the First World War, on the grounds that Italy needed bloodshed to renew itself. After the premiere of one of his plays, the patriotic 1908 drama *La nave*, rapt audience members spilled out into the streets of Rome, chanting lines from the play and calling for violent intervention in the *irredenti*.[6] Modern Italy, D'Annunzio contemptuously put it, had devolved into a desiccated "*pension de famille*, a museum, a horizon painted . . . for international honeymooners," rather than a "living nation."[7] In a parodic riposte to Jesus's famous Sermon on the Mount, which declared as blessed the poor, the hungry, and the oppressed, D'Annunzio announced that, instead, "blessed are the young who hunger and thirst for glory, for they shall be satisfied."[8] When

D'Annunzio marched on Fiume, he encouraged his followers to replace the contemporary Italian *hip, hip, hurrah* with the battle cry *eia, eia, alala*, which, he insisted (without historic evidence to back him up), was based on the Greek hero Achilles's battle cry in *The Iliad*.

D'Annunzio's external nationalism was intimately connected to his even more important project: creating himself as a work of art. D'Annunzio had been heavily influenced by the dandies and the Decadents of the fin de siècle. His first novel, the autobiographical *Child of Pleasure*, written in 1889, contained a classic dandy hero, the amoral Andrea Sperelli. The young nobleman is obsessed with art, and he is subsequently incapable of forming any real (and, D'Annunzio implies, inferior) human connections. But, far more than any of his contemporaries, D'Annunzio took the implicit ideology of dandyism—and aristocratic self-making—to its natural conclusion. If the modern world really was bleak and brutal and devoid of meaning, if *la foule* really did consist of sheeplike idiots, if the closest thing to divinity or transcendence really lay in the superior human being's exertion of artistic and aesthetic control over his stupefied audience, then that had political as well as personal implications.

The greatest form of self-making would demand not just the creation of oneself but also the creation of a whole populace. It necessitated political and aesthetic control of *la foule*, subdued in turn by D'Annunzio's false promises of heroism. *Follow me*, D'Annunzio's logic went, *and you, too, can be one of those special, chosen beings*. The audience had become a new canvas. And the self-maker had become the dictator.

For the eighteen months that D'Annunzio presided over Fiume—in a political regime that, it immediately became clear, was a dictatorship—he blended dandyist aesthetics and the kind of authoritarian political power that the rest of the world would soon come to understand as fascism. Under D'Annunzio, Fiume became, as one contemporary put it, a "permanent festival," a hotbed of bohemian hedonism, rampant drug use, and prostitution.[9] D'Annunzio mandated nightly poetry readings and concerts, along with fireworks meant to remind Fiume's citizens of his splendor. The constitution of Fiume insisted that every municipality of the province would be assigned a state-sponsored chorus and orchestra.[10] Another Fiume resident recalled eighteen months of "songs, dances, rockets, fireworks, speeches. Eloquence! Eloquence! Eloquence!"[11] The local bishop began to fret that the populace had abandoned Christ himself, preferring to worship the magnetic D'Annunzio, who had started staging elaborate political liturgies in the local Saint Vitus Church.[12]

There was, of course, a darker side to Fiume's carnival atmosphere. Members of Fiume's substantial ethnic Slavic minority were routinely detained, if not expelled from the city altogether. D'Annunzio suppressed political and journalistic dissent, becoming notorious for a particularly unorthodox method of humiliating his opponents: dousing their food with castor oil to ensure that they would soil themselves publicly. (This method would receive new life under one of D'Annunzio's most fervent admirers, Benito Mussolini.) D'Annuzio's Regency of Carnaro—though technically imagined as an "anarcho-syndicalist" corporatist state—was in practice a cult of personality for D'Annunzio himself. Like those of the many right-wing leaders who would follow D'Annunzio's playbook—from early fascists like Mussolini to our own contemporary reactionary strongmen like Donald Trump and Viktor Orbán— D'Annunzio's worshippers had no time for the people who would not or could not bolster his insistent narrative that he was not only *il vate* but also *il duce*, the leader who would restore Italy to greatness, whether Italy wanted him to or not.

After fifteen months, Italy intervened. The government became convinced at last that the dangers of letting D'Annunzio play in the sandbox of international politics outweighed the dangers of displeasing a man whom public opinion still hailed as a national hero. Diplomatic negotiations between Italy and the Kingdom of Serbs, Croats, and Slovenes—D'Annunzio, of course, was not involved—had finally produced a solution. Fiume would exist as an independent free state, controlled by neither country. D'Annunzio summarily ignored this decision. In the end, between Christmas and New Year's Eve of 1920, Italian troops marched on Fiume, and D'Annunzio, knowing better than to push his luck, promptly capitulated. The assault was well-timed. During the holiday period, the Italian government knew, the press and the Italian public would be distracted. D'Annunzio's greatest weapon, his ability to manipulate the media, had been temporarily muzzled.

D'Annunzio, rather miraculously, faced few consequences for his act of open sedition, in part because he remained discomfitingly popular with ordinary Italians. Rather than reprimand him, the Italian government decided to buy him off, allowing the perpetually broke D'Annunzio to live out the rest of his life in a magnificent, state-sponsored villa off Lake Garda, with all the cocaine, fine wine, luxury objets d'art, and age-inappropriate lovers he could possibly handle, on the condition that he stay out of politics for good. D'Annunzio grudgingly agreed, although he would spend the rest of his life defending the Fiume endeavor as a success of human artistic freedom over the mediocrity of the common rabble. "The supreme poetic effect," he was known to declare, "was accomplished in Fiume."[13]

❧

D'ANNUNZIO WAS NOT the only figure of the early twentieth century to see the potential of a "supreme poetic effect" in politics. But he was the one who most directly put into practice the dandyist ideology of the aristocratic self-maker: the naturally superior human being who has, by virtue of that very natural superiority, transformed himself into a god. D'Annunzio understood that, in a world of poses, where truth was less important than what people thought of you, the cultivation of a public image of strength, power, and thrillingly atavistic heroism could be enough to stir the hearts of a disaffected and lonely populace. The cult of personality could become, well, an actual cult.

In D'Annunzio, we find the moment that the dandy—the previous paradigm of aristocratic self-making—evolved into a new, and perhaps even more unnerving, figure: the Übermensch, or "overman," a concept first developed by the German philosopher Friedrich Nietzsche. Rather than shut himself off

from *la foule*, as the dandies did (or at least claimed to do), the Übermensch
used his supreme creative powers to reshape the populace, transforming it into
a reflection of his divine will.

Or, as one of the autobiographical protagonists of D'Annunzio's novels
tells himself, "There is no God if it is not I."[14]

The figure of the Übermensch, in various and often differing ways,
would come to dominate much of late nineteenth-century and early
twentieth-century political and philosophical discourse. It would, of course,
ultimately reach its natural conclusion in Nazi Germany, where Adolf Hitler
himself would use the term to justify the creation of an ostensibly superior
"master race" and with it the murder of millions of people who fell outside its
arbitrary boundaries. Nietzsche himself was not necessarily an anti-Semite,
unlike his sister, Elizabeth, who married a prominent member of the Nazi
Party and who edited several of Nietzsche's posthumous publications to serve
her political agenda. However, the Übermensch today is often equated exclusively with Aryan racial supremacy and Nazi propaganda: images of strapping,
virile, blond men with rippling muscles. At first glance, this distinctly masculine figure appears as quite the contrast to the countercultural, feminine,
queer-coded (if not outright queer) "man-woman" of fin de siècle dandyism.

But the two figures have more in common than it might seem. Both the
fin de siècle dandy and the Nietzschean Übermensch arose out of the same
set of late nineteenth-century anxieties, responding to the same fundamental
questions: Where do we find meaning in a world that seems devoid of it? And,
to use a phrase for which Nietzsche is justly famous, What do we do when
God is dead?

Nietzsche saw in modern European life a curious contradiction. People
said they believed in God. People maybe even showed up at church once in a
while. But, at least since the Enlightenment, the idea of a supreme, personal
God like the one described in orthodox Christian doctrine seemed ever more
implausible. People talked about God, sure, but nobody actually believed in
him, at least in any meaningful way. God functionally did not exist.

And yet, Nietzsche simultaneously believed that much of European culture—the way people fetishized self-denial, or sexual repression, or submissive meekness—was predicated on that very Judeo-Christian God whom nobody actually believed in. These cultural dictates were the ideological equivalent of a vestigial tail: outmoded ways of being and living, custom masquerading as morality. What was called for, Nietzsche argued, was a "transvaluation of values," a brave reimagining of what was good and what was bad.

Nietzsche had particular contempt for the Judeo-Christian tradition and what he saw as the "slave morality" that arose out of it. For Nietzsche, this culture, which put a premium on self-denial in the name of religious virtue, was actively hostile to life. Ideas of good and bad, at least as Western Europe often understood them, were all too often driven not just by social convention but by what he called "ressentiment": a blend of anger and envy used by the powerless against the powerful, those "masters" who valued life-affirming qualities like strength, pride, or sexual domination.

Underpinning Nietzsche's transvaluation of values were two interwoven and seemingly contradictory assumptions. The first was that human existence was inherently meaningless. Morality was simply a function of certain groups cannily exercising dominance over others by whatever means possible. "Whatever has value in our world," Nietzsche wrote in 1887's *The Gay Science*, "now does not have value in itself, according to its nature—nature is always value-less—but has been given value at some time, as a present—and it was we who gave and bestowed it. Only we have created the world that concerns man!"[15] If you couldn't exert power by, say, defeating someone in battle, you could exert power by convincing your stronger enemy that it was, in fact, immoral to defeat somebody in battle.

Nietzsche's second assumption, however, was that certain ways of being were, in fact, better than others and potentially even preferable. Nietzsche might have rejected traditional morality, and with it the notion of inherent moral value, but he also condemned certain ways of living that he deemed to be dishonest. "Once blasphemy against God was the greatest blasphemy,"

Nietzsche writes in *Thus Spake Zarathustra*, "but God died, and therewith also those blasphemers. To blaspheme the earth is now the dreadfulest sin."[16]

To "sin against the earth," for Nietzsche, was to live dishonestly. This was to deny truths of nature, truths that reflected both a broadly Darwinian ethos as well as the dandies' obsession with innate aristocracy. There were, Nietzsche claimed, natural hierarchical distinctions between people, which Christianity had falsely collapsed. Nietzsche condemns, for example, "the will of the weak to represent some form of superiority, their instinct for devious paths to tyranny over the healthy—where can it not be discovered, this will to power of the weakest!"[17]

"Health," for Nietzsche, wasn't just the absence of physical ailment. Rather, it meant adopting a pre-Christian worldview that he associated with the ancient Greeks, emphasizing strength, vitality, and the power of the human will. "What is good?" Nietzsche asked, before answering his own question: "Everything that heightens the feeling of power in man, the will to power, power itself."[18]

This power could not be reduced to either physical strength or social authority. Rather, this will to power was the process by which man became most truly, most authentically himself. It was a will to become oneself as a god.

Nietzsche's preferred value system, such as it was, required an unfettered honesty about the self and about its singular, powerful place in the world. Simultaneously, the self was both the arbiter of what was good—ascribing value to the world around him—and the measure of value. The greatest man was the one who most completely expressed his interior selfhood. Self-expression was not just allowable but obligatory. After all, those onetime goals of truth and ultimate reality were not to be found out there, in the empty world. So, a human being had two choices. He could either slavishly allow himself to be determined by other people's values and self-assertions, or he could look inward, refashioning reality in accordance with his own self.

ENTER THE ÜBERMENSCH. For Nietzsche, this is the ultimate aristocratic self-creator. He is both naturally superior to all other men, by virtue of his intellectual and physical qualities, and also capable of exercising that superiority by consciously creating himself, exerting his will upon the world.

This creation, for Nietzsche, was at least in part an artistic act, a conscious cultivation of an image of a unified self. Just as Balzac's "elegant man" arranged all elements of his external presentation—his wardrobe, his hair, his gestures—to suggest a fundamental unity, so, too, does the Übermensch arrange all aspects of his life in accordance with his superior will. "One thing is needful," Nietzsche writes, "to 'give style,' to one's character, a great and rare art. It is practiced by those who survey the strengths and weaknesses of their nature and fit them into an artistic plan."[19]

The Übermensch, furthermore, is a solitary figure. He must bravely determine his values for himself, rather than letting society tell him what to think. His individuality and his originality are attained by separating himself from the common herd. "During the longest period of human past," Nietzsche writes dismissively, "nothing was more terrible than to feel that one stood by oneself. To be alone, to experience things by oneself, neither to obey nor to rule, to be an individual—that was not a pleasure but a punishment; one was sentenced 'to individuality.'"[20] But the Übermensch knew that this aloneness was a virtue. It allowed him to understand that his individual existence was at the heart of the meaning of life itself.

"The overman is the meaning of the earth," Nietzsche insists. "Let your will say: the overman shall be the meaning of the earth!"[21] Life meant nothing outside of self-flourishing. Those who recognized that fundamental truth—and were willing to act on it—could shape reality in their image.

Nietzsche did not invent wholesale this new ideology of the self. We have seen already how many of its elements have suffused the ideology of self-making from the Enlightenment onward: the self's rejection of custom, the longing for new kinds of hierarchy, the belief that the world consisted of a binary between self-makers and *la foule*, and the sense that, in the absence of a God, the self was the only arbiter of value. But Nietzsche, far more than any other thinker, made these tendencies explicit, calling out European society for refusing to acknowledge the sea change that had already taken place. God was dead, Nietzsche insisted, adding—only partly ironically—that "I shall be ruling the world from now on."[22]

Nietzsche's philosophy echoes, albeit with different emphases, that of some of his American contemporaries, those post-transcendentalist proponents of New Thought who believed that human beings, by looking inward, could harness a mysterious energy running through the world and use it to their own ends. For Nietzsche, the only creative energy in the world comes from within, through the power of the self and, more particularly, the self's will. These fundamental desires and drives, Nietzsche believes, can help us transcend the illusions of custom and bourgeois Christian morality. What we want, Nietzsche suggests, makes us who we really are, far more than any other fact about our existence. If there is anything transcendent in this empty, brutal world, it is our own desires, our own hunger to flourish and to, in turn, become ever more ourselves.

The democratic strain of self-making insisted that anybody, theoretically, could become a self-maker so long as they worked hard enough. The aristocratic strain posited that only certain, special people possessed the qualities of an Übermensch. But in practice the two ideologies were more alike than they were different. Those who had acquired power or prosperity—whether through hard work or New Thought–style positive thinking or some inborn quality that set them apart from the common herd—were the people who understood that reality itself was malleable, that truth was flexible, and that life was simply raw material for the magician of personality to reshape into his desired image.

※

FOR WRITERS LIKE D'Annunzio, disillusioned with what they saw as the mediocrity of modern, industrial life, Nietzsche's philosophy was a revelation.

In D'Annunzio's 1892 novel *The Triumph of Death*, he celebrates the philosopher who has at last laid bare the truth of existence. Citing several figures in Nietzsche's writing, D'Annunzio urges his readers to "open the heart to the voice of the magnanimous Zarathustra . . . and we prepare in art with sure faith the advent of the übermensch, of the Overman."[23] In another novel, *La Vergine delle Rocce*, D'Annunzio harkens back to the Italian Renaissance as an era of "supermen," contrasting it with what he saw as the sclerosis of contemporary Italians.[24]

These aristocratic prophets of self-making reserved particular ire for self-makers of the more literal, economic kind: the middle classes. Ironically, these were the very people, of course, who were most likely to read their books in the first place. D'Annunzio and Nietzsche both, much like their dandyist forebears, reserved most of their criticism for the bourgeoisie. They saw them as inextricably linked with the social customs they so despised, as well as with the democratic institutions they saw as disingenuously rendering everybody equal. (Whether they actually did render everyone equal is quite another matter. A look at the astounding inequality and brutal poverty of Gilded Age New York suggests that the fantasy of equality was just that.) Yet, for Nietzsche and D'Annunzio, the despised bourgeoisie—and *la foule* more broadly—were not so much self-makers as sheep, people whose personalities existed exclusively to be formed and shaped by other, more powerful figures.

At worst, the bourgeoisie were total moral and aesthetic nonentities, seduced by the dull creature comforts of modern life. At best, they were second-rate imitators or fans, like D'Annunzio's "ten thousand young men," as one contemporary put it, "who hang on every word of Gabriele and scrutinise the knot of his tie and the length of his waistcoat with the same anxious affection as the colour of his adjectives and the cut of his phrases."[25] In a world where controlling one's poses meant controlling truth itself, these second-order followers proved their inferiority by their very willingness to be led.

At the same time, however, neither D'Annunzio nor Nietzsche believed in the literal, hereditary aristocratic system. D'Annunzio, like so many dandy theorists, was from a wealthy and landowning but not outright aristocratic family. The noble "D'Annunzio" particle, like that of "de Balzac," was self-chosen: in this case adopted by D'Annunzio's father, who got it in turn from a childless uncle.

What these modern would-be aristocrats hungered for, rather, was a new, better way of talking about innate superiority. They wanted a new way of establishing their individuality and originality in a world that seemed to foster similarity and reproducibility, an era of mass production where human beings were little more special than machines. Like the dandies, who lived in terror of being part of *la foule*, these prophets of the Übermensch saw self-assertion as the only bulwark against the anonymity of modern urban life. There were two choices for the modern, Western man, as they saw it: to declare himself an Übermensch or else to accept life as one of what Nietzsche called the "last men"—mere followers accepting bourgeois mediocrity as their fate.

～～～

AT THE DAWN of the twentieth century, the Übermensch became the strongman. While the dandies of the nineteenth century sought to retreat from the modern world through fantasies of a superior past, the would-be Übermenschen of the early twentieth century reimagined themselves as part of a promising future, where war, and the chance for self-assertion that it offered, would separate the courageous natural aristocracy from the cowardly last men. There were the futurists, followers of the Italian writer Filippo Tommaso Marinetti, whose 1909 *Futurist Manifesto* envisions war as "the only cure for the world—militarism, patriotism, the destructive gesture of the anarchists, the beautiful ideas which kill."[26] Like D'Annunzio, Marinetti decried what he felt modern Italy had become: a country infected by "smelly gangrene of professors, archaeologists . . . antiquarians . . . the numberless museums that cover her like so many graveyards."[27]

While the dandies had sought refuge in beautiful antiquities and gem-encrusted tortoises, Marinetti and his followers instead celebrated the twentieth century's technological possibilities. "The splendor of the world has been enriched by a new beauty," Marinetti writes, "the beauty of speed," waxing poetic about "a racing automobile with its bonnet adorned with great tubes like serpents with explosive breath."[28] Yet the futurists shared with their dandy forebears a sense that nature had had its day. The artificial, the man-made, the sleek, sexy results of human progress, all these were coming into their ascendancy. Like the dandies, the futurists were avowed misogynists—Marinetti's manifesto included a call for "contempt for women"—seeing the feminine as representative of the wider failure of the natural world. And, like the dandies, the futurists knew the power of producing an effect, however eccentric, on their audience. One of Marinetti's more outré theater pieces involved putting glue on his unwitting audience's chairs and trapping them in their seats. Mixing aesthetic outrageousness with an obsession with masculine virility, the futurists claimed their place as the aristocrats of the new world order.

For many futurists, the outbreak of the First World War represented a thrilling possibility: a chance to at last play out in real life their fantasies of vitality and vigor. Wartime, as one futurist poet put it—shortly before dying in battle—was "a battle with the infinite. Grandiose, intense."

Nearly all of the futurists, including Marinetti himself, joined up. Many joined the *arditi*—the "daring ones"—the same corps from which D'Annunzio would later rouse followers for his march on Fiume. These *arditi* saw themselves as the ultimate embodiment of the Übermensch. As one sympathetic newspaper described them, they were the new "aristocracy of character, muscles, faith, courage, blood, brains."[29] They were, the paper glowingly went on, "patricians dismounted from their chargers, aviators from their planes, intellectuals removed from their ideologies, sophisticates from their salons, mystics disgusted with churches," all willing to leave their world behind to subsume themselves into the only thing that mattered: bloodshed.

But few soldiers of World War I would reflect this new obsession with the aristocracy of character, and its relationship to allegedly cleansing violence, quite like one of D'Annunzio's admirers, a young political journalist named

Benito Mussolini. In 1914, Mussolini had founded a new political party: the Fascio d'Azione Rivoluzionaria (Band of Revolutionary Action), dedicated to encouraging Italian intervention in the First World War. Like D'Annunzio, Mussolini hoped that Italian reconquest of the "unredeemed" territories—places like Trieste, in what is now Italy, and Fiume—would restore national glory and vigor.

Once the war was over, Mussolini set his sights higher. In 1919, the same year D'Annunzio invaded Fiume, Mussolini founded a second political party, one with an even more ambitious stance. Boasting a manifesto coauthored by Marinetti himself, the Fasci Italiani di Combattimento (Italian Bands of Fighters, or fascists), understood themselves as participating in a twofold project. First, they were helping to restore (or, more accurately, invent) an Italy that would celebrate, rather than elide, the natural hierarchies among people in the service of a purer world. And, second, they were helping to create a new, secular spirituality, a kind of religion of the human will, to replace the vanquished world of old Christianity. After all, *la foule* needed a leader—and what better way to lead them than by the tantalizing promise of human greatness.

For Mussolini, fascism was "not only a party . . . but a faith, not only a faith but a religion that is conquering the laboring masses of the Italian people."[30] Mussolini wasn't just creating himself as a work of art. Rather, he was creating a work of art in his audience, shaping and forming them in his image by promising them a chance to participate in the wider spectacle he created. Fascism, for Mussolini, was an artistic and an aesthetic project. He, like D'Annunzio, believed in utilizing powerful pageantry and quasi-religious imagery to whip participants into an ecstatic frenzy. "When I feel the masses in my hands, since they believe in me," Mussolini once recalled, "then I feel like one of the masses."[31] He understood himself as an artist of humanity—even, and perhaps especially, when committing acts of violence. "Doesn't the sculptor sometimes break the marble out of rage, because it does not precisely mold in his hands according to his vision?" he insisted. "Everything depends on that—to dominate the masses as an artist."[32] (Some of Mussolini's touches—the use of the title Il Duce, the visual language of the paramilitary Blackshirts—he took directly from D'Annunzio himself.)

The promise of fascism, Mussolini insisted, was the promise of life as a work of art: reimagined for the common people. Follow Mussolini—or D'Annunzio—the promise went, and you, too, can be part of something special. "Fascism brings back 'style,' into people's lives," Mussolini insisted in 1922, a month before his March on Rome, arguing that democracy and equality had almost destroyed style altogether. (Balzac and Brummell would no doubt have agreed.) Fascism, for Mussolini, offered "a line of conduct, that is the color, the strength, the picturesque, the unexpected, the mystical." Here was a sense of a world that fit together in a beautiful, orderly, cohesive, whole: Balzac's "elegant man" expanded to encompass all creation.

The ultimate advertisement of fascism was that you could become a "natural aristocrat," or at least something close to one, by participating in a violent uprising at the behest of one of the actual (so-called) natural aristocrats who staged the whole performance in the first place. D'Annunzio and Mussolini were canny salesmen of the fascist aesthetic. They at once understood themselves as the world's aristocrats of blood and muscle and profited from their ability to make other people follow them in the hopes of becoming like them.

The fascist narrative—no less than the "humbug" of P. T. Barnum—lay in a clever rhetorical sleight of hand. The despised masses who wanted to be self-creators became convinced that they could be self-creators by those who despised them. They could live lives of true, meaningful originality rather than reproducible, bourgeois mediocrity, but only by giving themselves over to the power of another. They celebrated the triumph of the will—through violence and bloodshed—by subsuming their own will to the desires of their leaders. They operated as a single "nation, advancing, as one conscience and one will," while simultaneously understanding themselves as special. They were members of the group Mussolini, like his futurist forebears, called *aristocrazia trincee* (the aristocracy of the trenches, i.e., warriors). They were those who—as

Mussolini's own lover Margherita Sarfatti described him—"recognize . . . the privilege of the supreme aristocracies, as they were, are, and will be, gens and barons, ras and samurai."[33] God's bastards ascended to their rightful throne.

⁓⁓

AESTHETIC FASCISM BECAME not just a means for the most successful self-makers to gain power, but also to reshape their audience, making them believe that they, too, could participate in this aristocracy of spirit. Their individual struggle, their personal worries—all these, fascism promised, could be raised up to the level of transcendent myth.

As Mussolini wrote in a 1932 treatise: "Fascism wants man to be active and to engage in action with all his energies; it wants him to be manfully aware of the difficulties besetting him and ready to face them. It conceives of life as a struggle in which it behooves a man to win for himself a really worthy place, first of all by fitting himself (physically, morally, intellectually) to become the implement required for winning it."[34] What Mussolini was peddling, in other words, was an experiential fantasy. It was the chance to feel like you were an Übermensch, whether or not you actually were one. By joining the Blackshirts, his promise went, by participating in nationalist violence against Jews, Slavs, and other so-called undesirables, you, too, could set yourself apart from *la foule*. You, too, could be God, even if (especially if) you never exerted political power of your own.

And although Mussolini's 1919 effort at forming a fascist political party would fail miserably—he would be trounced in a November election—he continued to develop his theories. He also continued to form political alliances. By 1921, he would finally be elected to parliament, along with thirty-five other members of the Fascist Party, stoking resentment toward the weak-willed King Vittorio Emanuele III, an easily manipulated politician. And, in October 1922, just three years after the invasion of Fiume, Mussolini would lead a political assault of his own, mobilizing his supporters to march on Rome itself. "Let us, too, pure in spirit," Mussolini exhorted his supporters to raucous applause, "raise our thoughts to Rome . . . the city of our spirit, a city purged, cleansed, of all the elements that have corrupted and violated her; we aspire to make of Rome the pulsating heart, the active spirit of the imperial Italy of our dreams."[35]

Soon, fascist movements like Mussolini's would be spreading all across Europe. There was Austria under Engelbert Dollfuss, Spain under Francisco Franco, and, of course, Germany under Adolf Hitler. What these movements had in common was not just the power of particular dictators' personality cults. These dictators all understood that what people wanted, more than anything, was to feel special, to feel that they, too, had joined nature's aristocracy, that they, too, had a life that mattered in a world where nothing else seemed to. The fantasy of aristocracy, it turned out, was the most valuable commodity of all. And at Europe's rallies, no less than at P. T. Barnum's American circuses, it turned out that people were more than willing to go along with humbug—provided it made them feel good along the way.

## – eight –

# THE POWER OF *IT*

I T WAS 1933 IN HOLLYWOOD AND ONE YOUNG ACTRESS, BARBARA
Stanwyck, had decided to play by Nietzsche's rules. Or, more accurately,
Stanwyck's character Lily Powers had decided. Although, before long, it
would be difficult to tell the difference. Stanwyck would soon make a whole
career out of playing grimly determined femmes fatales in gritty noir films
like *The Lady Eve* (1941), *Double Indemnity* (1944, perhaps her signature role),
and *The Strange Love of Martha Ivers* (1946). They were women who were not
afraid to use their sex appeal to get what they wanted, as able as a Machiavelli
or a Vivian Grey to manipulate the people around them in order to change
their circumstances.

At the time, Stanwyck was best known on the silver screen for a few early
roles as virtuous heroines and damsels in peril. But Lily Powers was about to
change all that. The indefatigable antiheroine of *Baby Face* was determined
to lie, cheat, steal, and sleep her way to the top, no matter what it took to get
there. Released just before the institution of the Hays Code that would come
to censor so many of Hollywood's most salacious storylines, *Baby Face* was

willing to depict Lily's rise to glory in all its lurid detail. What's more, *Baby Face* was willing to bet that the audience would root for her.

Across America, the Great Depression had almost everybody feeling bleak. Wall Street had crashed, taking with it nearly half the country's GDP. As much as a quarter of the population was unemployed, with thousands displaced to shantytowns known as Hoovervilles, after the president presiding over the economic collapse. Poverty and despair seemed built into the country's social fabric. Lily Powers, we learn at the film's beginning, was one of America's unluckiest: pimped out as a teenager by her father, the alcoholic proprietor of a Pennsylvania speakeasy desperate to get money for his next bender. But Lily doesn't let anything, not even her personal trauma, not even an entire global catastrophe, get her down. She is, as one contemporary reviewer writes, "a cold, relentless creature," playing "her game with a cunning hand," using "her heel to grind down her victims."[1] Blonde, lithe, and leggy, Lily knows how to use the magnetic power she has at her disposal to claw her way out of poverty and enforced prostitution and into the life she feels that she deserves. Over the course of *Baby Face*, Lily moves to New York, sleeps her way to the top, bags a rich husband, and then leaves him when his fortunes wane (only to change her mind in an eleventh-hour romantic and redemptive reversal).

Her inspiration? Nietzsche's *Will to Power*, a shot of which opens the film. In *Baby Face*'s initial moments, Lily's closest friend and trusted mentor, the elderly cobbler Cragg, takes the book down off the shelf, reading it aloud to her. "A woman, young and beautiful like you," he muses, "can get anything she wants in the world. Because you have power over men." But, he warns her, she needs to learn to use that power wisely. "You must use men," he reminds her, "not let them use you. You must be a master, not a slave." Cragg makes the point obvious, quoting Nietzsche directly as he shakes his fist: "All life, no matter how we idealize it, is nothing more or less than exploitation." Nietzsche's moral, according to Cragg, is this, "Exploit *yourself*." Cragg tells Lily to head to New York and embark upon a career of seduction.

The camera, though, isn't paying attention to Cragg. Its focus turns over his shoulder to Stanwyck's vulpine, angular face. Every one of her expressions is lovingly rendered in celluloid: her dark eyes widening underneath her penciled brows, her painted lips parting in an expression between hunger and arousal. We watch her, lost in thought, as her gaze moves from Cragg to the book and back again. Cragg may be the one speaking, but our focus is entirely upon Stanwyck as she considers her options.

Lily raises her cigarette to her lips. She blows out smoke. The camera lingers a little longer.

"Yeah," she says.

Hays Code–era censors would ultimately water down the film's opening moments. The original *Baby Face*, however, is a celebration of Lily's determination to become an Übermensch—and, rarer and more thrilling still, a female one. She leaves behind a literal body count. One of her spurned lovers murders another and then commits suicide. A third wealthy lover attempts to kill himself before Lily finally marries him. (She tells him that his money no longer matters to her, but we don't exactly believe her.) For Lily, life is a "zoo." She refuses to be kept "like a dumb animal" inside its confines. She makes her own luck with the help of Cragg's guidance and a bit more Nietzsche to boot. Late in the film, just before the murder-suicide knocks out two of Lily's rival suitors, Cragg mails her a helpful reminder of her mission, a copy of Nietzsche's *Thoughts Out of Season*. The camera lingers on the quote: "Face life as you find it, defiantly and unafraid. Waste no energy yearning for the moon. Crush all sentiment."[2]

Across the Atlantic, the promise of Nietzschean self-creation was galvanizing many Europeans into a nationalist fervor, lured into submission by the promise of being part of a master race. Self-creation and glory alike were offered to those who fit the fascist mold. But here in Hollywood, where the narrative of self-creation had been bound up for a century with the amassing of wealth, and where good old capitalist grit had a moral and spiritual dimension, Nietzsche's dream was subsumed into an entirely different narrative.

Gods really did walk among us, Hollywood suggested. Individuals existed who had the power and the capacity to shape their own destinies, to trans- form the world to their will, to become the people they dreamed of being. But they were, as in Europe, a very particular sort of person, born with a very particular sort of quality, a modern-day answer to Beau Brummell's bon ton. They had something that nobody could quite name. It was what made man after man willing to kill or die for Lily Powers. It was, too, what made Barbara Stanwyck herself so impossible not to love, so impossible not to root for, even as she left a trail of bodies and broken hearts in her wake. These people had beauty, to be sure, but it wasn't just that. Plenty of people were beautiful. What these new contemporary deities, male and female alike, had was power. It was the ability to grab your attention, to control you, to captivate you, to make it impossible for you—or the camera—to ever look away.

They had, as the Hollywood magazines liked to put it, "it." And, as one tagline for *Baby Face* describes, they "made *it* pay."[3]

ONLY NOBODY WAS sure, exactly, what *it* was. The term first came into common usage in February 1927, when a British novelist named Elinor Glyn published an article on the subject in the women's magazine *Cosmopolitan*. According to Glyn, *it* was a blend of raw sex appeal, Wildean dandyism, and the kind of quasi-magical personal magnetism we've seen heralded already by the tradition of New Thought. *It* was, Glyn wrote, a kind of scientific maxim, a "quality possessed by some which draws all others with its magnetic force."[4] *It* was also a source of sexual attraction: "With '*it*,'" Glyn promised, "you win all men if you are a woman, and all women if you are a man."[5] But *it* involved something more, something special, and importantly something innate. Like sprezzatura and bon ton, *it* involved the presence, or at least the illusion, of authenticity. You didn't have to try to get it; it had to appear effortless. "'It,'" Glyn cautioned her readers, "must be absolutely un-self-conscious." Like the dandy, the possessor of *it* must display "an indifference to whether you are pleasing or not."[6]

In other words, *it* represented a kind of Hollywoodized, Americanized version of the narrative of the aristocratic self-maker. This person didn't have to try; they were simply better or superior or more powerful than other people. Yet, *it* was also curiously democratic. It made stars out of nobodies, mink-wearing glamor goddesses out of onetime shopgirls. Anybody could be discovered, could be the next Barbara Stanwyck or Jean Harlow or even the most successful it-girl of all, Clara Bow.

Shortly after Glyn's article came out, Paramount producer B. P. Schulberg paid a solid $50,000 for the rights to the article, convinced that the concept had, well, *it.* Less than a year later, the movie "*It*" (salacious quotation marks included) came out starring the bob-haired gamine revered as the "hottest jazz baby in movies," one Miss Clara Bow, as Betty Lou. Less explicitly cunning than her successor Lily Powers, Betty Lou nevertheless absolutely has *it* and makes *it* pay. Exuding charm, charisma, and a certain additional je ne sais quoi, Betty Lou, a lowborn but high-spirited shopgirl, catches first the eye, then the heart, of the heir to the department store where she works.

Stories about beautiful, impoverished young women who win the affections of wealthy, powerful men were of course hardly new. But what was new about "*It*" was Clara Bow's method. She didn't—like the virginal heroine of *Pamela* so derided by the Marquis de Sade—attract her man by her virtue, innocence, or youth. Nor did she attract him simply by being beautiful. Her romantic rival—a wealthy, blonde socialite—is also quite the looker. Rather, Betty Lou gets her man through *it*: her joyful, thoroughly effortless approach to life, a feminine answer to the Renaissance's sprezzatura. In one telling scene, the film cuts back and forth between Betty Lou's rival's preparations for a date—careful, studied, measured—and her own careless elegance. Unable to afford a fancy dress, Betty Lou takes a pair of scissors to the décolletage of one she already has, and looks incredible doing so. Almost overnight, Clara Bow became a sensation—not just as an actress, but as a star. Here was someone whose own personal possession of *it* had allowed her to make it onto the big screen and into the brand-new world of Hollywood celebrity. People didn't just fall in love with Betty Lou, the character. They fell in love with Clara Bow, the human being.

The rise of Hollywood, and the new kind of celebrity it engendered, marked a watershed moment in the history of self-creation. It blended, for perhaps the first time, the aristocratic and the democratic stories about self-making into a single account of stardom. Stars were—like the European dandies—demigods, born with *it* and therefore superior to mere mortals. But they were also, to a much greater degree than even an Oscar Wilde or a Jules Barbey d'Aurevilly, plugged into America's distinctly capitalist system. This system linked their possession of *it* to their attainment of untold financial success, and it dangled the possibility of acquiring (or appearing to acquire) *it* to a much wider audience. Stars like Clara Bow and Barbara Stanwyck were simultaneously coded as innately better than ordinary human beings and also as walking advertisements—often created and fashioned by the interests of powerful film studios—for the products and techniques that promised to make ordinary people a little bit better, too.

The rise of Hollywood also expanded the story of self-creation in another way. For the first time, it opened up a wider cultural narrative of self-making to women. That is not to say that there were no female self-creators before Hollywood. There were examples of both self-made female entrepreneurs—such as the cosmetics magnate Madam C. J. Walker, America's first Black self-made millionaire—and self-made dandies, such as the French cross-dressing novelist Rachilde. However, self-making as an aspirational myth rarely if ever included women, either in its aristocratic or democratic strains. Indeed, as we have seen, narratives of self-creation were often misogynistic, treating women as examples of the "natural" or "organic" humanity that the divine self-maker had the skill, ability, or sheer force of will to overcome. But *it*—charisma, sex appeal, the power to influence others through performance—and the cult of celluloid celebrity it engendered opened up the possibility of self-making to men and women alike. Anyone (at least, for most of Hollywood's racist history, anyone with the right skin color) could, just like Bow's Betty Lou, theoretically be transformed overnight into a god, someone a whole nation of fans could worship. And, people increasingly understood, controlling your image—how people saw you, on-screen or off—was essential to that chance at transformation.

THE BIRTH OF celebrity culture, of course, did not originate with Hollywood or even in America. As we have already seen, performers of the eighteenth and particularly nineteenth centuries had achieved cult status. Their public persona blended with their artistic work to such an extent that we can say that they achieved success, in part, by being themselves. There was, for example, the Hungarian pianist and composer Franz Liszt, whose largely female admirers regularly broke into hysterics and mass fainting fits at his concerts throughout the 1840s, to the extent that one contemporary, the German poet Heinrich Heine, invented the term "Lisztomania" to describe their intensity. There was, too, the storied feud between the American actor Edwin Forrest and his English rival William Macready, which grew so intense that in 1849 warring fans of the actors transformed an ordinary performance of Shakespeare's *Macbeth* at New York's Astor Place Theatre into a full-scale riot. There was, as we have already seen, Oscar Wilde, whose decision to wear a green (or was it a blue?) carnation started a decades-long fashion trend among London's theatrical set.

And, above them all, there was Sarah Bernhardt, the actress and diva whose many admirers sounded more like worshippers than audience members. Bernhardt, one admiring reviewer wrote, wasn't just alluring or attractive. She had "a magnetism . . . [which] attracts, interests, and finally enslaves." When it came to Bernhardt's charms, the reviewer wrote, "you are not simply snared; you are enchained."[7] Her magnetism had given her the kind of mesmerizing, quasi-magical power over her audience that Europe's strongmen exerted in the political sphere. To her admirers, she was not merely human but more than human, her alluring public image forceful enough to render her a kind of living god.

But these performers had a relatively narrow reach, attracting hundreds of audience members who could afford to see Bernhardt playing Hamlet, Liszt playing a concert, or a performance of *Lady Windermere's Fan*. It was only with the invention of film—and with it the ability to disseminate a single image, a single gesture, a single face to thousands and even millions of people—that the true star was born.

The device that would become the motion picture camera had a number of overlapping origins. As with the invention of the light bulb, the motion picture camera was not invented by a single person but rather developed by several often competing developers throughout the 1890s. In the United States, there was our old friend Thomas Edison, by then largely a figurehead at his own company, presiding over the day-to-day work of William Kennedy Laurie Dickson, who pioneered the Kinetoscope camera, and subsequent Kinetoscope viewing machine, in 1891. In France there were the aptly named Lumière brothers, Auguste and Louis, who patented the Cinématographe camera in 1895. In Germany, two more brothers, Max and Emil Skladanowsky, patented the Bioscop that same year.

Early films were, however, more celebrations of technical ingenuity than they were of human charisma. Among the earliest cinema hits were the Lumière brothers' 1896 *Demolition of a Wall* (the subject matter was exactly what you'd expect), along with their *Arrival of a Train at Ciotat Station* (likewise). While an infamous story about *Train*'s effect on its audience—that the sight of the incoming train spooked early moviegoers out of their seats—is likely apocryphal, it nevertheless speaks to a truth about early cinema. It was, like Edison's light bulbs before it, largely a celebration of human technical progress. Those few actors who did appear in cinema were mostly vaudeville or circus performers, people who could move their bodies in interesting or "freakish" ways like the contortionist Ena Bertoldi or the strongman

Eugen Sandow. And when stage actors finally began to make the transition to film—often because it paid better than "real" theater—they were derided as sell-outs by their peers. Film actors were merely stuntmen, proper theater actors insisted, existing only to shock an audience eager to be bowled over by the power of technology to depict the strangest and most outlandish things imaginable. "The repertoire actor," one 1907 article from *Moving Picture World* snipped, "has discovered a new use for his talents. . . . By lying down, rolling over, and jumping in front of the camera, he . . . [can] earn in three days a sum equal to a week's salary at his former industry."[8]

These performers were almost exclusively anonymous. Like the medieval craftsmen of centuries past, they existed only to provide a service to a wider corporation. In this case, it was not the church but the film studios, which not only funded film production but also held virtually exclusive monopolies by controlling the means—cameras and film stock—through which films could be made. These were less creative industries than they were technology companies: consortia of inventors whose products advertised their own ingenuity. Film studios would not cast actors for a particular project but rather hire actors on contract and use them at their discretion for multiple productions.

These early studios, furthermore, protected their monopoly on the industry by banding together. Under the aegis of Thomas Edison himself, the major studios created the Motion Picture Patents Company, also known as the Edison Trust, to protect their interests. The trust worked to prevent unauthorized outsiders from using these new inventions to create rival films. They held, for example, an exclusive contract with Kodak, the country's main film supplier, effectively rendering film stock difficult to acquire, if not downright unavailable, for any upstart outsider.

These early films may have been short on character and story. Nevertheless, audiences loved them and began flocking to their local cheap nickelodeons—so named for the affordable five-cent cost of a ticket—as a reliable, regular source of entertainment. In 1905, fourteen years after the invention of the Kinetoscope, there were just a small handful of nickelodeons in the United States, but by 1907, there were 2,500. By 1910, that number had skyrocketed further to a staggering ten thousand cinemas across the country.[9]

It's worth noting that for the first decade or so after film's invention, America was hardly the only country in which films were becoming the dominant form of entertainment, nor was it the only country to have wealthy and powerful film studios. Indeed, in the first decade of the twentieth century, it was European rather than American filmmaking that looked to become ascendant, as French film studios like Pathé produced films—like *A Trip to the Moon* and *The Great Train Robbery*—that proved hits on both sides of the Atlantic. But by the 1910s, and certainly by the 1920s, the American film industry would come to dominate not only films screened in America but a major market share of films screened in Europe as well. Part of this is due to obvious historical circumstances. The devastation wrought across Europe by the First World War destroyed a whole host of industries, not just filmmaking. But part of this, too, was due to the sheer size of American audiences. With such a wide potential viewership, after all, American studios could afford to invest in spectacular, high-budget productions (and lure high-quality international performers), confident that a blockbuster would recoup their costs. Ultimately, while the film industry would exist as a major source of entertainment in America and Europe alike, it was only in America that Hollywood as a cultural force reached anything like an apex of influence. It was only in America, too, that the ideal of the star—the superhuman individual, the democratized dandy carefully calibrated by a corporation behind the scenes—came into ascendancy.

For it was in America that, as they say, the star was born. Or, more accurately, it was in America that audiences first realized that stars were what they wanted. As nickelodeons spread across the United States, the cinema managers started noticing that something strange was happening. The audiences were getting curious. They wanted to know who, exactly, was in the pictures they were seeing. They were writing to industry magazines like *Moving Picture World*, as well as directly to studios themselves, clamoring for any tidbit they could get their hands on regarding their favorite performers, especially that detail studios had always hidden: their names. A 1901 letter addressed simply to "the lady who appeared in *The Ingrate*" begs the performer for a crumb of information. "Will you please answer this letter," the fan writes, "just telling me your name, your real name, not a stage one. I promise I won't tell no one."[10] Another fan letter from that time, directed to a mysterious "Biograph girl," informs the actress that fellow fans had joined together, in the absence of other information, to come up with a code name for her: the "Queen of Sheba."[11]

Even at this early juncture, audiences were drawn to a quality in their favorite performers that seemed to relate not to their skill as actors, strongmen, or contortionists but rather to who they *really* were, their (apparent) innate personalities. There is a reason, after all, that the *Moving Picture World* letter writer is so keen to get a real, rather than merely a stage, name for the *Ingrate* actress. The secret to *it*—the quality that made certain performers so tantalizingly magnetic—appeared to lie in something ostensibly real about their inner life and their ability to express that inner life outwardly. Stardom, in other words, seemed to audience members to be less about performance as a distinct skill than about a very particular kind of self-expression.

Early on, film studios were loath to reveal their actors' identities. Their reasoning was practical. If certain actors became known, loyalty to them might rival the audience's loyalty to the studios that employed them. The studio's name, as in the case with the "Biograph girl," substituted as brand recognition for the performer's own. With a few rare exceptions—Edison occasionally named performers of whom he was particularly fond—studios kept their actors as anonymous as possible.

Then Carl Laemmle came along.

A rarity among film producers, Laemmle wasn't part of the Edison Trust. Working-class and Jewish—in contrast with the trust's members, who were largely gentile and middle-class—Laemmle had come into the film world as a nickelodeon manager, and he had seen firsthand audiences' response to performers like Biograph's Queen of Sheba. Back in 1906, Laemmle had opened Chicago's first nickelodeon; since then, he had tried and failed to legally challenge the Edison Trust's monopoly on film in order to break into the industry himself. In 1909, he'd organized a group of would-be independent movie producers to counter the trust's influence, forming the Independent Moving Pictures Company—or, as the company's intentionally puckish logo would have it, IMP. That spring, Laemmle had managed to poach for IMP the mysterious Queen of Sheba herself, a young actress named Florence Lawrence.

At the time, Lawrence was desperate for work. Despite her relative success at Biograph, where she'd appeared in over a hundred films in eighteen months, Lawrence—and her actor husband Harry Solter—had been blacklisted by the trust after they'd tried to switch studios in an attempt to increase their salaries. But Laemmle was happy to snatch her up.

So, on March 12, 1910, Laemmle participated in the same tradition that Edison and Barnum had practiced before him: a clever bit of journalist-baiting humbug. Just as Barnum had done eighty years prior to drum up public interest in the enslaved Joyce Heth, Laemmle bought advertising space in a periodical, in this case *Moving Picture World*, in order to "nail a lie." The lie, in this case, had almost certainly been planted by Laemmle himself, if it had ever existed at all. Rumors were swirling, Laemmle insisted, that the Biograph Girl had been killed in a car accident. But—fear not!—these appalling rumors were untrue. The Biograph Girl was alive and well. Only she was no longer the Biograph Girl but rather an IMP. And, most importantly, she had a name: Florence Lawrence, a rising star whose best work—two IMP films cunningly advertised—was yet to come.

But Laemmle didn't stop there. He placed a second advertisement in the *St. Louis Post-Dispatch* informing readers that not only was Lawrence alive and working for IMP but also that Florence Lawrence, the Queen of Sheba herself, was coming to Saint Louis and could be seen in the flesh by any fans who wished to pay her homage. "You've Seen Them on the 'Screen,'" one of Laemmle's ads read, "Come See Them in Person."[12] And come they did. According to one Laemmle biographer, fans were so ecstatic to see the real-life

Florence Lawrence that they immediately began to mob her, desperate for any relic of this secular saint they could get their hands on.

Together, Laemmle's humbug and Lawrence's *it* factor combined to create the blueprint for what we now think of as celebrity stardom: a blend of individual (usually but not always female) personal magnetism and careful calibration behind the scenes. For the men and women lucky enough to attain it, and for the breathless audience members who treated Hollywood's royalty as their role models, stardom became a new way of thinking about the myth of self-creation, one that blended European artistic self-cultivation and American capitalist grit. You could make yourself into a work of art and also get rich doing so. Becoming better—more beautiful, more alluring, possessed of more personality, as it had come to be known by the 1920s—would allow you to practice the New Thought arts of personal magnetism in a new way, attracting the health, wealth, and happiness that was your birthright. Your own authentic personality, expressed to the public, could become the key to your material success.

The founding myth of Frederick Douglass and Andrew Carnegie alike—that of the hardworking young man who taught himself to read and then made millions—had been replaced. Now there was a new American dream: that of the undiscovered star, the young man or woman working in a shop or restaurant who overnight became the next it-girl (or, to a lesser extent, it-boy), swaddled in minks and dripping in diamonds. This new fantasy of discovery rested not merely on virtuous actions that anybody could at least theoretically perform—work hard, study, hustle—but rather on a fundamental inner truth about the discovered starlet in question. Her very innermost personality, who she really was (or at least could convince audiences that she was), was the key to her success.

It didn't hurt that most of the earliest film stars came, like Lily Powers herself, from backgrounds of poverty and deprivation. Their discovery narratives fit the mythic mold of the American rags-to-riches story. Bow had been born in a Brooklyn tenement, her childhood shaped by physical and sexual abuse.

Stanwyck's father had abandoned her weeks after the death of her mother in a streetcar accident, and Stanwyck and her siblings had largely grown up in a series of foster homes. Then there was Joan Crawford, another screen scion of the 1920s and 1930s—like Bow, both abandoned and abused by her parents— who in films like *Sally, Irene and Mary*; *Grand Hotel*; and *Sadie McKee* captivated audiences with characters who, like Crawford herself, had made good from difficult origins.

This modern fairy tale only grew more potent against the backdrop of the Great Depression of the 1930s, as the lives of Hollywood stars became ever more removed from those of their audience. It contained elements of both the democratic and the aristocratic fantasy of self-making. The myth of stardom promised that an ordinary person could transcend their material circumstances simply by being himself or, even more commonly, by being herself. It was a gloss on the traditional American narrative of WORK! WORK!! WORK!!!, one in which actual labor and conscious self-cultivation fused into a single practice.

Central to the success of the star was not simply her beauty or her ability to perform a character. Rather, it was in her ability to express what appeared to audiences to be some fundamental truth about her personality, about her inner glory. Different stars had their own distinct personae, each one linked indelibly with the actor themselves. There was "Little Mary" Pickford, who took up Florence Lawrence's mantle as the Biograph girl, and whose veneer of childlike innocence was central to her public appeal. There was Clara Bow, who, as *Photoplay* put it in 1926, "plays the reckless younger generation on and off the screen"—vamps and jazz babies modeled on her own persona as a hard-living flapper. There was Joan Crawford, portrayer of hardscrabble, working-class girls made good, alongside Barbara Stanwyck, the scheming femme fatale. Each of these stars projected a heightened analogue of authenticity, a sense that their personality was more real than real. As Pickford ruefully recalled of her infantile persona, "I became in a sense my own baby," a carefully cultivated reimagining of her allegedly innate self.[13] As one 1921 primer to screen acting reminded would-be actors: "It never pays to imitate anyone else's interpretation of any emotion. Each of us . . . have our own way of showing our feelings. This is one thing that is our very own."[14] The very thing that the dandies had sought—originality—as a reprieve from the world of commerce was now a marketable commodity.

If this originality of personality was the key to stardom, then stars' private lives took on a new significance for their audience. How they really lived could provide clues to how *it* could be attained. When Mary Pickford and matinee idol Douglas Fairbanks left their respective spouses for one another, their marriage became, in the words of one contemporary, "living proof of America's chronic belief in happy endings." Fan mobs and journalists alike besieged the couple's transatlantic ocean liner when they set off for England. Once in London, the honeymooners' every attempt at moving through the city brought traffic to a standstill. In one instance, their presence paralyzed the limousine of no less august a person than King George V himself. Like his great-great-uncle Prinny, he was no match for the appeal of this new kind of aristocrat.

The studio machine that helped produce stars soon learned that their lives and loves were as valuable a commodity as their faces. While in 1912 *Photoplay*'s inquiries department primly informed would-be snoops that "information as to matrimonial alliances and other personal matters will not be answered," by 1915, trade magazines were regularly running gossip features like "Who's Married to Who in the Movies." The inquiries department at *Photoplay* shortened its list of no-no's to "religion, scenario writing, and studio employment." As one early trade magazine mused, "There are several questions agitating the Great American public. But one of the most important of these questions is . . . What do [stars] do when they're not working?"[15] Left unsaid was the equally important corollary: And whom do they do it with?

Yet these private lives of the stars weren't exactly private. Rather, they were a conscious effort of cultivation, both on the part of the stars themselves and on the part of the businesses that supported them, creating as well as capitalizing upon the *it* that had become indelible from stars' self-expression. While a few luminaries were able to parlay their fame into corporate power—like Pickford, who started her own production company—most stars were at the mercy of the studios who cast, molded, and branded them. Each studio had a type that it marketed to the public: RKO was known for erudite charmers like Fred Astaire and Katharine Hepburn. Metro-Goldwyn-Mayer had powerhouse, glamorous stars like Joan Crawford and Judy Garland. Warner Brothers, by contrast, was famous for magnetically intense working-class hunks like James Cagney and Humphrey Bogart.[16]

Every stage in the life cycle of the average Hollywood starlet was, in fact, tailored by studios. There were the talent scouts who would haunt burlesque shows and nightclubs in the hopes of finding the next great it-girl. And there were vast production teams standing in wait to teach their new charges everything they needed to learn to project *it* successfully, from acting, singing, and dancing to horseback riding and fencing to skin care and fashion. Each star would have a media team, responsible not only for formal publicity but also for more casual forms of personal branding, such as leaking on-set stories—true or false—to gossip columns in order to feed a hungry public's appetite for backstage drama. *It* might have advertised itself as a mysterious, magnetic force innate in an individual, but in practice *it* could be (and usually was) cultivated by committee. A star's "authentic" personality was curated in accordance with public desire.

Meanwhile, behind the scenes, studios exerted control over their stars' relationships, ensuring that they would be—or at least seem—palatable to an American public who wanted sex and glamor, but not too much. Studios strictly enforced morality clauses in stars' contracts, ensuring that any actress whose private behavior risked bringing the studio into disrepute risked her own career as well. Studios scrupulously monitored the lives of the young men and women who had become their livelihood. According to critic Ty Burr, one studio, MGM, even went as far as monitoring the menstrual cycles of its various actresses.[17] Few studio interventions, however, were as extreme as

MGM's involvement in the pregnancy of Loretta Young, who'd had a back-stage affair with her *Call of the Wild* costar Clark Gable in 1935. Anxious to preserve Young's public image, MGM put its top fixer, Eddie Mannix, on the case. Soon, Young was taking a few months off from the public eye, while her daughter, Judy, was placed in an orphanage. Months later, Young would very publicly "adopt" Judy—a high-profile act of munificence from an actress struck by the plight of the hopeless poor—in order to be reunited with her biological daughter, who would only learn the truth of her parentage thirty years later.

*It*, in other words, was a more curious proposition than the simple truth of personality. Rather, it was the conflation of a star's imagined inner state and their outward persona. Like sprezzatura, *it* was as much about the perfor-mance of innateness as it was about innateness itself. *It* was reality reshaped and reimagined for public consumption. Or, you might say, *it* was a new way of thinking about reality altogether. Truth, for Hollywood and for Lily Powers alike, was what you made it—which is to say, what you could make other peo-ple think it was.

Stars may have been more adept at making *it* pay than most, but the Amer-ican public, too, soon became obsessed with the potential magic of their own personalities and how they, like the stars they idolized, might reimagine their faces, bodies, and ways of moving through the world in order to suggest that they had *it*. To ape the Hollywood starlet—an image of aristocratic glamor nev-ertheless democratically available to anyone who could afford a nickelodeon ticket—became, for many young men and women, a new kind of self-making. Anyone who wanted to dress like Mary Pickford or Clara Bow could use her adopted persona to disguise her actual social origins. "I used to be able to tell something about the background of a girl applying for a job as stenographer by her clothes," Burr reports one 1920s Indiana businessman lamenting, "but today I often have to wait till she speaks, shows a gold tooth, or otherwise gives me a second clew [*sic*]."[18]

Meanwhile, stars and studios were quick to capitalize on audiences' appetite to develop their own public personae. "If I could grow up to be one hundredth part as sweet and lovely as Mary Pickford," one early fan wrote in to *Photoplay*, "my dearest wish would be fulfilled."[19] By 1915, Pickford had launched her own brand of face cream, promising to help fans like the letter writer fulfill that very wish. Another early it-girl, Norma Talmadge of Vitagraph, launched a regular newspaper self-help guide, *Miss Talmadge Says*, in order to teach other would-be actresses how to move, speak, and dress like a matinee idol. And, by 1930, ordinary people could dress exactly like their idols. That year, a canny businessman, Bernard Waldman, founded the Modern Merchandising Bureau, which would license designs worn by popular cinema stars on-screen, then sell them to the general public. Within just a few years, Waldman's imitations could be found in 400 shops and a further 1,400 outlet stores.

But ordinary Americans didn't simply want to slavishly imitate stars. They wanted to become them. They wanted to celebrate their own individual, authentic selves, recognized at last by the public at large as the stars they deserved to be, with the help of the right cold cream.

Just as, a generation earlier, a cottage industry of New Thought self-help books had sprung up to teach Gilded Age Americans how to attract wealth, so, too, did a collection of New Thought–inflected guides to "personality" seek to help Americans develop *it*, or something like it, throughout the 1920s, 1930s, and 1940s. Less explicitly spiritual than their forebears, these new books and lectures focused less on positive thinking and visualization exercises than on personality as exterior presentation: how to act in the world in order to dominate others or bend them to your will. There was *Instantaneous Personal Magnetism*, which lured readers in by asking, "What marvelous force that raises the sick to glowing, vibrant health, the timid to a new confident personality, the unsuccessful to positions of wealth and astonishing power?"[20] The answer? "You, yourself—your manner—your own marvelous personal force . . . more necessary than good looks. More valuable than money."[21] Personality wasn't just necessary to become a star or even to attract a mate; it was also necessary to achieve success in business or any other economic endeavor. Paul Chapman's

*Your Personality and Your Job*, from the 1940s, reminded readers, using dubious numbers, that "technical training accounts for only 15 percent in the success of an individual, while personal qualities count for 85 percent."[22]

If New Thought had suggested that there was an innate magic in the universe that the right-thinking individual could access to exercise his power over the world, then these personality primers took that logic to its natural conclusion: *you* were the magic in the world all along. Echoing both New Thought and Nietzsche, another primer of the era, Orison Swett Marden's 1921 *The Masterful Personality*, reminded readers that "weak men wait for opportunities; strong men make them" and that "not learning, not culture alone . . . but personal power . . . make a man great."[23]

These personality guides built on the ideologies already formed in the nineteenth century: certain individuals could achieve success by turning inward, to their own selves, to make the world fit their vision. They also developed these ideas further, making explicit the implicit connection between internal self-shaping and outward presentation. The creation of the self was now, finally, understood as both an artistic and a commercial act. To become what you wanted to be (which was also, implicitly, what you always innately were) was to realize your fullest potential as a human being and, no less important, to receive material success. The world rewarded canny self-makers, these books suggested, no less than they rewarded entrepreneurs. They were, at last, rightly understood as the top of the evolutionary food chain.

These books also resolved the ultimate tension between the aristocratic and democratic models of self-making—whether *it* was something just a few people had, or whether it was available to anybody—by creating a striking proposition. As one 1928 advertisement for *Instantaneous Personal Magnetism* promised, "You have it [personal magnetism]—everyone has it but not one person in a thousand knows how to use it."[24] What separated the star, therefore, from the ordinary person was not just specialness but rather a powerful, even quasi-magical desire, their willingness to leverage their own innate personality to achieve their chosen ends.

So long, of course, as they were willing to pay $3 for a handbook to teach them how.

It is impossible, after all, to separate this new narrative of self-making—theoretically available to anyone who wanted it badly enough—from a wider capitalist system, one that cannily transformed desire into cold, hard cash. Self-making was no longer something solely available to a special few but rather something anybody could acquire—or buy. Within this paradigm, any self-respecting American man or woman might well have a claim to having *it*, so long as they bought the right products, presented themselves the right way, and otherwise capitalized on the innate specialness of their innermost selves.

From the 1920s onward, the advertising industry in the United States exploded. Each tagline, jingle, and maxim was predicated on the same fundamental principle: everybody is watching you, and you're responsible for what they see. As one 1922 advertisement for Woodbury Soap put it, "All around you, people are judging you silently."[25] Another contemporary advertisement, Williams shaving, framed it just as ominously: "Critical eyes are sizing you up right now."[26] After all, Williams reminded readers, people's perceptions of you were crucial to your success or failure in this world. "A favorable first impression is the greatest single favor in business or social success. . . . It is the 'look' of you by which you are judged most often."[27]

That look had to be carefully maintained and paid for. Every brand had its own story to tell about how perception of the right kind, when combined with its magical product, could lead to professional or social advancement for its users. Hinds Honey and Almond Cream assured readers that it was the secret behind "many refined and beautiful women," while Woodbury powder promised to make its users "somebody's dream girl."[28] Even Wrigley's Spearmint gum could help a lonely heart "get her man." Bad breath became one of the new collective anxieties of the 1920s after Listerine helped coin the faux-medical term "halitosis" in a series of advertisements tracing the romantic misadventures of one foul-smelling would-be lothario who "never knew why" he couldn't get the girl.[29] "Reducing," as dieting was euphemistically known, was all the rage in an era that increasingly fetishized the slender body. It was a literalization of the notion that if you worked hard enough, controlled your body intensely enough, you, too, could be like Clara Bow, who often reminded journalists that she was once a "fat little schoolgirl" who had exercised and dieted her way to movie stardom.[30]

But the promise of products to shape people's perception wasn't limited to the beauty and hygiene industries. Even an item as innocuous as stationery was—according to advertisers, at least—redolent with meaning, a meaning that any nosy onlooker could decipher. "Does your writing paper talk about you behind your back?" one particularly discomfiting advertisement reads. "Does it say to your friends what they are too loyal to you to say—that you lack taste or that you are indifferent to the taste of others?"[31] If *it* was, theoretically at least, about the external expression of internal personality, then, advertisers insisted, the clothes you wore, the cold cream you used, the stationery you wrote on could all be taken to express your possession of *it* or, troublingly, your lack thereof. Your personality, your mysterious inner quality, your *you*-ness, if expressed correctly, could lead to the same kind of social advancement that had once been promised by the moral call of hard work.

Yet in America, far more than in Europe, aesthetic self-making retained a quintessentially moral character. While the dandies had been relatively pragmatic, even nihilistic, about self-making—it was a way to exert power in a meaningless world—the Hollywood narrative rendered aesthetic self-making as much of a duty as hard work had been. After all, advertisers suggested, if you could look or act like a Barbara Stanwyck or a Clara Bow, wasn't it a dereliction of duty to remain slovenly, homely you? Advertisers presented themselves not as purveyors of Barnum-style humbug but rather as gracious ennoblers of mankind, helping Americans attain the same skills of deportment that, a century and a half earlier, had been found in gentlemen's guides like those of George Washington. Well-known artists like Norman Rockwell and Maxfield Parrish, lured in part by free-flowing advertising money, were commissioned for major ad campaigns.[32] As historian Roland Marchand notes, "respectable" cultural institutions like the Metropolitan Museum of Art created "liaison officers," people whose job it was to partner with advertisers to use the museum's collections in branding. And, in 1926, no less august a person than President Calvin Coolidge himself, addressing the American Association of Advertising Agencies, lauded the industry as the great reformer of America, making Americans not just into better-looking people but into better human beings. Advertisers brought to ordinary Americans the "cultivation of the mind and the social graces." They took on the "high responsibility of inspiring and ennobling the commercial world."[33] Advertising, Coolidge bombastically concluded, represented the "spiritual side of trade." It was "part of the great work of the regeneration and redemption of mankind."[34]

If the social Darwinists had envisioned human progress as a linear march toward perfection, then the advertisers of the early twentieth century helped clarify what, exactly, that perfection looked like: a whole nation of stars, all expressing their own singular, unique personality by using the same few products.

Across the Atlantic, fascism—an aesthetic politics designed to commodify the experience of specialness for the masses—was in the process of subduing nations. But, in a slightly different guise, the capitalist machine that animated Hollywood had learned the same lesson. The promise of being special could be bought and sold. And so, too, could the cold creams and breath mints and diet techniques and personal magnetism seminars necessary to a self-making, both economic and aesthetic, that was now a positive requirement for every American who'd ever been to a nickelodeon. If you wanted to make *it* pay, you first had to learn how to pay for it.

# "YOU BASICALLY JUST SAID YOU WERE"

T HE COOLEST CELEBRITY WEDDING IN NEW YORK CITY WAS about to commence. It was summer of 1969. A hundred people—artists, actors, members of the bohemian glitterati of the East Village— had thronged together on an Eleventh Street rooftop, eagerly waiting for the spectacle. Outside on the sidewalk, a chalk-scrawled announcement directed revelers to the nuptials, along with the couple's performance credits: "Superstars Jackie Curtis ('Flesh,' 'Cock Strong,' 'The Moke-Eaters') and Eric Emerson ('Chelsea Girls,' 'Lonesome Cowboys') to Be Married on July 21. Everyone Welcome!"[1] An even more ebullient press release had drummed up media interest for the ceremony, promising the wedding would "coincide, spiritually and metaphysically, with the Apollo 11 landing on the moon." Which of the two would be "the bigger event," the press release wryly added, "only history" would tell.[2]

Even the couple's officiant was a celebrity. The performance artist Louis Abolafia had made headlines one year earlier by challenging Richard Nixon for the presidency. Running as the "love candidate," Abolafia had made a habit of appearing in public naked, an easily legible way of expressing the hippie values of freedom, transparency, and rejection of social custom that would, no doubt, have made Montaigne proud. Today, however, Abolafia wore a different costume. He was dressed, rather incongruously (and sacrilegiously), in the vestments of a Roman Catholic priest.

The jazz band was waiting. The reception hall had been booked. Max's Kansas City—located in Manhattan's Midtown—was the customary mecca of the downtown artistic set that buzzed and fluttered around pop-art impresario Andy Warhol, who was there, too, as friend and sometime collaborator of both the bride and groom. In fact, the wedding reception would double as a canny piece of publicity for Warhol. It was also planned as a launch event for Warhol's *Blue Movie*, premiering that same night.

Such a venue would have been highly convenient for the groom. Eric Emerson worked as a waiter at Max's when he wasn't starring in Warhol's films, including *Chelsea Girls*, *Lonesome Cowboys*, and *San Diego Surf.* Not quite a superstar, Emerson had been a supporting player among the ranks of Warhol's handpicked performers, models, artists, and scene kids that made up his Factory studio set, at once artistic collaborators and nightlife co-revelers. Tonight, too, Emerson was on the sidelines.

The main attraction was Curtis herself, as resplendent as any Hollywood bride. A *Village Voice* article covering the occasion rhapsodized about the young performer-playwright as "stunning in a white ante-bellum gown, a beige shawl thrown over her right shoulder, her red-brown hair teased wildly, long simulated pearl earrings and white ribbons dangling from her ears, a bridal bouquet of daisies clutched in one hand."[3] If her girlish pre-wedding interviews with the press were anything to go by, she might have been another Elizabeth Taylor, seamlessly coordinating her professional and personal life with the help of MGM. To the *Village Voice*, Curtis was "a real bride, like in the movies, femme, a virgin, no less. Married and carried away into a Honeymoon Sunset in the arms of her Superstar."[4]

This wasn't the first time, after all, Curtis had put on the mantle of the old-school Hollywood starlet. Curtis had first come to the attention of Andy Warhol for playing a fictional 1930s film star in *Glamor, Glory and Gold*, a play she'd also written.

But Curtis and Emerson's nuptials hadn't been designed by a major Hollywood film studio. The artistic projects they were trying to promote were not big-budget affairs but somewhat ramshackle endeavors, funded and promoted through sui generis happenings around New York City. And Jackie Curtis wasn't exactly a traditional Hollywood starlet. Nor was she, exactly, a woman.

Born John Curtis Holder Jr., Jackie Curtis rejected throughout her life the notion that she could be limited to a single gender or a single form of gender expression. She was as fond of mixing up her aesthetic as she was of switching her pronouns. She was, she insisted, neither male nor female but rather "just me, Jackie."[5]

Sometimes Jackie would appear as James Dean, in a leather jacket with a boyish swagger. Sometimes Jackie would be Marlene Dietrich, androgynous and camp. Sometimes, like on the day of her wedding, she would imagine herself in full femme regalia.[6] In this, Curtis had joined a number of other gender-bending performers, many of whom were associated with Warhol's Factory. Some of these performers understood, and talked or wrote about, their gender in ways that prefigured contemporary understandings of the transgender experience. Others, like Curtis, took a far more freewheeling approach to the question of identity. They treated gender, as the dandies of the nineteenth century had done, as another opportunity for self-creation, a performance animated by aesthetic and artistic impulse and, most of all, by *it*. "You never knew if he would show up as a girl or as a boy," one contemporary recalled, praising Curtis's "amazing energetic aura of boundless creativity that drew others to him like moths are drawn to a source of light."[7] To her admirers, as biographer Craig Highberger put it, Curtis was "an artist whose greatest creation was his own persona."[8]

Curtis dreamed of living life a certain way, with a certain style, and she was going to make reality fit the image she had in her head. "I always wanted a formal wedding," she told the *Voice*, and by God, she was going to have one.[9]

~~~

NEVER MIND THAT Curtis and Emerson were not, and had never been, romantically involved and that the whole happening was, in fact, something between performance art and a publicity stunt for the pair's artistic ventures. Never mind, too, that Emerson himself had not bothered to show up. He was, the crowd would later learn, working a last-minute shift at Max's, where he'd run into the remaining revelers later that night. Curtis was undeterred. Within minutes, a backup groom—a pornography producer named Stanley Sweetheart—was procured, and the wedding ceremony went on without a hitch. The crowd celebrated, then went on to Max's as planned, where Curtis waved away Emerson's sheepish attempt at an apology.

"I have a show to do now," Curtis told him while mugging for the *Village Voice* reporter covering her every move. "My reception."[10]

Curtis's truncated wedding to Emerson was not to be her last. Between 1969 and 1985, when she died from a heroin overdose at the age of thirty-eight, Curtis would go on to have seven more weddings, none of which was genuine in the traditional sense. Each of Curtis's marriages—to hungry-for-fame performers with whom she had no romantic or sexual connection—was an opportunity for a new public performance. The weddings were a celebration of Curtis as a transcendently powerful being, one who did not need a man— or anyone else, for that matter—to give birth to her most valuable offspring: herself.

Throughout her life, Curtis would hunger to be taken seriously as a playwright and a poet. Her best works are prophetic explorations of the need to invent oneself. One of Curtis's poems, "Mom Eternal," reads: "'It is the work one does himself,' my mother told me / 'and not what is handed to him ready made / that has the constructive power.'"[11] Ultimately, however, Curtis would be primarily remembered for the work she did on herself, the public image that she so cannily constructed. Curtis, like many superstars who moved around Andy Warhol in 1960s and 1970s New York City, was famous for being famous.

~~~

CURTIS AND THE set she moved in represented the birth of a thoroughly modern way of thinking about self-making, one that drew on elements of the earlier aristocratic and democratic strains of the narrative, added in the mythos of the Hollywood starlet, and thoroughly subverted them. Just as the wider social and political upheavals of the late 1960s had heralded a revived suspicion of the custom and social mores that defined the optimistic conservatism of America's postwar boom, so, too, did the era herald a break from the studio-based model of the corporate star. Offbeat and anarchic, this new kind of celebrity didn't need a team of fixers or an office of professional publicity hacks or MGM cash to express her inner truth. Creativity, eccentricity, and individuality could easily replace the sheen of a studio budget or even improve upon it. Curtis herself became infamous for altering the high-end designer gowns she'd borrowed from prestigious labels like Halston, Oscar de la Renta, and Yves Saint Laurent, ripping them up or tearing into them with scissors before declaring, "They look better now."[12] Such was the wider ethos of the post-1960s mood, which rejected institutions and their claims to authority (moral and aesthetic alike) in favor of a renewed focus on the creative power of individual self—a power available, in theory if rarely in practice, to anybody willing to cut up a designer gown.

This new crop of self-proclaimed superstars finally made explicit the implicit promise of every self-help book from *Instantaneous Personal Magnetism* to *How to Win Friends and Influence People* and the Gilded Age New Thought handbooks that preceded them. Truth and desire were indistinguishable from one another. Want something badly enough, want to be someone badly enough, and it will become true. You really are—in the deepest, truest, and most profound sense—who you want to be. As one contemporary described the atmosphere at Warhol's Factory: "If you wanted to be an artist, you basically just said you were. Like with punk, if you wanted to be a musician . . . you didn't really have to learn how to play an instrument."[13] Saying and believing you were something, or someone, was enough to make you the person you claimed to be.

As Curtis put it, "I wanted to sing, dance, talk, be a man, be a woman. . . . I was a 'Superstar.' I showed everyone you could change your sex, you could be male or female without surgery."[14] Her performances of different personae weren't instances of Curtis pretending to be a boy one day, a girl another day, or a Hollywood star on a third. Rather, Curtis suggested, she really was all of these things, precisely because truth itself could be shaped by her own artistry, an artistry predicated on desire.

Self-creation and self-expression would soon become inextricable from one another. After all, what was creating a public persona but working to make your exterior presentation, the way you were with and around other people, match what you felt to be true within? And it was work. The cultivation of public presentation—whether for aesthetic pleasure, economic gain, or, more often than not, a bit of both—had already become as much a moral obligation for your average American as the hard work and discipline Franklin and Douglass had once preached.

But figures like Warhol and Curtis understood something else, too, something already implicit, if less obvious, in the mythos of Hollywood stardom. Self-making wasn't just morally necessary work. It was also economically necessary. Your public image, your persona, your you-ness—these were commodities that could be developed and cultivated.

Locke and the other fathers of the liberal political tradition had imagined the ideal Enlightenment man as a kind of farmer-cultivator, transforming untrammeled forests into orderly fields. The new twentieth-century luminaries were understanding that the interior landscape could be a commodity, too. In her diaries, Curtis refers to one of her public presentations as "the product I have always been selling and will always be selling."[15] Her body was a canvas that could bear advertisement as well as art. She'd coyly tattooed Warhol's name onto her shoulder, thus cementing for life her association with her even more famous collaborator.

As early as the 1970s, Warhol himself had figured out how marketable his handpicked commodities were. Once his superstars had begun generating buzz among New York's social scene, he started renting them out as party guests to wealthy Manhattan socialites looking to enliven their gatherings. They would pay up to $5,000 a week for the privilege of having some of New York's most notorious eccentrics pretend to be their friends for a few hours. "This way," Warhol boasted, "they can take the art [i.e., Warhol's superstars] home, have a party for it, show it to their friends, take Polaroids of it (which I will sign), take recordings. And after the week is over, they'll still have anecdotes."[16] The relationship between Warhol and the superstars was not necessarily a healthy one. He was infamous for paying the muses who made him famous in exposure and fleeting social capital but little in the way of cash. But both Warhol and the flamboyant eccentrics who flocked to him understood that the world was changing and that attention was on the verge of becoming, potentially, the most valuable currency of all. In this new, increasingly media-saturated world, creating the right image—and marketing it well—was the only way to survive.

WARHOL, CURTIS, AND the superstars were, perhaps, extreme examples of this new understanding of self-making as self-expression. But they represented shifts in the broader culture, which was newly obsessed both with authenticity and with the power of performance.

It is impossible, of course, to consider the cultural shifts of the late 1960s without looking first at the postwar decades that preceded them. The chaos of the Second World War years had given way—in the United States, at least—to a generation in which custom once more seemed to reign supreme. Religious faith and adherence, conformity to gender roles, fervent patriotism—all these were, on the surface, the governing myths of postwar America. They were celebrated and reinforced in wholesome media like *Father Knows Best*, *The Donna Reed Show*, and *Leave It to Beaver*.

In practice, however, this myth of American splendor was just that. For starters, it was profoundly unequal. Its optimistic vision of the American dream was rarely available to people of color, particularly Black Americans, to queer people, or to women who did not fit the Hollywood-shaped molds of virginal ingenue Doris Day or loyal housewife Donna Reed.

In addition, this postwar restoration of custom demanded from those who would profit from it intense conformity. The stodgy, nine-to-five-working "man in the gray flannel suit"—to quote the title of a 1955 novel on the theme by Sloan Wilson—became as indelible in the American popular conscious-ness as the submissive housewife. These were men who went to work, came home, and did what they were supposed to without questioning their own desires. They were the men who, as Wilson's protagonist reflects, "pursu[ed] neither ideals nor happiness . . . [but] routine."[17] They were likewise the men (and women) who had been lulled by the promises of Hollywood into passive consumerism, believing that the right cold cream or stationery or car would finally allow them to shape their lives as they saw fit. Capitalist consump-tion in America, a warped mirror image of the fascist cult of personality in Europe, had provided ordinary human beings with a means of simultaneously self-creating and handing over their selfhood to another. They embraced the simulacra of agency and self-determination their economic and political supe-riors provided.

The late 1960s saw a variety of concrete political responses to the per-ceived insufficiency of the postwar years: the burgeoning civil rights move-ment, the feminist awakening then known as "women's liberation." But it also saw the rise of a far more inchoate cultural rebellion: a vague, shared sense that what the culture was lacking was authenticity. In this, the members of counterculture were joining a long tradition within modern thought. From Montaigne and the Enlightenment to the American transcendentalists and beyond, as we have already seen, would-be celebrators of individual liberty condemned custom (and the sexual and social repression that went along with it) as a way of dampening the personal, individual spirit. For Beat poets and writers like Jack Kerouac and William S. Burroughs, abstract painters like Jackson Pollock, and free-love-espousing, nature-worshipping hippies like Curtis's Louis Abolafia, being authentically, really yourself could only happen once you were liberated from society's expectations.

As the characters in the 1967 musical *Hair* (book and lyrics by James Rado and Gerome Ragni, music by Galt MacDermot) sang it: "Harmony and understanding / Sympathy and trust abounding / No more falsehoods or derisions / Golden living dreams of visions / Mystic crystal revelation / And the mind's true liberation."[18]

The counterculture warriors believed that the promise of the American dream—individual freedom against a stratified and hypocritical society—had been turned against itself. Now, they feared, economic self-making was no longer an avenue toward freedom but rather a descent into further repression. Whatever made people really themselves, it could not simply be reduced to the work they did for the Man or even to their success in doing it. Likewise, the Hollywood studios, once the chief creators and propagators of the aesthetic ideal of self-creation, were similarly suspect. The stars they created no longer seemed to be mysterious gods, animated by a force mere viewers could not understand, but rather repulsively over-polished products. Hollywood's meticulously coiffed screen sirens, to the countercultural mind, resembled less the effortlessly chic Clara Bow than they did her stodgy socialite rival.

Intensifying this cultural dissatisfaction was a growing sense that new technological developments were making the world less authentic. Just as, half a century earlier, the development of the film camera had made it possible to disseminate an alluring image to millions of people, so, too, did newer inventions make such dissemination ever more democratic. Cassette recorders (invented in 1963), portable movie cameras (first invented in the nineteenth century but not perfected until the 1950s), and Xerox copiers (patented in

1948) had all taken the act of lifelike reproduction out of the hands of major film and production studios and put it into those of ordinary Americans.

And, of course, there was television. In just a few years, it had gone from a luxury product to an everyday necessity. In 1950, less than four thousand American households had a television. By 1960, they could be found in almost nine out of every ten American homes.[19] Americans no longer needed to flock to the nickelodeon to see their favorite performers—or to learn what was happening in the world around them. All they had to do was switch on the news.

This democratization of technology was thrilling. But it was also, for many Americans, destabilizing, as more and more areas of their lives and their homes were saturated with images. There were images of performers, actors in hit television shows like *I Love Lucy* and *The Dick Van Dyke Show.* There were images of products, sold in commercials between episode segments. And there were images of the global news, including of the Vietnam War (1955–1975), the first war in history to be completely televised.

Less than a century earlier, the aristocratic dandies of Europe had posited that the whole world was simply a pose, one where reality was little more than what the powerful made of it. Now, every American with a television set had access to a world where reality and its representation were no longer easily dissociated. As one critic of the era, Harold Rosenberg, reflected in a March 2, 1973, issue of the *New Yorker,* "We have entered an epoch in which nothing is real until it has been reproduced. . . . Facts no longer enjoy any privilege over various renderings of them."[20]

Politics at home as well as abroad morphed to reflect this new vision of reality. From 1960 onward, entertainment and governance became inextricable from one another, at least on the small screen. That year, a televised presidential debate between candidates John F. Kennedy and Richard Nixon was broadcast to seventy million people. Nixon, then the vice president to Dwight D. Eisenhower, had been the favorite to win the election that year, but he had performed astoundingly poorly in front of the cameras. While Kennedy—glowing with the aid of cannily applied stage makeup—came across as virile, healthy, and confident, a barefaced Nixon looked to the camera, and to more than a third of Americans, as jaundiced and haggard, his now notorious five-o'clock shadow presenting Americans with an image of slovenly disarray. By the next day, polls would shift in Kennedy's favor. He would go on to win the election and, at forty-three, become the youngest man to ever hold the office.

The Kennedy years saw JFK transform the White House into a kind of Hollywood spectacle. It was a Camelot of chivalric ideals and splendid glamor, aided by the keen fashion sense of Kennedy's socialite wife Jackie, who played a radiant Guinevere to her husband's magnanimous and charming Arthur. Never mind that, behind the scenes, Kennedy was a notorious philanderer whose political team had to work around the clock to keep his infidelities from hitting the press, or that Kennedy's actual administration was as marked by spectacular failure—the catastrophic near miss of the Cuban Missile Crisis and the imploded attempt to overthrow Fidel Castro—as by the success displayed on television.

Yet it was Nixon himself who, five years after Kennedy's assassination, would learn the most from his earlier misstep. By 1968, when Nixon defeated Hubert Humphrey to succeed Lyndon B. Johnson, the candidate had meticulously assembled a team steeped in the images and rhetoric of television advertising. In the 1969 book *The Selling of the President 1968*, Joe McGinniss, a young reporter who had embedded with the Nixon campaign, published a blistering account of Nixon's attempts to manipulate and rehabilitate his public image.

"Television," McGinniss wrote, "was the only answer. . . . But not just any kind of television. . . . [Experts] would have to find the proper settings for him, or if they could not be found, manufacture them."[21] What the American public needed was not a real-life president but rather someone who could convincingly play one on television. Or, as McGinniss records one of Nixon's speechwriters saying, "It's not what's there that counts, it's what is projected . . . [and] what the viewer receives. It's not the man we have to change but rather the received impression. And this impression often depends more on the medium and its use than it does on the candidate himself."[22] Even a presidential candidate was fundamentally a commodity, a product to be advertised and sold to a people hungry for the emotional experience of someone else's personality. "It is not surprising," McGinniss wrote, "that politicians and advertising men should have discovered one another . . . [for] they recognized that the citizen did not so much vote for a candidate as make a psychological purchase of him."[23]

In many ways, television had helped the American political establishment discover what D'Annunzio and his successors had learned across the Atlantic fifty years before: that political and aesthetic power were inextricable from one another. To attract the love and loyalty of the common people, you had to sell them the fantasy that you were a godlike being, superior to ordinary mortals, and also that your superiority was somehow attainable, that anyone who followed you could become like you. In writing about this new generation of televised politicians, another cultural critic, Marshall McLuhan, describes them in a manner that echoes the dictates of the Renaissance courtier: "The success of any TV performer depends on his achieving a low-pressure style of presentation. The harder a man tries, the better he must hide it. The TV politician cannot make a speech; he must engage in intimate conversation."[24] Ultimately, McLuhan concludes, the secret is "carefully studied nonchalance"—sprezzatura, by a different name.

Yet, McGinniss's speechwriter suggests, selling a fantasy wasn't exactly the same thing as telling a lie. Rather, it was the reshaping of reality itself. To present himself as a viable, Camelot-style president, Nixon didn't have to tell a falsehood. Nor did he have to change who he really was. Rather, according to his speechwriter's logic, he had to effectively convey a particular kind of truth to ensure that his received impression was consistent with the image of himself he wanted to display. Whether Nixon really was or wasn't presidential was beside the point and perhaps even nonsensical. He was presidential if, and only if, people watching him on television agreed he was and voted for him accordingly. Reality was what people made it.

As early as 1962, some scholars and writers were expressing concern with this new, television-saturated vision of reality. That year, the historian Daniel Boorstin published a chilling book called *The Image: A Guide to Pseudo-Events in America*, a condemnation of what he called a "national self-hypnosis," in which Americans had lost their ability to distinguish reality from fantasy. Boorstin tried to separate real history from what he called "pseudo-events" or publicity stunts, happenings like Jackie Curtis's abortive wedding (or, say, a presidential press conference) that existed only to court media attention. The ubiquity of this new form of mass media, Boorstin argued, had made it impossible for Americans to live life authentically. Instead, they sought to fulfill their emotional needs by participating in a culture of celebrity. They had outsourced their fantasies and desires to these new gods, those who in many cases were not renowned for any particular talent or virtue but merely "well-known for well-known-ness."[25]

Boorstin's hypothesis was specific to the television era and to the particular new challenges that it presented to the American experience of truth, reality, and the allure of advertising. But the culture of unreality that he describes did not occur spontaneously. Rather, we can see it as the expansion and proliferation of centuries of earlier understandings of self-making, of the idea that it is the self, and not the world around him (or her), that determines truth. In a world in which divesting from custom and deciding upon and developing one's own identity are the markers of a fully actualized human being, the line between event and pseudo-event becomes ever thinner.

The rise of television, in other words, did not give birth to this collective sense of unreality. It did, however, democratize it. Ordinary Americans had learned the lesson preached by prophets of self-making from Sade to Nietzsche. Reality was only ever determined by the person holding the camera. When the Watergate scandal revealed in 1972 that the Nixon campaign had been secretly bugging its political opponents, Americans began to conclude that, as Warhol once quipped, "everyone, absolutely everyone, was tape-recording everyone else."[26]

AT FIRST GLANCE, hippie authenticity (long hair, nudity, freedom, self-expression) seemed like the polar opposite of Factory girl artificiality. But the two in fact came from the same philosophical place: the idea that externalizing our innermost desires is an act of both creativity and honesty. You really are, deep down, who you want to be. The trick is in making sure the world knows that, too.

It is precisely this fusion of the authentic and the artificial that defines the Warholian superstar. This has, in turn, come to define how we think about self-creation in the contemporary era. From Jackie Curtis to Holly Woodlawn to Candy Darling to Warhol himself, the Warholian celebrity understood that reality, fundamentally, was shaped by desire. Want something badly enough, want to *be* something badly enough, and reality—if it ever existed in the first place—will succumb. Our powers to create, to imagine, and, most important, to desire are as close as we can get, in this chaotic and meaningless world, to divinity. We are the only gods—Warhol's muses suggested, following in the footsteps of self-makers from Pico to Sade to Nietzsche—and our greatest power is to fashion ourselves. At the same time, Warhol understood that, once you started self-creating, it was impossible to know what "real" self-expression looked like. Reflecting about his tenure running *Interview* magazine, during which Warhol coaxed minor celebrities and ordinary people alike into sharing—some might say oversharing—their personal problems, Warhol wrote in his 1975 collection of musings *The Philosophy of Andy Warhol*, "An interesting problem was an interesting tape. Everyone knew that and performed for the tape. You couldn't tell which problems were real and which problems were performed. . . . The people telling you the problems couldn't decide any more if they were really having the problems or just performing."[27]

For the Warholian superstar, self-creation was simultaneously an expression of authenticity and one of studied artificiality. It was a playful celebration of how the unreal could become real through the force of human desire. They were the democratizers of *it*. They showed the world the truth already implicit in the logic of Hollywood: the difference between stars and everyday people was the power of the hustle, the place where desire, creativity, and hard work came together.

Warhol praised the drag queen—by which he meant superstars like Woodlawn and Darling who would today likely be understood as transgender women—as "living testimony to the way women used to be . . . living archives of ideal movie star woman." For Warhol, drag queens were secular saints, "consecrating their lives to keeping the glittering alternative alive."[28] After all, he argued, "it's hard work to look like the complete opposite of what nature made you and then to be an imitation woman of what was only a fantasy woman in the first place."[29] For Warhol, the superstar who put effort into her feminine appearance wasn't simply playing pretend. Rather, she was revealing the very truth of femininity, if not of the whole world. All of life was a pageant of appearances, and that those who were willing to work for it would inevitably be granted the spoils. "Drag queens," Warhol insisted, "are the reminder that some stars still aren't just like you and me."[30] Yet the difference between stars and ordinary people wasn't some innate, mystical force that came from without. Rather, it came from within.

The same hunger that animated Stanwyck's Lily Powers animated each of Warhol's superstars, one with the power to reshape reality. "I am not a genuine woman," Darling was known to say, "but I am not interested in genuineness. I'm interested in the product of being a woman."[31]

∼∽C∼∽

THE SUPERSTARS' FUSION of artificiality and authenticity would come to have repercussions far beyond their narrow artistic circle. The idea that you not only could but should create a persona for yourself—and that this persona was the most authentic thing about you—would soon become a maxim of American culture.

Ultimately, it wasn't one of Warhol's outré Factory girls who brought these ideas firmly out of the New York subculture and into the American mainstream. Rather, it was another one of Warhol's admirers and another one of Jackie Curtis's would-be grooms: a young man named Lance Loud.

In 1973, Loud made his first television appearance, along with the rest of his family, in an experimental new documentary premiering on television channel WNET. Craig Gilbert, previously best known for producing anthropologist Margaret Mead's *New Guinea Journal*, had set his scientific sights closer to home. What Gilbert wanted to present to the American people was the American people themselves—or, more specifically, the American family. The world, Gilbert felt, was in flux. It was time to investigate what that meant for the average, nuclear American family in the 1970s. "What is the current American dream?" Gilbert asked in his voice-over introduction to the show. "Why has marriage become less than a permanent arrangement? What is left of the parent-child relationship? Where are America's children going?"[32] *An American Family*, Gilbert promised, would solve those very questions by exploring authentically what all-American television shows like *The Brady Bunch* and *Leave It to Beaver* had falsely promised to display: the real family, unvarnished, unadorned.

The Loud family seemed, at first glance, to be the perfect "authentic" subject. They were upper middle class; they were conventionally attractive (it almost goes without saying that they were white); they were Californian, with just a touch of Hollywood. And, no less important, they were willing to allow television cameras unfettered access into their homes and into the lives of their children for six months straight. Not that they were the only ones. Gilbert would later claim that nearly all of the fifty-odd families he'd considered for the project had agreed to let cameras film their every move. But the Louds were telegenic and perhaps hoped that television would allow them to build their own personal brands. As Andreas Killen reports in his extensive treatment of the Loud family in his history of the year 1973, patriarch Bill would later ruefully recall his hope that *An American Family* would transform him and wife

Pat into "West Coast Kennedys."[33] They hoped to become aspirational avatars of elegance and success, who had achieved the glamorous American dream through hard work (Bill was an independent businessman) and perfectly manicured physical presentation. And so, in pursuit of their dream of fame, they let cameras into their lives, gathering three hundred hours' worth of material that would ultimately be whittled down into twelve hour-long episodes.

Every family has its secrets. But what soon shocked America is that a family with quite as many secrets as the Louds had agreed to share them with the American public. Bill Loud, it soon became clear, was chronically unfaithful to Pat. Yet it was Pat who would scandalize the public further by asking her husband for a divorce on-screen.

And then there was their son Lance. Lance, America soon learned, wasn't just a slightly risqué downtown artist, living among the Warhol set at New York's Chelsea Hotel. He was also an openly gay man at a time when acknowledging homosexuality on television was virtually unthinkable. Yet there Lance was, owning his camp aesthetic ("I love to live with style and a certain phony put-on elegance," he told cameras, informing them that "I want to be a superstar") without fear or shame.[34] In *An American Family*'s most famous episode, an astounded but ultimately supportive Pat visits Lance in New York, where he introduces her to both Jackie Curtis and Holly Woodlawn.

Lance had always wanted to be a star in the Curtis/Woodlawn mode. As a teenager, he'd dyed his hair silver in an homage to his idol, Andy Warhol, and the pair had corresponded by letter for a time. And although they'd fallen out of touch, Loud had moved to New York City as soon as he could, anxious to make his dreams of a certain kind of stardom a reality—or, at least as close to reality as you could get in Warhol's orbit.

Lance thrilled and appalled his audience in equal measure, as did the Louds as a whole. This new genre of documentary—it had not yet become known as reality television—seemed to have laid all of America's neuroses bare. It was one thing for the Jackie Curtises and Andy Warhols of the world to live life as a work of art. But, *An American Family* suggested, living life onstage was now something everybody did. Worse still, it was something everybody enjoyed.

Critics were appalled and fascinated in equal measure. Anthropologist Margaret Mead marveled at the invention of a new genre of art, "as new and significant as the invention of drama or the novel—a new way in which people can learn to look at life, by seeing the real life of others interpreted by the camera."[35] Other critics, as author Andreas Killen notes in his cultural history of the year 1973, were less forgiving. *Time* magazine diagnosed the Louds as victims of a cultural "compulsion to confess."[36] The *New Republic*'s Roger Rosenblatt called this new type of television an "attempt . . . to create its own brand of realism, and to destroy our idea of reality in the process."[37] All of the Louds (not just the flamboyant Lance), critics felt, suffered from the primary cultural sickness in America: a false consciousness of the self as celebrity.

Or, as writer Abigail McCarthy put it: "In public life one learns very quickly that everyone wants to be on television. There are very few private people left. Let a television crew appear. . . . A crowd gathers almost at once, pushing each other, pressing close so that they, too, will be on screen. Appear on a talk show, and you take on new reality, even for close friends. In recent months we have seen the wife of a prisoner of war allowing her husband's first phone call to be recorded by television sound and camera crew—without his knowledge."[38]

But it was Lance Loud who put it most clearly: "TV swallowed my family."[39]

~~~~~~

*AN AMERICAN FAMILY* had touched a nerve, making plain that Warhol's fifteen minutes of fame no longer applied to just would-be superstars. Rather, Americans were coming to recognize that everyone—people who looked and acted like Bill as well as those who looked and acted like Lance—could be famous. "With innumerable variations," another critic lamented, "the Louds are all around us."

The furor around *An American Family* would die down, and it would be decades until MTV's *The Real World* brought reality television back into American public life. Lance Loud would go on to become a vocal LGBT rights advocate and journalist. Bill and Pat would indeed divorce, although they would ultimately reconcile following Lance's death from AIDS-related complications in 2001.

But if there was a breakout character of *An American Family*, it was not the superstar Lance but rather Pat herself. She was an ordinary California housewife who credited the reality show with giving her the courage to end her marriage and, in so doing, to at last find out who she really was.

Pat would move to New York, befriend the Warhol set, and function as a kind of den mother for the city's queer glitterati for decades to come. But it was precisely the experience of thinking of herself as a character, of performing Pat Loud for an audience, she suggested, that motivated her to leave her philandering husband in the first place. Becoming a character, she told one interviewer, had helped her think about who she was deep down. She had learned the same lesson that the Warhol crowd knew so intimately: true authenticity means becoming who you want to be.

"So now instead of going into analysis or getting my MA or boozing or running off with a beach bum," she said, "all in search of my real self, apparently I've acquired a real self just by being on channel 13."[40]

# ten

# "DO IT YOURSELF"

I N SPRING OF 1994, A FEW INTREPID SEEKERS WERE TRYING TO work out how to transcend their bodies. All across California, particularly around the technology hub that would come to be known as Silicon Valley, entrepreneurs were obsessed with the power of human technological potential and, in particular, the potential of the networked community known as the World Wide Web. Even by these standards, however, the idealistic members of the Extropian movement were extreme.

They had, as a contemporary *Wired* magazine article reported, their own secret handshake: spreading out their fingers and pointing to the stars. They had their own language, Extropia, for use in any small community of like-minded Extropians. There was Extropolis, the imaginary outer-space city where Extropian principles would come into being as a wider political community. Extropiates were the psychedelic or ability-enhancing substances that, once taken, would maximize their Extropian potential.[1] They had their own sacred text, *Extropy* magazine. And, most important, they had their own theology: a new vision for humankind.

Founded in 1988 by the British-born futurist and philosopher Max More (originally Max O'Connor), then just a twenty-four-year-old Oxford graduate with a passion for science fiction, the Extropian movement was dedicated to a new, optimistic dream of human potential. Extropy, for More, was the opposite of entropy, a description of the disorder that physical systems—including living ones—inevitably tend toward, according to the fundamental laws of physics that held that all of life's processes would ultimately descend into disorder and decay. Rather, More believed that with the help of human ingenuity and technological development, life could be not just improved but perfected. Extropy, as More wrote in a 1990 manifesto, meant "boundless expansion."[2] It was a process by which human beings could attain "more intelligence, wisdom and personal power, an unlimited lifespan, and removal of natural, social, biological, and psychological limits of self-actualization and self-realization."[3] It meant "self-transformation," "dynamic optimism," "intelligent technology"—all bullet points in More's manifesto. It meant freedom, not just from outmoded human custom but from outmoded human biology. Nature really had had her day.

"No longer is biology destiny," the *Wired* journalist Ed Regis breathlessly wrote of the movement. "With genetic engineering, biology is under human control. And with nanotechnology, smart drugs, and advances in computation and artificial intelligence, so is human psychology. Suddenly technology has given us powers with which we can manipulate not only external reality— the physical world—but also, and much more portentously, ourselves. We can become whatever we want to be: that is the core of the Extropian dream."[4]

And maybe, just maybe, the Extropians could defeat death itself.

By the first major Extropian conference in Sunnyvale, California, in April 1994, More's followers had already come to the conclusion that indefinite life extension, if not outright bodily resurrection, was achievable. Among the presentations at the conference, which billed itself as a "joyful celebration of humanity's limitless potential and how it will be achieved," was a talk by Mike Perry, a onetime computer science PhD who now presided over twenty-seven cryogenically preserved corpses (seventeen heads, ten unsevered bodies) at the Arizona-based Alcor Life Extension Foundation.[5] Perry assured his eager listeners that "immortality is mathematical, not mystical."[6] Cryogenics could help anyone with the cash to freeze their corpse shortly after death and wait out the decades until the inevitable discovery of how to bring the dead back to life. Furthermore, Perry went on, the true Extropian needn't worry about what happened to their body, even if they were to die in a particularly grisly, hard-to-restore way. Soon, he insisted, it would become possible for enterprising Extropians to upload their entire consciousness to a computer. After all, if human beings were little more than composites of information, then it should be easy enough to preserve that information long beyond the body's lifespan. Just keep rebooting yourself from your last save point, and you could keep your information alive in the world indefinitely.

But the Extropians weren't just interested in defeating death. They were interested in optimizing every aspect of human existence, transforming the body into the best possible machine. More had written extensively on what he viewed as "morphological freedom"—the right, if not the duty, of human beings to change their bodies in order to cast off the limitations of being mere *Homo sapiens*. Quoting heavily from Nietzsche, More argued that self-transcendence was a moral responsibility and, furthermore, the very foundation of the human condition. "Self transformation," he wrote, "is a virtue because it promotes our survival, our efficacy, and our well-being. As a dynamic process of self-overcoming, an internally generated drive to grow and thrive, it is the very essence and highest expression of life."[7] That self-overcoming could mean life extension. It could mean the abolition of aging, sickness, depression, and other physical ailments. Or it could mean getting rid of the human body altogether, instead adopting "the creation of faces and voices as synthetic means of expression."[8] It could mean "transhumanism": transcending the human condition by transforming the body into equal parts flesh and machine.

The possibilities for transhumanism were limitless, at least in theory. As another article in *Extropy* magazine put it, "You can be anything you like. . . . You can be big or small; you can be lighter than air, and fly; you can teleport and walk through walls. You can be a lion or an antelope, a frog or a fly, a tree, a pool, the coat of paint on a ceiling."[9] Human beings, for the first time, would be able to choose—with the help of neural implants or mechanical limbs or cryogenic corpses or anything else that they could dream of—what their species' future would look like. If Herbert Spencer's social Darwinism had predicted that the clever and the enterprising would make it to the top of the evolutionary food chain, the Extropians wanted to do away with the evolutionary order altogether. What human beings became was for human beings, not nature, to decide. More excoriated those who cautioned against such seeming hubris as being parochial, just as driven by custom and superstition as was *la foule* of a century past.

"We will ignore," More proclaimed, "the biological fundamentalists who will invoke 'God's plan,' or 'the natural order of things,' in an effort to imprison us at the human level. . . . To fully flower, self-transformation requires a rebellion against humanity."[10] The idea already implicit in so much of the post-Enlightenment narrative of self-creation—that to become your truest and best self, you had to cut yourself off from society at large—had here become explicit. Nature, custom, society—all of these phenomena paled in comparison to what individual human beings could do to rewrite the story of humanity itself.

Yet the Extropians weren't just interested in liberating their bodies from the so-called human condition. They wanted to liberate themselves from a society and political community they saw as hopelessly mired in centuries' worth of custom, superstition, and obligation. They, like More, made a habit of changing their names. They abandoned those names handed down to them by their parents in favor of monikers to, in More's words, "project what they value, rather than retaining a label connecting them to an unchosen background."[11] There was More's wife, the aptly titled Natasha Vita-More (born Nancie Clark). Another Extropian, Mark Potts, upgraded his name to Mark Plus, according to Regis's 1994 *Wired* article on the movement. Yet another, Harry Shapiro, went with the alliterative Harry Hawk, while Iranian transhumanist

Fereidoun M. Esfandiary dispensed with human names altogether and went instead by the legal name FM-2030.

"Conventional names define a person's past: ancestry, ethnicity, nationality, religion," FM-2030 told Larry King in a 1989 episode of King's eponymous talk show. "I am not who I was ten years ago and certainly not who I will be in twenty years. The name 2030 reflects my conviction that the years around 2030 will be a magical time. In 2030 we will be ageless and everyone will have an excellent chance to live forever."[12] Our ethnic origins, our family's choices, our traditions—in other words, the things that typically go into naming a child—do nothing but hold us back, occluding our real personalities. Only by naming ourselves can we express to the world who we really are.

To evolve as a species, these transhumanists believed, we needed to leave all vestiges of custom and collectivism behind. Humanity had to dispense with everything that was not chosen, was not actively willed, was not a conscious part of the ascent toward self-optimization. After all, in this new technological landscape—where people could for the first time communicate instantly and easily with like-minded people all over the world—the old arbiters of custom, such as place, parents, or even governments would soon become irrelevant. At the Extro 1 conference, participants shared a deep suspicion of the bureaucratic sclerosis of the state and the Clinton administration. One Extropian told Regis that the US leadership was simply a bunch of "entropic deathworkers," putting unnecessary restrictions on human ingenuity.[13] Tom Morrow, the movement's in-house legal theorist, proposed that Extropians band together to form a sovereign libertarian state, "Free Oceana," by creating a network of artificial islands in the middle of the ocean.

~~~⚭~~~

EVEN AT ITS height, the Extropian movement was a small one. There were about seventy-five attendees at the Sunnydale conference, and the movement's email list—its primary method of communication—hovered under four hundred members. The Extropy Institute remained active, publishing *Extropy* magazine and related manifestos, until 2006, when More, Vita-More, and Morrow all departed for other libertarian and transhumanism-adjacent ventures. (More later served as CEO of cryogenics company Alcor.) But the Extropian movement heralded the alliance between centuries-old narratives of self-making and the new technologies that would launch them into overdrive.

The Extropians understood that the technological developments of the late twentieth century—the personal computer, the World Wide Web— would irrevocably change how we think about our bodies, our desires, and what counts as our real selves. They understood that the incipient Internet culture offered the freedom to exist beyond our physical bodies and beyond our geographic communities. This, then, would embed the moral and even spiritual call toward self-creation in every aspect of our ordinary lives. This new Internet-infused culture would draw on both the aristocratic tradition of Nietzschean self-making—with its obsession with powerful individuals whose desire for power would allow them to reshape a fundamentally meaningless world—and the democratic, capitalist American obsession with self-optimization as a moral calling.

The ideology of these techno-utopians would affect not just the transhumanists and death defiers of Silicon Valley but also the millions of ordinary Americans whose daily lives and livelihoods are now shaped by smartphone apps and network algorithms. The mystic optimism of the Extropians—their faith in human perfectibility, their contempt for those unwilling or unable to transform themselves according to their will, their libertarian distrust of a state synonymous with the sclerosis of custom—is integral to the ideology of today's tech founders, from Google's Larry Page and Sergey Brin and the late Steve Jobs of Apple, to Twitter's cofounder and former CEO Jack Dorsey, PayPal's Peter Thiel, and Tesla's Elon Musk.

THE TECHNO-UTOPIAN OBSESSION with self-optimization arose out of the same landscape of distinctly American postwar cultural anxieties about authenticity, truth, and the role of the self in society that gave birth to Warhol's superstars. The 1960s counterculture, with its rejection of conformity and its obsession with human liberation through self-expression, saw in the promise of technology the potential for a transcendence of human nature. Humanity could leave behind its biases, its customs, its outmoded frailties and instead reimagine itself as part of a newer, better community linked by love, not blood. As the media theorist Marshall McLuhan wrote in his 1964 book *Understanding Media*, "Today, we have extended our central nervous system itself in a global embrace, abolishing both space and time as far as our planet is concerned."[14]

Ironically, the earliest technological developments toward personal, networked computing did not occur in countercultural spaces at all but rather in the hierarchical, heavily bureaucratic world of the Cold War–era military-industrial complex. Painfully conscious of the danger of nuclear war and the threat posed by the USSR, military scientists and analysts were racing against time to develop effective computing technologies that would allow, for example, senior military and government officials to communicate with one another in case of nuclear strike, or else to simulate the flight path of an enemy missile. Several of the United States' earliest computing companies—among them Intel and Hewlett-Packard—were founded by military scientists who had transitioned into the private sector. The world of computational technology was, in its early decades at least, a world of bourgeois expertise and men in gray flannel suits performing rote calculations to hold society together.

The early counterculture, naturally, treated such technology and the system that produced it with suspicion. In the winter of 1964, according to Fred Turner's history of American techno-utopianism, an early student protest in favor of free speech at the University of California, Berkeley, saw activists wearing blank computer cards around their necks: a symbolic rejection of the notion that the university saw them not as living, breathing human beings but as mere data points. Another 1967 editorial in a San Francisco newspaper Turner cites urged its bohemian readers to "beware of structure freaks. . . . What the system calls organization—linear organization—is a systematic cage, arbitrarily limiting the possible. It's never worked before. It's always produced the present."[15] Computing technology, like the military-industrial complex that fostered it, could only ever serve as an authoritarian mechanism of control, one that would alienate ordinary people from their own authentic experiences.

As the writer and philosopher Theodore Roszak wrote in his influential 1969 manifesto, *The Making of a Counter Culture*, the "primary project" of the counterculture was nothing short of a rebellion against the technocratic system itself, against the bureaucrats and so-called experts who demanded human experience contort itself to fit into the demands of custom. The counterculture, Roszak insisted, must instead "proclaim a new heaven and a new earth so vast, so marvelous that the inordinate claims of technical expertise must of necessity withdraw in the presence of such splendor. . . . To create and broadcast such a consciousness of life entails nothing less than the willingness to open ourselves to the visionary imagination on its own demanding terms."[16]

Yet, for some writers and thinkers of the counterculture, technology had the promise to create that new heaven and earth. More specifically, they looked to the kind of highly individualized technology that would take informational power out of the hands of the military-industrial complex and put it into the hands of the ordinary person (or at least the person with the intellectual and imaginative capacity to harness their power). Just as, a century earlier, electricity had become synonymous with a mysterious, quasi-magical force running through and animating human creative power, so, too, did information take on a new, divinized significance. Whoever could figure out how to harness information the way Edison had harnessed electricity would play a vital role in reimagining this new, countercultural world.

One such idealistic prophet of the information age was the architect and philosopher Buckminster Fuller. Nephew of the transcendentalist thinker Margaret Fuller—a colleague and contemporary of such spiritually inclined Romantics as Ralph Waldo Emerson and Henry David Thoreau—Fuller inherited from his aunt a fascination with human creative potential and its power to change the world. Like the transcendentalists, Fuller saw human creativity and social custom as enemies. True creativity demanded looking inward, toward the self, and expressing the self's fundamental originality.

For Fuller, the promise of new technology lay in its ability to take power away from the experts and institutions and put it instead in the hands of the people. The sort of person best equipped to handle this new power, Fuller believed, was not a functionary or a civil servant or a government scientist but rather an individual genius—a "comprehensive designer," in his terminology— capable of seeing from a wider artistic perspective the nature of the world and what it most needed.

The comprehensive designer, for Fuller, was an analogue to God himself, creating that new heaven and earth precisely because of his ability to under- stand the world as a self-enclosed system that he alone had the power and insight to hack. The comprehensive designer, Fuller wrote, was the "answer to the greatest problem ever addressed by mankind." He was, furthermore, the epitome of man's destiny, an evolution from mere created being to divine creator. "If man is to continue as a successful pattern-complex function in universal evolution," Fuller rhapsodized, "it will be because the next decades will have witnessed the artist-scientist's spontaneous seizure of the prime design responsibility, and his successful conversion of the total capability of tool-augmented man."[17] Fuller's inventions—including a geodesic dome structure known as the Fuller dome and the optimized Dymaxion (dynamic maximum tension) car—reflected his optimistic faith in the power of human genius, not just to improve human life but to reimagine it altogether. In this brave new world of progress, human beings could not only decide their own destinies but shape those of all mankind, once and for all displacing any ves- tige of a divine creator.

Yet few figures of the counterculture married spiritual certainty and mod- ern technology quite like Fuller's most influential devotee, Stewart Brand. A writer and onetime rock producer—he'd featured a then unknown band called the Grateful Dead at one of his early concerts—Brand was fascinated by the

potential that network and computing research held for his other major obsession: back-to-the-land communal living. Brand was far from the only member
of the counterculture fascinated by the prospect of creating new, intentional
community—during the movement's heyday in the 1960s and 1970s, about ten
million Americans lived in communes—but he was certainly its most fervent
advocate. Brand imagined a world in which hippies, artists, and other innova-
tors could leave behind the technocratic bureaucracy and the hopelessly outmoded rabble for good. Using the powers technology offered, they would form
their own self-sustaining communities, liberated from society at large. To aid
in this goal, Brand began publishing the *Whole Earth Catalog*. The *Catalog*,
which first appeared in 1969, was a regularly updated list of items that an enterprising communalist might need to leave society behind. It included both primal necessities (deerskin jacket, hunting equipment, psychedelic drugs) and
newly invented amenities (synthesizers, Hewlett-Packard calculators).

Like Fuller before him, Brand had a clear sense of his mission: to harness
the energies of a population finally come of age. No longer could humanity
accept its fate as that of mere submissive animals, blindly following church,
state, or society at large. It was time for human beings—all human beings—to
accept their new divine status. They were the creators and sustainers of the
world around them. Brand's mission statement appeared in every issue of the
*Catalog*: "We are as gods and we might as well get good at it."

Brand's mission statement continued: "So far, remotely done power and
glory—as via government, big business, formal education, church—has succeeded to the point where gross defects obscure actual gains. In response . . . a
realm of intimate, personal power is developing—the power of the individual
to conduct his own education, find his own inspiration, shape his own envi-
ronment, and share his adventure with whoever is interested."[18]

With this statement, Brand made explicit centuries of implicit connection
between the human need to shape our own existence and the worldview that
made such shaping possible. Human beings weren't simply created by God
for a particular purpose, living out their fated lives within the social order.

Nor, Brand insisted, was it the case that only a few select humans might have the opportunity to transform their destinies by playing God—the argument underlying the aristocratic self-making tradition from Sade to Brummell to Nietzsche. Rather, for Brand, self-divinization represented the fundamental apotheosis of what it meant to be human, the natural end of human evolution. We were called to embrace our destiny as gods. All of us. Only then, Brand suggested, with a moral fervor that echoes the entirety of the American self-making tradition, could a new world order come into existence, one predicated on harmony and love rather than warfare and social strife.

Of course, Brand had a very particular kind of human-god in mind: one who looked and sounded a lot like Stewart Brand. The ideal reader of the *Whole Earth Catalog* was a "Thing Maker," a "Tool Freak," a "Prototyper." He was a committed autodidact, suspicious of social norms, fervent in the pursuit of his own self-fulfillment. He was a modern-day swashbuckling entrepreneur with a talent for programming. He was simultaneously part of a new community—that of his fellow commune members, who had, like him, opted out of society at large—and more independent than ever before. He was untethered by the obligations and expectations into which he had been born.

But the *Whole Earth Catalog* didn't just express an ideology. It also helped to spread it. Its articles and advertisements helped counterculturally minded entrepreneurs and communards across the United States get in touch with one another. Just as, a few generations prior, handbooks promising readers the tips and tricks of "personal magnetism" or "thought-force" had made an industry out of Gilded Age notions of self-improvement, so, too, did the *Catalog* capitalize on the cultural miasma of the late twentieth century to pioneer a new vision of the self-made man. In 2005, Steve Jobs—one of many tech entrepreneurs inspired by Brand and his mission—described the *Catalog* as "Google before Google."[19]

Brand's influence and the libertarian utopianism he pioneered would come to shape the next generation of computing entrepreneurs. While the *Catalog* itself would only run regularly until 1972 (it would appear in more sporadic form until 1996), Brand ultimately reimagined it as a proto-online community, the Whole Earth 'Lectronic Link (better known as the WELL). In 1985 it was one of the first digital communities; the World Wide Web itself, which pioneered the use of the URL system we know today, would not be developed for another five years. The WELL managed to connect like-minded tech enthusiasts who might never have met one another in so-called real life. Early members included the founders of America Online and Craigslist.

By the 1990s, the dream of a few countercultural radicals—that personal computing and networked devices could be part of ordinary American life—seemed poised to become a reality. In 1990, Tim Berners-Lee and his colleagues at CERN (the European Center for Nuclear Research) developed the information transfer system known as the "World Wide Web." Three years later, two computer scientists at the University of Illinois, Urbana-Champaign, Marc Andreessen and Eric Bina, developed Mosaic, one of the world's first web browsers. It was made available to the public in November 1993, and within months, forty thousand people had downloaded it. By the end of 1994, that number had skyrocketed to over a million.[20] That same year, Apple released the Apple Macintosh, improving upon its previous personal computer, the Apple II, which had already found a home in four million American households. Meanwhile, Apple's biggest rival, Microsoft, was set to release its own watershed in personal computing: the Windows 95 operating system. Several other companies, among them Dell, IBM, and NeXT, had released their own personal computer models.

Brand's prophecy seemed to have come true. With the help of a device that could untether them from their geographic and social obligations and maximize the power of their creative potential, denizens of the new world order could collectively live up to the promise of the counterculture. In a 1995 essay for _Time_ (titled "We Owe It All to the Hippies"), Brand celebrated the dawning of the Internet age as the triumph of creative individualism. "Our generation proved in cyberspace," Brand wrote, "that where self-reliance leads, resilience follows. . . . If that dynamic continues, and everything so far suggests that it will, then the information age will bear the distinctive mark of the countercultural '60s well into the new millennium."[21] The maxim of that information age, Brand predicted, would be a new spin on JFK's famous inaugural exhortation: "Ask not what your country can do for you. Do it yourself."[22]

Like the Extropians, other pioneers of this new information age celebrated its political potential. The disembodiment that the Internet fostered, after all, could make those old sources of strife and inequality—race, gender, nationality—utterly irrelevant, as useless as a vestigial tail. In this vast Internet landscape, digital citizens could enter a realm in which—no less than in Warhol and Curtis's fever dreams—they were exactly who they wanted to be and liberated from all that they did not. The year after Brand's *Time* essay, another futurist, the author and activist (and Grateful Dead lyricist) John Perry Barlow, released a fervent panegyric to the potential of this new digital reality. In his 1996 "Declaration of the Independence of Cyberspace"—first published as an email and then swiftly shared across the burgeoning net—Barlow excoriated the "governments of the Industrial World," whose time had come to an end. Instead, he argued, world history would play out in "cyberspace: the new home of the mind."[23] The digital realm, for Barlow, was a place where governments, laws, and customs had no sway. It was a "world that all may enter without privilege or prejudice accorded by race, economic power, military force, or station of birth . . . a world where anyone, anywhere, may express his or her beliefs, no matter how singular, without fear of being coerced into silence or conformity."[24]

For Barlow, the World Wide Web had allowed humanity to ascend to another, higher plane of existence, one in which human beings could be liberated not merely from social custom but from their own bodies. Barlow uses language that echoes the optimistic idealism of the American liberal tradition, but he takes it even farther. He reimagines this new digital landscape as undiscovered terrain ripe with promise for cultivation. "Your legal concepts . . . do not apply to us," Barlow writes. "They are all based on matter, and there is no matter here. Our identities have no bodies."[25] Who we really are, Barlow suggests, consists only of our ideas, our longings, our desires—the people we are inside our minds.

"We must declare our virtual selves immune to your sovereignty, even as we continue to consent to your rule over our bodies. . . . We will create a civilization of the Mind in Cyberspace."[26]

⁓⁓⁓

In many regards, this techno-utopianism inherited the best of the American promise of self-making. No matter where or how you were born, no matter what you looked like or what socioeconomic group you belonged to, you could, through work and ingenuity, transform yourself into the person you wanted to be. But it also inherited that tradition's shadow side. If you had failed to thus make yourself, you had been derelict in some moral or spiritual duty. You had, in other words, ended up a little less human than those who did. It inherited, too, some of that tradition's inchoate mysticism in the way that it rendered human desire a kind of fundamental animating force. The world, techno-utopianism promised, would look the way you wanted it to, so long as you wanted it badly enough.

In one article on morphological freedom, published in *Extropy* in 1993, More posits the idea of the "optimal persona": basically, the *you* that you are supposed to want to be and are, at least in some sense, morally obliged to become. The optimal persona is, for More, "the ideal self, the higher (and continually developing) individual," whom he links explicitly to "Nietzsche's conception of the Ubermensch."

To become that optimal persona, More tells readers, in language that would not be out of place in the New Thought–era get-rich-quick guides of William Walker Atkinson or James Allen, it is necessary to "bring into focus a picture of your Optimal Persona . . . seeing yourself behaving as you want, achieving your goals. Practice until you can use all sensory modalities: Make your internal image clear and moving, and hear what is being said, even imagining the smells and sensations of the situation."[27]

Not everybody was uncritical about the developments of this new techno-utopianism. In 1995, the same year as Brand's *Time* essay, English media theorists Richard Barbrook and Andy Cameron published a searing critique of what they called the "Californian Ideology." This was a blend of countercultural libertinism and tech culture that, they predicted, would result in a wave of cultural individualism. This ideology promised "liberation" that would, in practice, be fulfilled only for the limited few capable of making their fortunes among this new "virtual class."

Sure, Barbrook and Cameron wrote in their "Californian Ideology," many of the techno-utopians believed in the potential for unfettered human freedom to overcome political tyranny and oppression. But, they warned, by "championing this seemingly admirable ideal, these techno-boosters are at the same time reproducing some of the most atavistic features of American society, especially those derived from the bitter legacy of slavery. Their utopian vision of California depends," they argued, on what Barbrook and Cameron saw as "a willful blindness towards the other—much less positive—features of life on the West Coast: racism, poverty and environmental degradation."[28] The success of the "virtual class," they argued, would be predicated on the cheap manual labor of those without computer science degrees or Internet access, a source of labor they predicted would be all too easy for some to exploit. After all, they wrote, "white people in California remain dependent on their darker-skinned fellow humans to work in their factories, pick their crops, look after their children and tend their gardens."[29]

Barbrook and Cameron worried, too, that this obsession with technological innovation was little more than a modern-day version of social Darwinism, one that would reward the ostensibly deserving (hardworking entrepreneurs) and punish those unwilling or unable to get with the program of perfection.

～～～

NEARLY THREE DECADES later, the promise of self-optimization and the conviction that we have a moral obligation to create and become our best and truest selves is encoded into nearly every facet of contemporary Western society. The distinctly American narrative of moral self-cultivation has made its way into a global economic system predicated on the notion that we can, and indeed must, transform ourselves into the hottest commodities. Untethered to our biological bodies, to our geographic communities, to custom both social and physical, we are simultaneously free to reimagine ourselves as who we want to be and constrained by an economy that demands this constant reimagining.

Sometimes this reimagining is literal. Tech investors have poured millions of dollars into biotech companies whose sole purpose is to hack human biological development—optimizing the human body, the human mind, or both. PayPal founder Peter Thiel, for example, has invested heavily in the anti-aging research conglomerate known as the Methuselah Foundation, as well as in Halcyon Molecular, a company devoted to genomic sequencing technology. Google cofounder Larry Page, likewise, has partnered with former Apple chairman Arthur Levinson to cofound Calico Labs (short for the California Life Company), which exclusively focuses on researching the biological basis of aging and how it might be stopped or even reversed. Google's other cofounder, Sergey Brin, partnered in 2014 with both Levinson and Facebook founder Mark Zuckerberg to fund the Breakthrough Prize in Life Sciences, which promises $3 million annually to those carrying out the most promising life-extension research. Amazon founder Jeff Bezos has invested in Altos Labs, a company pursuing "biological reprogramming technology" to fight aging.[30] What each of these quixotic programs has in common is the faith that human technology can be used not merely to improve the human condition but to reimagine it: to change at the level of both biology and society what it means to be human.

Yet it's not all attempts to avoid death (or, for that matter, taxes). The idea that we can, and should, reprogram ourselves to optimize our life on this earth has also suffused contemporary American (and global) culture in more subtle, everyday ways. From the step counters and fitness trackers we wear around our wrists (or, in the case of smartphones, in our purses and pockets) to the proliferation of apps and techniques designed to help us life hack—learning mindfulness or meditation through apps like Headspace or cultivating our powers of attention with work-timer apps like Pomodoro—our daily lives are defined by the expectation that we can, and will, use the powers technology affords us to become our best and most productive selves. We can track our sleep schedules and weight fluctuations; we can monitor our heart rates and our distance traveled and, in something of a productivity ouroboros, our screen time. This is supposedly all in the service of doing more, better. As of 2020, one in five Americans reported using a smartwatch to track their exercise.[31]

And, no less important, we can share that data with the world, presenting our improved productivity as part of our personal brand. New York Times technology columnist David Pogue gave a 2013 interview on the then nascent "quantified self" movement, defending the practice of life hacking and displaying that data to your social network. "Everybody behaves differently when they're on stage versus when they're off stage," he said. "You want to be your best self. You want to put your best foot forward. And that's what sharing your data with a few other people does for you."[32]

Over the past few decades, life hacking has taken the place once occupied by manuals of personality cultivation, reiterating the promise that, by looking inward and focusing your energies on developing yourself, you, too, can live the unfettered life of Barbrook and Cameron's "virtual class." There is David Allen's Getting Things Done (2001), Gina Trapani's Lifehacker (2003), Merlin Mann's 2003 blog 43 Folders, and entrepreneur Tim Ferriss's series of "four-hour" promises (The 4-Hour Workweek, The 4-Hour Body, and The 4-Hour Chef, among others), all promising to teach readers how to optimize their lives with the minimal amount of effort, simply by hacking the norms of human existence. There is, too, psychologist Daniel Kahneman's Thinking, Fast And Slow (2011), which has become a de facto handbook in some Silicon Valley circles, who see it as a guide to identifying and overcoming evolutionarily derived, instinctive patterns of thinking in order to see the world more accurately.

What all of these techno-utopian manuals and manifestos share is their belief in both the divine power of human ingenuity and the moral urge toward self-betterment. If we do not optimize ourselves, whether by sleeping the ideal number of hours a night or by maximizing our work productivity or by consuming the right amount of macronutrients, it is because we have failed to participate in the collective self-improving of the human race. Technologically assisted self-actualization marks the next step in the Spencerian vision of human progressive betterment.

Consider, for example, the advice given by Peter Thiel and his onetime protégé (and failed Senate candidate) Blake Masters in their manual for would-be entrepreneurs, *Zero to One*. The book's title doubles as a paean to human ingenuity: to go from zero to one is to create something ex nihilo, the prerogative of geniuses rather than ordinary men. *Zero to One* sees the start-up founder as the ultimate creator, a secular inheritor to both the Renaissance genius and the mature Enlightenment man, cutting himself off from custom's leading strings. "The most contrarián thing of all," Thiel and Masters write, "is not to oppose the crowd but to think for yourself."[33] The ideal founder has learned the lessons of Nietzsche and New Thought alike: it is necessary to reject *la foule* and look inward in order to succeed. Other people are, at best, an irrelevant distraction. At worst, they are an albatross, interfering with the supremacy of genius.

In its ideal form, start-up culture allows the founder to engage creatively with the world, untethered by physical or social restriction. "A startup is the largest endeavor over which you can have definite mastery," Thiel and Masters write. "You can have agency not just over your own life, but over a small and important part of the world."[34]

Central to Thiel's view of the world is a rejection of "the unjust tyranny of Chance." Like many in Silicon Valley, he argues that inequality of circumstance is little more than an illusion. Anyone willing to harness the power of genius can overcome seeming obstacles of birth and position. "You are not a lottery ticket," Thiel insists.[35] Elsewhere, he quotes Twitter founder Jack Dorsey: "Success is never accidental."[36]

Thiel is hardly singular in preaching the gospel of self-reliance or in seeing the power of technology to liberate ingenuity from the cage of human contingency. *Zero to One*, perhaps ironically, is less a manifesto than it is a recapitulation of centuries' worth of narratives about the power of the individual to decide his own fate—and the moral inferiority of those who are unable to do so. The idea that thinking for one's self is preferable to being shaped by the mores of the herd is hardly a contrarian one. We are all called now—to paraphrase Norman Vincent Peale—to picturize, prayerize, and actualize our optimal personae.

This calling is the basis of a new kind of religious sense, a reimagining of our values, our obligations, and our purpose in a world where we have replaced God as the ultimate creators. In her 2022 book *Work Pray Code: When Work Becomes Religion in Silicon Valley*, journalist Carolyn Chen shows how ubiquitous the cult of "spiritual wellness" has become at several tech companies, where coaches and spiritual leaders are employed to help workers maximize their productivity. Google, for example, sponsors a program called Search Inside Yourself, which teaches employees Buddhist meditation, while tech company Euclid pioneered a program called Be Your Best Self, which encouraged employees to practice meditation and self-examination.[37]

It would be possible, of course, to read this tendency cynically, as a craven attempt to maximize workers' productivity by making them feel more inspired in the workplace. But it's also true that, from Stewart Brand onward, the work of Silicon Valley has always had a spiritual bent. If we are gods, then it stands to reason that we, as Brand famously said, better get good at it. Focusing on our innermost selves—whether through life hacking or mindfulness—and turning away from the pernicious influence of the outside world has for centuries been a necessary part of the liberatory doctrine of self-creation.

As early as 1990, the Extropians understood their philosophy as a successor to the outmoded "irrationalist-fantasy," as More put it, of organized religion. Paradise was not "in another realm," one that removed "from us the necessity and point of taking responsibility for our condition," but rather in the here and now. It was something that human beings could achieve in their own right.[38]

"Religion," More concluded, "justifies complacency and stagnation. The religionist has no answer to the extropian challenge put by Nietzsche's Zarathustra: 'I teach you the overman. Man is something that is to be overcome. What have you done to overcome him?'"[39]

That overcoming, for all of us who are heirs to the Extropians' sense of promise, is not just a tantalizing possibility for a chosen few. Rather, it has become an obligation for us all.

# – eleven –

# "BECAUSE I FELT LIKE IT"

I N JANUARY 2007, A PORN STUDIO CALLED VIVID ENTERTAINment had just nabbed one of the most scandalous tapes in the business. Five years before, when the tape had originally been filmed for private use during a raucous holiday at the Esperanza Resort in Cabo, Mexico, its participants—a young couple in love, or something like it—were hardly celebrities. Willie "Ray J" Norwood, then twenty-one years old, was a minor singer, known to audiences, if at all, as the kid brother of far more popular R & B phenomenon Brandy.

His girlfriend at the time was even less notable. A twenty-three-year-old socialite at the margins of Hollywood, Kim Kardashian had forged a minor career for herself organizing the closets of her better-connected Hollywood friends, among them Brandy herself, as well as hotel heiress Paris Hilton, who was about to make it big. The following year, 2003, Hilton would appear alongside Nicole Richie, daughter of singer Lionel, on *The Simple Life*, a reality television show devoted to exploring, and mocking, the contrast between Richie and Hilton's privileged upbringing and the down-to-earth mores of ostensibly real America. Kardashian would make regular cameo appearances on the show as Hilton's long-suffering personal assistant.

At the time, Kim Kardashian hardly seemed poised to become a household name. She was wealthy and well-connected, to be sure, but hardly on the scale of a Richie or a Hilton. Her father, Robert Kardashian, was the lawyer who had successfully defended football player O. J. Simpson on the charges of killing his then girlfriend (and ex-wife) Nicole Brown. Her stepfather, Bruce Jenner (now known to the world as Caitlyn) was a celebrated Olympic decathlete. She was certainly good-looking, but, by the standards of Hollywood at least, she had stiff competition for the sorts of roles and spokesperson gigs generally peopled by professionally beautiful ingenues. She had no particular ambitions toward acting or singing or any of the other performance-adjacent fields common in the Hollywood expanded celebrity landscape. (Even Paris Hilton made a brief, ill-fated attempt at a pop career.) And so the sex tape she'd made with her then boyfriend, for their private enjoyment, was hardly of interest to anyone besides the couple themselves.

Fast forward five years, and the constellation of celebrity had shifted. Ray J and Kim Kardashian had broken up. Ray had embarked upon a stable, if unremarkable, career as a supporting actor, playing the brother of his real-life sister Brandy on the UPN television show *One on One*. And Kim Kardashian was about to become one of the most famous women in the world.

Her star was already on the rise. Kim, along with her sisters Kourtney and Khloe, had parlayed her closet-organizing experience into a career in fashion. The three ran a well-regarded boutique, Dash, in Calabasas. Kim's four-time guest stint on *The Simple Life* had garnered her a few tabloid appearances—aided, rumor had it, by her willingness to tip off the paparazzi as to her location. She'd been linked romantically to a few more minor celebrities, although—according to one editor at *In Touch Weekly*—she'd failed to seduce her most well-known target, the 98 Degrees singer Nick Lachey, fresh off a breakup with country star (and fellow reality TV actress) Jessica Simpson.

Plus Kardashian was poised to star in her own equivalent of *The Simple Life*: a television show devoted to her whole family, including her sisters, brother Rob, half-sisters Kylie and Kendall, stepfather Bruce, and, presiding over all of them, mother and "momager" Kris Jenner. *Keeping Up with the Kardashians* was scheduled to premiere on E! network in the fall of 2007.

The show wasn't guaranteed to be a hit. More likely, it would wind up as network filler. At that time, there were scores of nearly identical reality television shows about the "real" lives of minor celebrities. These shows straddled the tantalizing line between the old tabloid canard "Stars—they're just like us!" and carnival fascination with the most extreme or idiotic of celebrity antics, fulfilling the American public's burgeoning hunger for "authentic" stars. Audiences were encouraged to simultaneously laugh at the foibles of celebrities—as when, also in 2007, Jessica Simpson had infamously misidentified the tuna brand Chicken of the Sea as actual poultry on her and Lachey's show, *Newlyweds*— and to relate to them as ordinary people dealing with ordinary-person problems like negotiating marriage or establishing family boundaries. There had been *The Osbournes*, a family show about Ozzy, patriarch and has-been metal singer, and his clan. There had been, of course, Hilton's *The Simple Life*, along with its spin-off *Filthy Rich: Cattle Drive*, on which the Kardashian sisters had briefly appeared. These shows at once exalted and mocked celebrity. Whatever star quality Paris Hilton and Nicole Richie had or didn't have, there was little sense, on the part of the editing room, that they might wield the same kind of mystical power as Barbara Stanwyck or Clara Bow once did.

*Keeping Up with the Kardashians*, furthermore, appears to have been something of a last-minute addition to E!'s celebrity-show roster. According to one oral history of the show, it was commissioned only after another planned series featuring Lindsay Lohan, the far better-known star of *Mean Girls* and *The Parent Trap*, fell through, apparently as a result of the actress's well-documented struggles with alcohol and drugs at the time.[1]

Kardashian's ambitions, at least at first, seemed equally modest. A stint on reality television would, at minimum, raise the profile of Dash or lay the groundwork for her to launch something straightforward like a perfume line. Even more importantly, it would help her maintain the tabloid presence she seemed to crave.

Other would-be performers and entrepreneurs had long courted the tabloids, to be sure, but generally there was a pragmatic purpose in mind. Celebrity was a currency that could kick-start a Hollywood career. Appear in Us Weekly one day, get cast in a blockbuster the next. Be photographed with Hollywood's latest heartthrob, then land a lucrative advertising gig. But what Kardashian seemed to want—with a desperation that disarmed even the paparazzi—was fame for the sake of fame, untethered to any specific career or monetary goals. "[Kim Kardashian] would give me stories every week," one gossip magazine writer claimed, but editors would refuse to run them. She wasn't important enough to gossip about. Getting screen time, the writer recalled, was "one of the conditions we gave her to be able to write about her. . . . You have to be on TV."[2] And, by 2007, reality television seemed a viable path to celebrity in its own right. While reality TV had been a boon for already famous or semi-famous figures like Hilton or Simpson, it had also made low-level stars out of ordinary people who had captured the public imagination on other kinds of shows. These were people like Andy Davidson of Big Brother, Omarosa Manigault of The Apprentice (more on this show later), Lauren Conrad of Laguna Beach, or Jon and Kate Gosselin, who had allowed a crew to film their experience parenting eight children (including one set of sextuplets) in Jon & Kate Plus Eight.

Then the sex tape got out.

It still isn't clear how exactly a five-year-old sex tape—one made, ostensibly, for private use—found its way to the offices of Vivid Entertainment. Plenty of Kardashian biographers and celebrity journalists, to say nothing of Ray J himself, have put the blame on the Kardashians, suggesting that they leaked the tape themselves. This is something Kim Kardashian and the Kardashian family, as well as Vivid's own founder, have strenuously denied. At least in the beginning, the Kardashian family seemed intent on keeping the tape private.

Weeks after Vivid's announcement, Kardashian's lawyers sued the company to block its release.

Regardless of the provenance of the video, the Kardashians seemed to be aware that a controversial sex tape could do wonders for a D-list career. Hadn't the career of Paris Hilton—Kim's perpetual role model—received a similar boost three years earlier, after she appeared in another originally private sex tape, titled 1 Night in Paris, that had been released under similarly dubious circumstances?

Ultimately, Kim and her family made the decision to embrace the sex tape's release on their own terms. She made a deal with Vivid, the precise terms of which have never been made public, to authorize the tape's release for a fee. (One disputed account puts the figure at $5 million.)[3] And so, on March 17, 2007, Kim Kardashian, Superstar entered the world.

It was one of the most-viewed pornographic films in history. Vivid's cofounder described it as "the number-one movie for us of all time." Over the next decade, Kim Kardashian, Superstar would rack up 210 million views.[4]

Yet, if Kardashian benefited from the deal, her windfall wasn't just financial. The transgressive popularity of her sex tape had catapulted her, virtually overnight, from minor-league social figure to major-league celebrity. Keeping Up with the Kardashians, languishing in development, was immediately green-lit. When the show premiered just a few months later, in October 2007, the sex tape was the focus of its very first episode. It was the defining incident that would introduce Kardashian's insouciant inscrutability to the whole world. Kim, or at least the character of Kim Kardashian, exists in a realm of her own, simultaneously blissfully out of touch and winkingly self-aware. She gyrates on a stripper pole in Louboutins during a "fitness" class. She giggles when Khloe corners her, at last, about the sex tape scandal, blithely refusing to justify herself. "I was horny," she shrugs, "and I felt like it."[5]

KUWTK didn't just live up to the promise of its predecessors. It eclipsed them. Over twenty excruciating seasons, Kim and her family fought, made up, fell in love, got married, got divorced, and got what appears to an outside eye to be uncanny-valley levels of plastic surgery (Kim disputes this). With each passing season, the female members of the Kardashian-Jenner clan almost uniformly morphed in appearance. They lost weight and slimmed down their noses, pioneering the highly contoured, long-lashed, full-lipped, thick-browed aesthetic that would soon come to be known as "Instagram face," designed as much for photographic clarity as for real-life interactions.

Audiences loved it. At the show's peak—a 2010 episode dealing with the fallout of Kim's divorce from Reggie Bush—nearly five million people were watching her real life play out as, if not exactly art, then high camp. The sisters fell in and out of love and marriage. Kim married the rapper and impresario Kanye West shortly after the birth of their daughter North West in 2013, becoming one half of a celebrity power couple that seemed to rival in reach—and far exceed in flamboyance—old Hollywood pairs like Mary Pickford and Douglas Fairbanks.

The Kardashians, and Kim in particular, became a cultural juggernaut, beloved not so much for any discernible abilities but because they seemingly lacked them. As a flabbergasted Barbara Walters put it in one 2011 interview with the family for her annual special on the world's *10 Most Fascinating People*, "You don't really act, you don't sing, you don't dance. . . . You don't have, forgive me, any talent."[6]

But what the Kardashians did have was *it*. Or at least, they had the highly distilled version of *it* that Barbara Stanwyck and Jackie Curtis alike had predicted. What they understood—and what Kim understood most of all—was that *it* was not something you were lucky enough to be born with but rather something you could acquire for yourself. Through cosmetic intervention and shameless self-promotion, you could celebrate yourself as simultaneously the most artificial and most authentic version of you. Whatever Kim Kardashian is or is not, there is little doubt that she is exactly the person she wants to be. From her enhanced-seeming hourglass figure to her flat affect to her extravagant (and often seemingly intentionally tasteless) costume choices, Kardashian's every public expression is an unapologetic celebration of herself as a product she has designed. She is—as Mary Pickford once ruefully described herself—her "own baby." Her public persona is a celebration of the potential of living as an advertisement. What Kardashian sells to the public is the fantasy of selling yourself.

If the techno-utopians of Silicon Valley represent the modern-day culmination of what we have called the democratic strain of self-making—the idea that there is moral purity in transforming and perfecting ourselves—then Kim Kardashian represents the apex of the nihilistic, aristocratic tradition. Although she is an unlikely successor to Beau Brummell and Oscar Wilde, to say nothing of Gabriele D'Annunzio, her apparent conviction that truth is only ever what you want it to be has shaped not just her own public image but the whole cult of the influencer that has succeeded her. As journalist Danielle Pergament wrote in a 2022 *Allure* profile, "If you look back 10, 15 years, you can almost see a bright generational divide delineating the moment that Kim Kardashian's body became the Platonic ideal of a body. But . . . Kardashian wasn't born with it, she created it. What we admire in her isn't the idea that she was born with it; we are admiring an act of creation. . . . Her body is her canvas."[7]

Kardashian can hardly be said to possess any of the traditional qualities of the dandy-style, aristocratic self-creator. Nothing about her looks effortless. Her famously flat affect—perhaps a modern-day answer to Brummell's nonchalance—is so extreme as to border on camp. Rather, she embraces—with every (seeming) alteration of her ever more chiseled features—the quintessentially American notion that hard work and naked ambition make you who you really are. Her authenticity and her artificiality are one and the same.

Early in 2022, Kardashian was roundly mocked by Internet commentators for blithe remarks she made in an interview with *Variety* magazine. "I have the best advice for women in business," she told journalist Elizabeth Wagmeister. "Get your fucking ass up and work. It seems like nobody wants to work these days."[8] The Internet, fairly, pointed out that Kardashian and her siblings came from substantial wealth and privilege. Yet this outrage missed the point. Kardashian's image, and her appeal, has always been based on her willingness to publicly hustle, not from a place of financial necessity but of profound emotional thirst. She has transformed her body into a monument to the power of plasticity. It is an acknowledgment that *it* comes not from divine favor, or from bon ton, or from innate charisma but simply from the willingness, to quote another hardworking pop diva, to "work, bitch." She sells the fantasy that total transformation is possible and accessible for anyone who can tap into their own innermost desire. "If I'm doing it," she told *Allure*, "it's attainable."[9]

It's little surprise, therefore, that the bulk of Kardashian's fortune comes from the products she sells. These products, in turn, transform the bodies and faces of her fans. There is KKW, Kim's cosmetics and fragrance company, so profitable that, when she sold a mere 20 percent stake to Coty Inc., she allegedly netted $200 million. Her shapewear brand, Skims—trading off the infamy of her exaggerated figure—was projected to bring in $400 million in 2022.[10] With a gleeful disregard toward the prevalent contemporary discourse about wellness and self-acceptance, she has hawked appetite-suppressing lollipops, diet pills, waist trainers, and sneakers that are supposed to tone your rear end.

Among her most notable ventures is a mobile game, *Kim Kardashian: Hollywood*, which lets players participate in a fantasy version of Kardashian's own rise to fame: booking club appearances, going on socially advantageous dates, and courting the attentions of in-game fans (Kardashian herself occasionally makes a cameo in the digital universe). Launched in 2014, the game made nearly $45 million in its first quarter alone and was downloaded at least forty-five million times in its first two years of operation.[11]

⌁

IT IS IMPOSSIBLE to separate Kardashian's appeal from the rise of the new technologies and social systems that made self-creation an even more seemingly democratic proposition. Three years after *KUWTK* premiered on E!, a new social media site, Instagram, debuted. Founded in October 2010 by Kevin Systrom and Mike Krieger, Instagram allowed anyone with a smartphone to share photographs of their daily lives, or what they pretended were their daily lives. While other social media websites such as Facebook (founded in 2004) and Twitter (founded in 2006) had already begun their journey toward ubiquity, Instagram—with its minimal text and aesthetically pleasing photograph filters—proved particularly popular among people whose livelihood, or desired livelihood, was looking good or getting famous. You could post a picture of your breakfast, the view from your window. Or you could use the new front-facing cameras on the latest smartphones to photograph yourself, in what became immediately known as a selfie. (The first iPhone to offer this feature, the iPhone 4, came out three months before Instagram's release.) Within a month, one million users had signed up.[12] Kardashian joined the app in early 2012, posting, predictably, a selfie blowing kisses to the camera.[13]

The Kardashians' initial fame preceded Instagram. But the whole family had a knack for using the platform, with its veneer of authenticity alongside its possibility for careful curation. Soon Kim and her siblings (and parents) had eclipsed the reach of reality TV rivals like Paris Hilton. Whether through luck or a talent for cultural augury, the clan had cottoned on to a shift in the celebrity landscape. Television—in Warhol's day, the engine of democratic stardom—was out. Social media—even more intimate, even more (seemingly) unmediated—was in.

It was now possible for celebrities to tell, or at least to appear to tell, stories about their daily lives, liberated from any competing demands that could be made by, say, a publishing house or TV network. No less importantly, *anybody* could become a celebrity simply by telling a story that enough people were willing to "like" or view. The earliest celebrities on Instagram tended to be people with at least some name recognition: a Kardashian, say, or a Hilton. But soon, fashion bloggers, fitness models, and anyone with an easily recognizable aesthetic soon found that they, too, were gaining not just reciprocal "friends"—the model Facebook had used to allow for personal connections—but "followers" or, more succinctly, fans. Kim Kardashian could parlay her existing fame into a public image and millions of dollars (and over 300 million

Instagram followers). But so, too, could someone like Dubai-based makeup artist Huda Kattan, who garnered over fifty million followers with Instagram posts of beauty advice and aspirational photographs.[14] Or twenty-two-year-old fashion blogger Danielle Bernstein, whose account WeWoreWhat had almost a million followers by the end of 2015.[15] While ordinary people gaining online followings was not new—plenty of the earliest crop of Instagram celebrities had already built up substantial followings on other social media platforms, like Tumblr or LiveJournal, or on bespoke blogs dedicated to beauty or fashion—Instagram gave would-be celebrities an even wider reach, using dedicated algorithms to bring them into potential followers' orbit (and, more importantly from Instagram's point of view, to keep viewers engaged and using the app). Kardashian levels of celebrity were—in theory, if not necessarily in practice—available to anyone who knew how to transform their seemingly authentic life, as she had, into compelling art. With that engagement might come enough money to make being an influencer, if not an automatic path to dazzling success, then at least a potential career in its own right.

This pretense of authenticity, after all, allowed for a far more enmeshed form of advertising, in which celebrities could present the products they were paid to hawk as part of the everyday lives they documented on social media. Sponsored content, or sponcon, collapsed the distinction between personal branding and public endorsement. By using and documenting a particular waist trainer, clothing brand, or piece of hiking equipment, social media influencers, as they came to be known, could inspire their followers to do the same thing, collecting a fee in the bargain. Celebrities like the Kardashians, of course, could charge up to $1 million for a single Instagram post. But influencing could prove profitable even for people without a Kardashian's reach. Bernstein of WeWoreWhat, for example, regularly earned between $5,000 and $15,000 a post.[16] These "ordinary" influencers offered advertisers an even stronger impression of authenticity. A successful influencer (or even a micro-influencer, who had a smaller but dedicated fan base within a particular niche community) could sell products as part of her (or, more rarely, his) complete lifestyle. They made the same promises as did, say, Mary Pickford's cold cream—*Buy this and you can be like me*—only in a more subtle fashion. Like reality television stars, social media influencers were real people, sort of. Yet their authenticity and their artificiality, like Kim Kardashian's, fed into one another. They lived their lives "for the 'gram," and in so doing transformed their fantasies (sponsored beach vacation, high-end fashion, perfect skin) into a new, monetizable kind of reality. They had learned the lesson of the old dandies—reality is what people think it is—and improved upon it: reality is whatever you want it to be.

In this new Internet economy, attention has become more than simply a prerequisite to selling a product. Rather, it has become a currency itself. Attention translates into clicks, which translate in turn into advertising dollars— money that doubles as the literalization of desire. Our ability to tell our own stories about ourselves, and to convince other people that those stories are true, sustains us not only culturally but economically. The carefully constructed presentation of our personal brand, after all, is no longer exclusive to those who wish to be Kardashians. All of us whose lives are lived online, in whole or in part, now spend our time wandering a digital landscape where our attention is the building block of reality.

Selling yourself has become an integral part of American professional life. For example, upper-middle-class high school students must write personal essays promoting their life experience as part of the college admissions process. Then there are the 16 percent of Americans who do paid gig-economy work through services like TaskRabbit, which allows would-be employers to choose from a competing array of handymen and housekeepers. Nearly a third of Americans work, at least in some capacity, as freelancers, a career path that requires constant self-pitching.[17] (This is to say nothing of the personal branding necessitated by dating apps, by far the most common way that Americans now meet partners.) As early as 1997, at the dawn of the Internet age, marketing experts were predicting that self-commodification would become a major part of the American economy. "We are CEOs of our own companies, Me Inc.," wrote management guru Tom Peters in *Fast Company* in October of that year. "To be in business today, our most important job is to be head marketer for the brand called You."[18] Yet it's doubtful even Peters could have predicted the ubiquity of self-branding in the social media age, when ostensibly ordinary people can sell products using the power of their personal narratives.

Professional influencers—those who consciously use social media as a major part of their career ambitions and financial security—are more ubiquitous and powerful than ever. By 2018, eleven years after *Keeping Up with the Kardashians* first premiered, influencer culture had become so ubiquitous that some ordinary social media users started labeling their personal posts as "sponsored" or "ad" in the hopes that they might be mistaken for influencers, and perhaps asked by brands to collaborate in the future.[19] "People pretend to have brand deals to seem cool," one teenager, who herself had faked a sponsored collaboration with a water company, told the *Atlantic*'s Taylor Lorenz in 2018. "It's a thing, like, I got this for free while all you losers are paying."

A year later, another pair of would-be influencers, Gabriel Grossman and girlfriend Marissa Casey Fuchs, went viral when Grossman treated Fuchs to a surprise engagement via scavenger hunt followed by an equally lavish (if not legally binding) surprise wedding ceremony. Soon, it emerged that the whole outing seemingly had been concocted, at least in part, as a preplanned marketing scheme to launch the couple's relationships with various brands; a pitch deck detailing Grossman's plans to prospective brand partners leaked to the press. (The couple maintains that Fuchs was unaware of the extent of the preparations, telling the *New York Times* that one of their mutual friends, a social media strategist, handled meetings with potential sponsors without Fuchs's knowledge.)[20]

As of 2021, influencing had become a $13.8 billion industry; 75 percent of American brands now budget separately for influencer marketing.[21] There are fitness influencers, fashion influencers, music influencers, gaming influencers, parenting influencers. There are influencers for colleges and for individual building-management companies, paid to advertise their experience on a particular campus or in a particular luxury development. There are even medical influencers, paid by pharmaceutical companies to hawk products they promise have relieved their ailments. The "psoriasis influencer" Louise Roe (698,000 followers), for example, has a partnership with Celgene, maker of the psoriasis medication Otezla.

According to one survey of the rising Generation Z, a full 86 percent say that they would post sponsored content for money, given the opportunity. Over half would gladly become full-time influencers.[22] Meanwhile, "social media star" is now the fourth most desirable career for contemporary teenagers.[23]

What could be more desirable, after all, than that fantasy once promoted by Hollywood studios? That your distinct, authentic personality could be enough to propel you to the heights of fortune and fame. All you have to do, social media suggests, is show the world a cultivated, curated, and color-filtered exterior self that matches your innate superiority within.

In such a paradigm, buying and selling the right product takes on a new, loaded cast. As well as hawking products that align with the narrative of themselves that they're selling, influencers and ordinary people alike can help bolster their hyper-specific personal brands through what they buy, be it a *New Yorker* tote bag for the hipster intellectual, a "Notorious RBG" T-shirt for the feminist liberal, or Glossier makeup for the simple-yet-elegant "clean girl."

The ubiquity and relative diversity of Internet influencers—as opposed to the monolithic standards of beauty and charisma represented by the it-girls of Hollywood past—make self-creation an increasingly open-ended proposition. No matter who you want to be, there is a product that will help you become it. Such aesthetic diversity can be liberatory. After all, old Hollywood tended to favor the white, the able-bodied, and the thin. But it also risks reducing any closely held lattice of personal identities into a hyper-specific brand—lesbians who like "dark academia," say —ripe for a canny micro-influencer to define and sell. In practice, Instagram influencers, like their forebears, do still tend toward the white, the slim, and the well-heeled. Yet the fantasy of the narrative that anyone can (and should) become a celebrity persists. Our private lives are raw material for public presentation, one that, in turn, purports to be more authentic and more reliable than any other fact about who we are.

By 2022, nearly 67 percent of Americans—including 76 percent of those born between 1978 and 1986—report that they "are more likely to buy from someone who has an established personal brand."[24] When it comes to how we spend our money, we trust influencers. Or at least, we buy into the idea that we, like them, can change our reality by purchasing the right products and presenting ourselves the right way to the world.

The Internet has merged once and for all the ideas of authenticity and artificiality, of innate genius and hard work—binaries that the narrative of self-creation has always held in uneasy tension. We live, now more than ever, in a disembodied reality shaped by other people's attention, by their perception, by the algorithms that track our desires, our clicks, and our engagements and transform them into a literalization of our interior longings. A Twitter news feed is populated by the headlines we already agree with. Instagram provides updates from our friends, acquaintances, and strangers, all bombarding us with images of their best selves. What we want, what we're willing to pay attention to (and click on), how we present ourselves, the stories we tell—all these shape what has become our new reality. In this world, we can not only make (and remake) ourselves. We can make everything else.

❧

YET FEW INFLUENCERS have understood or capitalized upon this increasingly fungible sense of reality quite like the man who might well be the twenty-first century's canniest self-creator of all.

In 2004, *Survivor* producer Mark Burnett had chanced upon a reality television hit with *The Apprentice*, which featured real-estate mogul Donald Trump as simultaneous host and judge, challenging fourteen seasons' worth of contestants to compete in various challenges in order to win a role in the Trump Organization.

Although Trump was already well-known in developer circles, as well as in New York tabloid society, he was hardly a titan of industry. In fact, he was experiencing what might very well have been the worst decade of his career. His real estate investments were flagging. In 2004 alone, he'd managed to lose nearly $90 million out of his $413 million inheritance.[25]

But Trump had always had a knack for self-promotion, even in the absence of substance, and this time he knew a good opportunity when he saw one. "My jet's going to be in every episode," he is reported to have mused to his onetime publicist, calling the possibility "great for my brand."[26] Like Kim Kardashian, Trump saw the potential of television exposure to bolster the narrative he wanted to present to the world: that of the shrewd and brilliant investor who had written (or, at least, hired someone to ghostwrite) such get-rich-quick self-help books as 1987's *The Art of the Deal*.

Regardless of what was going on behind the scenes, Trump knew how to play a hotshot businessman on TV. *The Apprentice*'s Donald Trump was a wealthy, wildly successful straight shooter, equal parts Andrew Carnegie and Gordon Gekko. And his contestants and underlings played their necessary parts, cooing in astonishment at the sight of Trump's gold-plated sinks. "Oh, my God," one breathed. "This is so rich—this is, like, really rich!"[27] Throughout his tenure on *The Apprentice*, Trump featured dozens of Trump-branded ventures. In one episode, contestants were asked to promote his Atlantic City casino; in another, they sold Trump-branded bottled water. (Meanwhile, Burnett and Trump cut a clever deal with NBC to split the proceeds of other endorsement deals from companies who wanted the man who supposedly had everything to mention them on-air.)

That off-air Donald Trump was not, in fact, that rich (let alone "like, really rich") didn't matter. He would become far richer as a result of *The Apprentice*, collecting $423 million from a combination of direct earnings, endorsements, and newly lucrative licensing deals, in which Trump would lend his increasingly notorious name to luxury international properties built by other developers. And the Trump mythos—that of a dazzlingly successful, uncannily brilliant businessman—became inculcated in the American consciousness.

It wasn't that people believed Trump, exactly, when he boasted of being the cleverest or the handsomest or the most magnetic or the wealthiest man in the world. Yet somehow, Trump had the power to convince people that he was honest and authentic, in spite of his increasingly well-documented tendency to tell outright lies. His appeal seemed to be in the fact that he was simultaneously making everything up and somehow also disclosing his truest self. Beyond the slogans, beyond the gold-plated toilets, beyond the claims he made to greatness, Donald Trump really was a manifestation of his own desires, a kind of golem constructed out of his hunger to be as rich, smart, and successful as he claimed to be. Drawing on the traditions pioneered by P. T. Barnum and Gabriele D'Annunzio alike, Trump didn't just sell products; he sold himself. Or, more accurately, he sold the fantasy of being like him, of participating in an act of self-creation as gleefully camp as Kardashian's apparent plastic surgery. Like Kardashian, Trump offered his fans the tantalizing promise that they, too, could transform their lives through the sheer force of their desire, so long as they opened up their wallets.

As Trump himself put it (via ghostwriter Tony Schwartz) in *The Art of the Deal*, in language that recalls Barnum's writing on humbug, "The final key to the way I promote is bravado. I play to people's fantasies. . . . A little hyperbole never hurts. People want to believe that something is the biggest and the greatest and the most spectacular. I call it truthful hyperbole. It's an innocent form of exaggeration, and a very effective form of promotion."[28]

It would be possible to understand this kind of "truthful hyperbole"— something that was not literally true but nevertheless felt true—as simply a statement about the power of effective illusion to convince uncritical Americans of falsehoods. One could see it as Trump endorsing lying to get what you want.

But Trump tapped into something deeper and more primal about the American cultural consciousness, something that felt truer than ever in the era of

Instagram. Things that were not true, especially about yourself, could become true if you said them loud enough and with enough conviction. After all, if human beings were as gods—as Stewart Brand had insisted—newly capable of reshaping reality in the age of technological possibility, and if truth itself was only ever what you could convince other people to believe, then "truthful hyperbole" wasn't, in fact, a lie. Rather, it was a way of exercising that fundamentally human power of reshaping reality itself until the lie (that Trump's business deals were singularly successful) became the truth.

If Trump's conviction in the power of his own mind to reshape reality sounds suspiciously like the gospel of New Thought, that's not entirely a coincidence. Among Trump's most trusted mentors was one of the twentieth century's most influential proponents of New Thought: the preacher Norman Vincent Peale. Peale had been the Trump family's pastor at Marble Collegiate Church in Manhattan and would go on to officiate Trump's first wedding. In books like his 1952 bestseller *The Power of Positive Thinking*, Peale exhorted readers to imagine and focus on their goals so that they would spiritually manifest in the world.[29] Reality, Peale insisted and Trump would come to insist after him, was something for human beings to determine. "What you are," Peale wrote, "determines the world in which you live, so as you change, your world changes also."[30]

In the lead-up to the 2016 presidential election, Trump certainly changed himself. While he had always sold the fantasy of himself as a brilliant businessman, from 2012 onward his brand began to sharpen. He peddled conspiracy theories, including the notion that then president Barack Obama was secretly born abroad and thus ineligible for the office. Borrowing (no doubt unconsciously) from D'Annunzio's playbook, he posted incendiary, nationalist rhetoric on Twitter, framing himself as a virile defender of (white) American civilization from the noxious forces of feminism, racially conscious political correctness, and socialism. Trump promoted himself as the only person capable of delivering America from the globalist hypocrites and making the country "great again." By the November 2016 election, Trump had thirteen million Twitter followers. By the time Twitter suspended his account, in the aftermath of the riots of January 6, 2021, he had almost eighty-nine million.[31] Those numbers might not quite match Kardashian's, but given the proportion of Americans who despised Trump and actively avoided engaging with him on social media at all, they nevertheless speak to the influential ubiquity of a man who was a celebrity first and a politician second.

As Donald Trump parlayed his reality television show into a Twitter personality cult, and his Twitter personality cult into an underdog political campaign and then a shock 2016 presidential victory, flabbergasted viewers blamed America's fascination with reality TV for Trump's ascendancy. "Thanks to Mark Burnett, we don't have to watch reality shows anymore," comedian Jimmy Kimmel announced, "because we're living in one."[32] How else, it seemed, could a buffoon best known for his bad taste have so successfully converted his media appearances into the highest office in the United States? But to blame reality television for Trump's election was to miss the point. What had changed in America, by 2016, was an understanding of reality itself.

~~~

BOTH KIM KARDASHIAN and Donald Trump managed to capitalize on the transition between reality television and the social media age. As pop-culture icons, they may be the two most prominent self-creators of the past twenty years. They are influencers whose combination of purported authenticity and exaggerated artificiality allowed them to capture the imaginations and finances of millions of Americans, inspired by the promise they presented. They have managed to fuse together the underlying ideologies of both the aristocratic and the democratic traditions of self-making: the idea that the only meaning available to us in the world is the meaning that we create, and the idea that our thoughts and desires have the power to transform reality and give us the lives we feel we deserve. Yet, as representatives of our contemporary world, Kardashian and Trump may already be obsolete.

Donald Trump is a statesman-in-exile. After being banned from Twitter, he started his own social media platform, Truth Social, with a fraction of his previous audience. Kim Kardashian's reality show (now Hulu's *The Kardashians*, after *Keeping Up with the Kardashians* was canceled in 2021) no longer draws the viewership it once did. Twitter and Instagram are starting to cede their cultural relevance to new apps, like TikTok, popular with Gen Z. TikTok has over one billion monthly active users, coming up strong behind Instagram's 1.3 billion.[33] Today's newest influencers are often ordinary people who got lucky going viral. Charli D'Amelio (follower count: 146 million), a teenage dancer who achieved overnight fame lip-synching to pop songs, was TikTok's most popular user from mid-2020 to mid-2022. Addison Rae (follower count: 89 million) parlayed similar viral dance videos into both a pop single and an incipient acting career. Content collectives—groups of young influencers and would-be influencers, often funded by a managing label, who live together and film their lives for social media—have become ubiquitous, building on the successful model of the LA-based Hype House, which counted both Rae and D'Amelio as former residents.

Meanwhile, over the past few years—particularly during the move to wider digitization necessitated by the COVID-19 pandemic—the lines between celebrity social media, manufactured intimacy, and more prosaic kinds of self-selling have become increasingly blurred. Pornography-adjacent site Only-Fans, founded in 2016, allows sex workers, burlesque performers, and aspiring influencers alike to sell custom (and usually explicit) photographs and videos of themselves to paying subscribers. OnlyFans and similar sites have become a newly respectable income stream for would-be influencers; as of summer 2022, there were over a million content creators on the platform.[34] The idea of a sex tape causing a scandal now seems embarrassingly passé—almost as passé as the idea of the private life itself. Our desires, our longings, our creativity, our power to shape the world around us—all these, in the 2020s, are ripe for the public expression that doubles as the fulfillment of our purpose as human beings. We are the content we create.

Today, self-creation is no longer something some of us can do to set ourselves apart from the people we see as the masses, the crowd, or *la foule*. Instead, it has become something that all of us *must* do in order to maintain our financial and social position in a culture that sees reality as up for grabs, to garner the attention central to so much of our Internet-driven economic system. Our identities, who we "really" are, have become what we choose and commodify. Reality is what we have made it. We have, at last, become gods.

# EPILOGUE:
## "HOW TO BE YOURSELF"

I F THERE IS A SELF-CREATOR FOR OUR CURRENT MOMENT, IT IS
not Donald Trump or Kim Kardashian but rather a seemingly ordinary
young woman named Caroline Calloway.

Born Caroline Gotschall, Calloway came to Instagram prominence in the
early 2010s as an American student at England's University of Cambridge, gaining a substantial following by posting picturesque, *Brideshead Revisited*-style
photographs of May Balls and other posh Cambridge parties, accompanied
by lyrically breathless captions (later revealed to be ghostwritten by her friend
Natalie Beach). Calloway parlayed her Instagram fame into a reported $500,000
book deal with Flatiron Books for a memoir, which never materialized.[1]

Instead, Calloway turned her hand to advertising a series of $165 creativ-
ity workshops on "how to be yourself," before promptly canceling the bulk of
the tour and initially delaying processing refunds. Meanwhile, the few 2019
sessions that did occur barely resembled the ones advertised. In lieu of making orchid crowns, participants were allowed to place a single flower in their
hair for a photo op, then had to return the flower.[2] Undeterred by the bad
publicity—intensified by the fact that Beach published a *New York* magazine
article taking credit for Calloway's captions—Calloway embraced the image

of herself as a "scammer," announcing that she was writing a new memoir of the same name (to be self-published) and selling a $210 skin-care line she termed Snake Oil. During the coronavirus pandemic, she briefly debuted an OnlyFans page, ostensibly to fund the repayment of her memoir advance to Flatiron, and as of summer 2022, she has deleted her social media and left her New York City apartment with several thousand dollars of back rent unpaid (Calloway disputes the debt on the grounds that she says she made improvements to the property, including the installation of a $3,000 Venetian chandelier). *Scammer* is still available for preorder.

"I'm chaotic," Calloway insisted on Twitter. "I love my work. My work is writing, painting, photography, posting on social media, and living inside a Truman Show of my own making—performance art."[3]

<hr />

IT WOULD BE possible to blame the advent of social media for our contemporary cultural landscape, for everything from the alienating nature of influencer culture to the ubiquity of Twitter conspiracy theories to a Tinder-saturated landscape that encourages us to treat one another as currency in the sexual marketplace.

It would be possible, too, to name as the culprit of today's social ills—in the United States, at least—unfettered and Internet-saturated hyper-capitalism. This system has pushed millions of Americans into the often grueling and unprotected world of the gig economy. During the COVID-19 pandemic, countless ordinary Americans were left at the mercy of the attention economy, forced to craft narratives of their own lives to get sufficient support on crowdfunding websites like GoFundMe to pay emergency medical bills or to make the next month's rent. Back in early 2021, during the pandemic's winter wave, the *New York Times* ran a piece about the staggering growth—from a little over one hundred thousand to over a million—of erotic content creators on OnlyFans, many of whom used the site to make up for lost in-person income.[4]

Yet it is impossible to understand contemporary capitalism—predicated as it is on the quite literal transformation of our desires into currency—apart from a much wider and older cultural shift in how we think about human beings and our place in the world. It is, likewise, impossible to understand the ubiquity of today's social media without understanding those same wider and older ways in which modern life treats self-cultivation and self-expression as inextricable from one another. Our authentic personal truth and our artificially curated image are two sides of the same coin.

Our personal lives and our economic lives—and the two are perhaps more closely intertwined than ever—are now predicated on the assumption that artful self-expression is not just a moral requirement but a teleological one. It is what we, as human beings, are *for*. We are creators of ourselves, of our lives, of the world around us. We take on the divine role of constructing and shaping reality. What we want, and who we want to be, has become the key to who we really are. In the process, we have lost sight of other elements of our shared reality, not just the customs that shape us against our will but all the other things we do not necessarily desire and do not choose. Other people—their traditions, their customs, their stories, their narratives—are treated as existential threats to our authentic inner self-hood. We ignore the inconveniences and insufficiencies and imperfections of our bodily existence. We have, in celebrating the quintessentially human trait of self-invention, neglected that other great human trait: our fundamentally social nature as creatures who depend upon one another. If once we erred on the side of assuming that who we "really" are could be reduced to our role in community or hierarchy—treating our interior impulses as sources of intellectual, moral, or social danger—now we are far more likely to make the opposite assumption: that our desires are somehow more "real" than our relationships, and that they are a more authentic part of who we truly are.

I AM NOT arguing that the story of self-creation is a straightforwardly tragic one, a decline from the good old days of the Thomistic medieval world to the decrepit present of Caroline Calloway's OnlyFans account. The idealistic promise of self-creators from Pico to Montaigne to Benjamin Franklin to Frederick Douglass to Stewart Brand is that human beings have the right to choose for themselves the life that they will live, that mere accidents of birth or blood or race should not determine our destiny, and that social tradition and custom are never above questioning or reproach. This promise offers the potential for genuine liberation. The early Americans' call to "self-cultivation," and the ideal that if we learn to govern ourselves emotionally we can better govern ourselves politically, is and should remain an inspiring one. Our ability to create, to imagine, to dream better lives for ourselves and those around us, and our freedom to transform those dreams into social realities are among the most vital and human parts of ourselves.

But the seemingly liberatory promise that we can create ourselves has, as often as not, been warped into an excuse to create, implicitly or explicitly, two classes of people: those who are capable of shaping their destinies (and who thereby deserve their success) and those who are not (and who deserve nothing). This classification invariably places those who do not fit the dominant physical or cultural mold—women, people of color, the poor, the disabled—in the second category.

That is not to say that it would be preferable to reinstate the image of a divine creator-monarch, Thomas Aquinas's vision of a universe where the laws of the natural world and of the social world are inextricable from one another, where the right of kings to rule is as ingrained in the functioning of our earth as the propensity of heavenly bodies to fall. But we must all ask ourselves what it means—politically, ethically, socially—to live up to Stewart Brand's predictions that we are as gods, that the world is nothing but what we make of it, and that our choices, our desires, our wanting to be or to have, are the *only* things that make us human, that make us *us*. We must, too, ask ourselves how often our desires are stoked by those with a financial interest in making us think that we both can and should shape ourselves, whether they're selling us self-help manuals or Snake Oil skin cream. How can our desires be the truest parts of ourselves when, all too often, they are shaped by others? And how can we be sure we even *know* our desires—or our motivations, or our goals—to begin with?

The dream of Pico—that the very thing that makes us human is the power to tell our own stories, to choose our own destinies—is not wrong. It is, however, incomplete. We are also, as no less authoritative a person than Aristotle once argued, social animals. We live in communities; our very method of telling stories, language itself, depends on learning from, listening to, and engaging with one another. We can and should escape those inequalities and injustices that come from thinking that how, when, and where we are born should dictate our opportunities in life. But to forget our own vulnerability to one another, to forget the fact that we do shape (and, hell, influence) one another, and that there is something more to reality than what we say it is—be it on Twitter, Instagram, or in the Oval Office—is to forget self-making's wisest prophet.

"Properly understood," Frederick Douglass warned, "there are in the world no such men as self-made men. That term implies an individual independence of the past and present which can never exist."[5] We all help make one another.

The story of self-creation, at its core, is not only a story about capitalism or secularism or the rise of the middle class or industrialization or political liberalism, although it touches upon all these phenomena and more. It is, rather, a story about people figuring out, together, what it means to be human. It is a story about trying to work out which parts of our lives—both those parts chosen and those parts we did not choose—are really, authentically *us*, and which parts are mere accidents of history, custom, or circumstance. It is, in other words, a story about people asking, and answering, and asking once again the most fundamental question human beings can ask: Who am I, really?

And it is the story of how one answer—in my view, the wrong one—became dominant: I am whoever I want to be.

It is, too, a story about how that answer has brought us to a still-imperfect place. It is a place where far more of us than in da Vinci's day can dream of becoming a great artist, or a great statesman, or a great businessman. Yet, at the same time, it is a place where we are increasingly liable to mistake our ordinary human desires, and ordinary human efforts, for spiritually potent forces with the psychic or moral power to bring us fame, riches, or superiority to others. We are less likely to think that there is divine providence at play in a king being born a king. But we are perhaps more likely than we would want to admit to think that there is some magical order at work in the universe that lets billionaires be billionaires or movie stars be movie stars. We are less likely to think that our social class is really who we are, and more likely to think that our desire for fame or fortune or sex says something real about us and our relationship to others.

This is not, in other words, only a story about how we became gods. It is also a story about how we have always been, and remain, human beings: caught between facticity and freedom, trying imperfectly to work out how to relate ourselves to both. We are—as *Hamlet* still reminds us—kings of infinite space, bounded in nutshells. We are bound to a natural world we do not fully understand, to our bodies that so often betray us, to the communities that give us language and culture and shared senses of meaning, and to the interior longings and yearnings that vex and confuse us as often as they provide us with hope, joy, and purpose. Which part or parts of that tapestry of identity "count" as real? And which do we leave behind? And what do we lose once we do?

The yoke of custom and the promise of the modern self-maker alike converge, at least, on this one point. All of us—from Classical philosophers to medieval saints to Renaissance geniuses to modern self-makers to the millions of ordinary people whose lives are often less bombastically recorded—are trying to work out the answer to that same question. When we lose sight of that, I think, we lose sight of what makes us really, authentically human in the first place.

# Acknowledgments

I AM SO grateful for the support—practical and intellectual—of so many wonderful colleagues, including my editors, Clive Priddle and Anupama Roy-Chaudhury at PublicAffairs and Juliet Brooke and Charlotte Humphery at Sceptre, and agents Emma Parry and Rebecca Carter. I'm also grateful to the Robert Novak Fellowship and to Dr. William Wood and Oriel College, Oxford, for their support of my ongoing research. I also owe a debt of gratitude to my husband, Dhananjay, whose intellectual and moral support (and keen copyediting eye) has been invaluable at every stage of the process.

# Notes

INTRODUCTION: HOW WE BECAME GODS?

1. "Equinox: Make Yourself a Gift to the World," Droga5, https://droga5.com/work/equinox-make-yourself-a-gift-to-the-world/.

2. David Gianatasio, "Self-Love Is a Good Thing, Equinox Says in Wild New Year's Ads By Droga5," *Muse by Clio*, January 6, 2020, https://musebycl.io/advertising/self-love-good-thing-equinox-says-wild-new-years-ads-droga5.

3. Oscar Wilde, "The Critic as Artist," in *The Artist as Critic: Critical Writings of Oscar Wilde* (Chicago: University of Chicago Press, 1984), 389.


CHAPTER ONE: "STAND UP FOR BASTARDS"

1. Quoted in Joan Stack, "Albrecht Dürer's Curls: Melchior Lorck's 1550 Engraved Portrait and Its Relationship to Dürer's Self-Fashioned Public Image," *MUSE*, vol. 42 (2008): 63.

2. Quoted in Helmut Puff, "Memento Mori, Memento Mei: Albrecht Dürer and the Art of Dying," in *Enduring Loss in Early Modern Germany: Cross Disciplinary Perspectives*, ed. Lynne Tatlock (Leiden, Netherlands: Brill, 2010), 131.

3. Joseph Leo Koerner, *The Moment of Self-Portraiture in German Renaissance Art* (Chicago: University of Chicago Press, 1993), 212.

4. Stack, "Albrecht Dürer's Curls," 50.

5. Koerner, *The Moment of Self-Portraiture*, 103.

6. Quoted in Andrea Bubenik, *Reframing Albrecht Dürer: The Appropriation of Art, 1528–1700* (Farnham, UK: Ashgate, 2013), 89.

7. Quoted in Robert Brennan, "The Art Exhibition Between Cult and Market: The Case of Dürer's Heller Altarpiece," *Res*, vol. 67–68 (2016–2017): 115.

8. Saint Thomas Aquinas, *Summa Theologiae*, part 1 (Q93).

9. Noel L. Brann, *The Debate over the Origin of Genius During the Italian Renaissance: The Theories of Supernatural Frenzy and Natural Melancholy in Accord and in Conflict on the Threshold of the Scientific Revolution* (Boston: Brill, 2002).

10. Quoted in Stack, "Albrecht Dürer's Curls," 45.

11. Corinne Schleif, "The Many Wives of Adam Kraft: Early Modern Workshop Wives in Legal Documents, Art-Historical Scholarship, and Historical Fiction," in *Saints, Sinners, and Sisters: Gender and Northern Art in Medieval and Early Modern Europe*, eds. Jane Carroll and Alison G. Stewart (Aldershot, UK: Ashgate, 2003), 214.

12. Shakespeare, *King Lear*, 1.2, line 1.

13. Quoted in Albert Rabil, *Knowledge, Goodness, and Power: The Debate Over Nobility Among Quattrocento Italian Humanists* (Binghamton, NY: Medieval & Renaissance Texts & Studies, 1991), 41. Rabil's compendium of writing on true nobility has been invaluable to my work.

14. Ibid., 48.

15. Ibid., 109.

16. Ibid., 141.

17. Ibid., 115.

18. Ibid., 79.

19. Ibid.

20. Giovanni Pico della Mirandola, "Oration on the Dignity of Man," in *Renaissance Humanism: An Anthology of Sources*, ed. Margaret King (Indianapolis, IN: Hackett Publishing Company, 2014), 57.

21. Baldassare Castiglione, *The Book of the Courtier* (New York: Scribner's, 1903), 35.

22. Ibid.

23. Giorgio Vasari, *Stories of the Italian Artists* (New York: Scribner and Welford, 1885), 134.

24. Castiglione, *The Book of the Courtier*, 34–35.

25. King, *Renaissance Humanism*, 270.

26. Niccolò Machiavelli, *The Prince* (1532; Munich, Germany: BookRix, 2014).

27. Ibid.

## CHAPTER TWO: "SHAKING OFF THE YOKE OF AUTHORITY"

1. Michel de Montaigne, *Essays of Montaigne*, trans. Charles Cotton (London: Navarre Society, 1923), 1.

2. Ibid., 21.

3. Ibid.

4. Michel de Montaigne, *The Essays of Michel de Montaigne, Translated into English*, trans. Charles Cotton, 9th ed. (London: A. Murray & Son, 1869), 184.

5. Ibid., 184.

6. Catherine Kovesi, "Enacting Sumptuary Laws in Italy," in *The Right to Dress: Sumptuary Laws in a Global Perspective, c. 1200–1800*, eds. G. Riello and U. Rublack (Cambridge: Cambridge University Press, 2019), 190.

7. Montaigne, *The Essays of Michel de Montaigne*, 235.

8. Ibid., 326.

9. Immanuel Kant, "What is Enlightenment?," in *Princeton Readings in Political Thought: Essential Texts from Plato to Populism*, ed. Mitchell Cohen, 2nd ed. (Princeton, NJ: Princeton University Press, 2018), 354.

10. Quoted in Anthony Gottlieb, *The Dream of Enlightenment: The Rise of Modern Philosophy* (New York: Liveright, 2016), ebook.

11. Quoted in Anthony Pagden, *The Enlightenment: And Why It Still Matters* (Oxford: Oxford University Press, 2013), 151.

12. John Locke, *An Essay Concerning Human Understanding: In Four Books* (London: Printed for A. and J. Churchill and S. Manship, 1694), 19.

13. Quoted in David Adams, *Enlightenment Cosmopolitanism* (London: Routledge, 2017), ebook.

14. Ibid.

15. Quoted in Ritchie Robertson, *The Enlightenment: The Pursuit of Happiness, 1680–1790* (London: Penguin UK, 2020), 600. The translation is my own.

16. Pagden, *The Enlightenment*, 28.

17. Quoted in ibid., 89.

18. Paul Henri Thiry, Baron d'Holbach, *Nature, and Her Laws: As Applicable to the Happiness of Man, Living in Society; Contrasted with Superstition and Imaginary Systems* (London: J. Watson, 1834), x.

19. Montesquieu, *Persian Letters: With Related Texts* (Indianapolis, IN: Hackett, 2014).

20. Jean-Jacques Rousseau, *Discourse on the Origin of Inequality* (1755; e-artnow, 2018), ebook.

21. Ibid.

22. Quoted in Marvin Perry, *Sources of the Western Tradition*, vol. 2, *From the Renaissance to the Present* (Boston: Cengage, 2012), 91.

23. Ibid.

24. Margaret C. Jacob, *The Secular Enlightenment* (Princeton, NJ: Princeton University Press, 2019), 90.

25. Quoted in John Phillips, *The Marquis de Sade: A Very Short Introduction* (Oxford: Oxford University Press, 2005), 34.

26. Quoted in Lorna Berman, *The Thought and Themes of the Marquis de Sade: A Rearrangement of the Works of the Marquis de Sade* (Kitchener, Ontario: Ainsworth Press, 1971).

27. Marquis de Sade, *120 Days of Sodom* (1904; General Press, 2022), ebook.

28. Quoted in Laurence L. Bongie, *Sade: A Biographical Essay* (Chicago: University of Chicago Press, 2000), 205.

29. Quoted in Phillips, *The Marquis de Sade*, 116.

30. Neil Schaeffer, *The Marquis de Sade: A Life* (Cambridge, MA: Harvard University Press, 2000), 381.

31. Tony Perrottet, "Who Was the Marquis de Sade?," *Smithsonian*, February 2015, www.smithsonianmag.com/history/who-was-marquis-de-sade-180953980/.

32. Denis Diderot, *Rameau's Nephew*, trans. Ian C. Johnston (2002; e-artnow, 2013), ebook.

33. Ibid.

34. Ibid.

35. Ibid.

36. Ibid.

## CHAPTER THREE: "A SNEER FOR THE WORLD"

1. Marquis de Vermont, *London and Paris, or, Comparative Sketches* (London: Longman, Hurst, Rees, Orme, Brown, and Green, 1823), 132.

2. John Feltham, *The Picture of London: Being a Correct Guide to All the Curiosities, Amusements, Exhibits, Public Establishments, and Remarkable Objects in and near London for 1809* (London: Lewis & Co., 1809), 268.

3. Ibid., 268.

4. Ian Kelly, *Beau Brummell: The Ultimate Dandy* (London: Hodder & Stoughton, 2005), 190.

5. Ibid., 55.

6. William Jesse, *The Life of George Brummell, Esq., Commonly Called Beau Brummell* (London: Clarke and Beeton, 1854), 87.

7. Thomas Raikes, *A Portion of the Journal Kept by Thomas Raikes from 1831–1847* (London: Longman, Brown, Green, and Longmans, 1856), 86.

8. Baron Alexander Dundas Ross Wishart Cochrane-Baillie Lamington, *In the Days of the Dandies* (United Kingdom: Blackwood, 1890), 15.

9. Thomas Moore and Nathan Haskell Dole, *Thomas Moore's Complete Poetical Works* (New York: T. Y. Crowell & Company, 1895), 573.

10. *The Cornhill Magazine* (London: Smith, Elder & Co., 1896), 769.

11. Max Beerbohm, *The Works of Max Beerbohm* (London: J. Lane, the Bodley Head, 1921; Project Gutenberg Canada, 2008), ebook.

12. Kelly, *Beau Brummell*, 2.

13. Ibid., 3.

14. Jesse, *The Life of George Brummell*, 58.

15. Quoted in Kelly, *Beau Brummell*, 180.

16. Ellen Moers, *The Dandy: Brummell to Beerbohm* (New York: Viking Press, 1960), 44.

17. Ibid., 51.

18. Jerry White, *London in the Eighteenth Century: A Great and Monstrous Thing* (London: Random House, 2012), 168.

19. Ibid., 173.

20. Ibid.

21. M. de Voltaire, A *Philosophical Dictionary: From the French* (London: John and Henry L. Hunt, 1824), 309.

22. Pierre Terjanian, ed., *The Last Knight: The Art, Armor, and Ambition of Maximilian I* (New York: Metropolitan Museum of Art, 2019), 28.

23. Quoted in Philip Mansel, *Dressed to Rule: Royal and Court Costume from Louis XIV to Elizabeth II* (New Haven: Yale University Press, 2005), 1.

24. Quoted in David Kuchta, *The Three-Piece Suit and Modern Masculinity: England, 1550–1850* (Berkeley: University of California Press, 2002), 24.

25. Ibid., 238.

26. Jesse, *The Life of George Brummell*, 59.

27. Quoted in Kelly, *Beau Brummell*, 150.

28. Elizabeth Amann, *Dandyism in the Age of Revolution: The Art of the Cut* (Chicago: University of Chicago Press, 2015), 167.

29. Quoted in ibid., 179.

30. Ibid., 174.

31. Jules Barbey d'Aurevilly, *Of Dandyism and of George Brummell* (London: J. M. Dent, 1897), 57.

32. Quoted in Kelly, *Beau Brummell*, 5.

33. Honoré de Balzac, *Treatise on Elegant Living* (Cambridge, MA: Wakefield Press, 2010), ebook.

34. Ibid.

35. Ibid.

36. Ibid.

37. Ibid.

38. Mrs. Gore [Catherine Grace Frances], *Cecil: Or, the Adventures of a Coxcomb, a Novel* (1860), 16.

39. Edward George E. L. Bulwer Lytton, *Pelham: Or, the Adventures of a Gentleman* (1854), 129.

40. Ibid., 116.

41. Quoted in Christopher Hibbert, *Disraeli: A Personal History* (London: HarperCollins, 2010), 24.

42. Benjamin Disraeli, *Vivian Grey* (New York: Century Co., 1906), 18.

43. Ibid.

44. Ibid., 37.

45. Ibid.

46. Quoted in Moers, *The Dandy*, 85–86.

47. Quoted in ibid., 102.

CHAPTER FOUR: "WORK! WORK!! WORK!!!"

1. Quoted in Waldo E. Martin Jr., *The Mind of Frederick Douglass* (Chapel Hill: University of North Carolina Press, 2000), 25.

2. Frederick Douglass, *The Speeches of Frederick Douglass: A Critical Edition*, eds. John R. McKivigan, Julie Husband, and Heather L. Kaufman (New Haven, CT: Yale University Press, 2018), 240.

3. Ibid., 431.

4. Ibid., 447.

5. Ibid.

6. Ibid.

7. Ibid.

8. Ibid.

9. Frederick Douglass, *The Life and Times of Frederick Douglass, Written by Himself* (Hartford, CT: Park Publishing Co., 1881), 217.

10. Ibid., 140.

11. Ibid.

12. Frederick Douglass, *The Essential Douglass: Selected Writings and Speeches*, ed. Nicholas Buccola (Indianapolis, IN: Hackett, 2016), 336.

13. Quoted in David W. Blight, *Frederick Douglass: Prophet of Freedom* (New York: Simon & Schuster, 2018), 113.

14. Frederick Douglass, *Great Speeches by Frederick Douglass* (Garden City, NY: Dover Publications, 2013), 148.

15. Ibid., 147.

16. Ibid.

17. Ibid.

18. "Declaration of Independence: A Transcription," America's Founding Documents, National Archives, www.archives.gov/founding-docs/declaration-transcript.

19. Alexander Hamilton, "The Federalist Papers," in *Classics of American Political and Constitutional Thought*, Vol. 1, ed. Scott J. Hammond, Kevin R. Hardwick, and Howard L. Lubert (Indianapolis, IN: Hackett, 2007), 454.

20. Quoted in Anthony Pagden, *The Enlightenment: And Why It Still Matters* (Oxford: Oxford University Press, 2013), 712.

21. Quoted in Domenico Losurdo, *Liberalism: A Counter-History* (London: Verso, 2011), 9.

22. Abraham Lincoln, "Temperance Address," in *The Methodist Review* (New York: G. Lane & P. B. Sandford, 1899), 15.

23. Ibid., 16.

24. Frederick Douglass, "Temperance Meeting [October 20, 1845]," in *Frederick Douglass and Ireland: In His Own Words*, ed. Christine Kinealy (London: Routledge, 2018), 204.

25. Quoted in Daniel Walker Howe, *Making the American Self: Jonathan Edwards to Abraham Lincoln* (Oxford: Oxford University Press, 2009), 153.

26. Quoted in Losurdo, *Liberalism*, 11.

27. Quoted in ibid., 10.

28. John Locke, *Two Treatises of Government* (London: C. and J. Rivington, 1824), 146.

29. John Locke, *Locke: Political Essays* (Cambridge: Cambridge University Press, 1997), 180.

30. John Stuart Mill, *The Collected Works of John Stuart Mill* (e-artnow, 2017), ebook.

31. Douglass, *The Speeches of Frederick Douglass*, 431.

32. Quoted in Jim Cullen, *The American Dream: A Short History of an Idea that Shaped a Nation* (Oxford: Oxford University Press, 2004), 47.

33. William Cowper, *The Poetical Works of William Cowper* (London: William Smith, 1839), 142.

34. Quoted in Richard L. Bushman, *The Refinement of America: Persons, Houses, Cities* (New York: Vintage, 2011), 31.

35. Quoted in Ron Chernow, *Washington: A Life* (New York: Penguin, 2011).

36. Quoted in Willard Sterne Randall, *George Washington: A Life* (New York: Henry Holt & Company, 1998), 30.

37. Harriet Beecher Stowe, *The Lives and Deeds of Our Self-Made Men* (Hartford, CT: Worthington, Dustin & Co., 1872), 17.

38. Harriet Beecher Stowe, *Men of Our Times* (Hartford, CT: Hartford Publishing Company, 1868), vii.

39. William Ellery Channing, *The Works of William Ellery Channing* (London: Chapman, 1844), 113.

40. Ibid.

41. Ralph Waldo Emerson, *The Portable Emerson* (New York: Penguin, 2014), 320.

42. Channing, *Works*, 130.

43. Quoted in David Robinson, *Apostle of Culture: Emerson as Preacher and Lecturer* (Philadelphia: University of Pennsylvania Press, 1982), 55.

44. Benjamin Franklin, *The Autobiography of Benjamin Franklin: 1706–1757* (Carlisle, MA: Applewood Books, 2008), 124.

45. Ibid., 128.

46. Ibid.

47. Quoted in Howe, *Making the American Self*, 30.

CHAPTER FIVE: "LIGHT CAME IN AS A FLOOD"

1. Quoted in Randall E. Stross, *The Wizard of Menlo Park: How Thomas Alva Edison Invented the Modern World* (New York: Crown, 2008), 81.

2. Ibid., vi.

3. Quoted in ibid., 80.

4. Quoted in ibid., 83.

5. J. B. McClure, ed., *Edison and His Inventions* (Chicago: Rhodes & McClure, 1889), 153.

6. Quoted in Stross, *The Wizard of Menlo Park*, 83.

7. Quoted in ibid., 105.

8. Quoted in ibid., 247.

246   Notes

9. Quoted in Benjamin M. Friedman, *Religion and the Rise of Capitalism* (New York: Knopf, 2021), 228.

10. Nathaniel Hawthorne, *The House of the Seven Gables: A Romance* (Boston: Ticknor, Reed, and Fields, 1851), 283.

11. Henry Adams, *Education of Henry Adams* (Boston: Houghton Mifflin, 1918), 380.

12. Henry Adams, *A Henry Adams Reader* (New York: Doubleday, 1959), 341.

13. Ernest Freeberg, *The Age of Edison: Electric Light and the Invention of Modern America* (New York: Penguin, 2013), ebook.

14. Ibid.

15. Quoted in Robert W. Rydell, *All the World's a Fair: Visions of Empire at American International Expositions, 1876–1916* (Chicago: University of Chicago Press, 2013).

16. Gershom Huff, *Electro-Physiology* (New York: D. Appleton, 1853), iv.

17. Ibid., 412.

18. John Bovee Dods, *The Philosophy of Electrical Psychology: In a Course of Twelve Lectures* (New York: Fowler & Wells, 1850), 209.

19. Adams, *Education*, 34.

20. Ibid.

21. Quoted in Richard Hofstadter, *Social Darwinism in American Thought, 1860–1915* (Philadelphia: University of Pennsylvania Press, 2017), 24.

22. Ibid.

23. Herbert Spencer, *Herbert Spencer: Collected Writings* (London: Routledge, 2021), 5.

24. Igor Semenovich Kon, *A History of Classical Sociology* (Moscow: Progress Publishers, 1989), 54.

25. Quoted in Hofstadter, *Social Darwinism*, 21.

26. Quoted in Geoffrey Russell Searle, *Morality and the Market in Victorian Britain* (Oxford: Clarendon Press, 1998), 100.

27. William Graham Sumner, "The Challenge of Facts," in *Philosophy After Darwin: Classic and Contemporary Readings*, ed. Michael Ruse (Princeton, NJ: Princeton University Press, 2021), 116.

28. Quoted in Hofstadter, *Social Darwinism*, 44.

29. Sumner, "The Challenge of Facts," 117.

30. Henry Ward Beecher, *Beecher: Christian Philosopher, Pulpit Orator, Patriot and Philanthropist* (Chicago: Belford, Clarke & Co., 1887), 194.

31. Henry Ward Beecher, *Evolution and Religion* (New York: Fords, Howard & Hulbert, 1885), 97.

32. Ibid., 296.

33. Ibid., 26.

34. Hofstadter, *Social Darwinism*, 31.

35. Andrew Carnegie, *Autobiography* (Frankfurt: Outlook Verlag, 2018), 266.

36. James Allen, *James Allen: The Complete Collection* (n.p.: A Yesterday's World Publishing, 2018), 99.

37. Charles Fillmore, *Prosper* (Auckland, New Zealand: Floating Press, 2009), 7.

38. Charles Benjamin Newcomb, *All's Right with the World* (Boston: Lee & Shepard, 1899), 78.

39. Ibid., 79.

40. William Walker Atkinson, *The Secret of Success: How to Achieve Power, Success & Mental Influence* (e-artnow, 2017), ebook.

41. Ibid.

42. Quoted in Robert Wilson, *Barnum: An American Life* (New York: Simon & Schuster, 2020), 43.

43. Quoted in ibid., 12.

44. Phineas Taylor Barnum, *The Humbugs of the World & The Art of Money Getting* (n.p.: Musaicum Books, 2017), 2.

45. Phineas Taylor Barnum, *The Colossal P. T. Barnum Reader: Nothing Else Like It in the Universe* (Champaign-Urbana: University of Illinois Press, 2005), 99.

46. Barnum, *Humbugs*, 3.

CHAPTER SIX: "THE DANDY OF THE UNEXPECTED"

1. Quoted in Karl Beckson, "Oscar Wilde and the Green Carnation," *English Literature in Transition, 1880–1920* 43, no. 4 (2000): 387, muse.jhu.edu/article/367465.

2. Ibid., 389.

3. Ibid.

4. Ibid., 388.

5. Quoted in Jonathan Faiers and Mary Westerman Bulgarella, eds., *Colors in Fashion* (London: Bloomsbury, 2016).

6. Beckson, "Oscar Wilde," 390.

7. Robert Smythe Hichens, *The Green Carnation* (New York: Mitchell Kennerley, 1894), 14.

8. Ibid., 5.

9. Ibid., 23.

10. Quoted in Nicholas Freeman, *1895: Drama, Disaster and Disgrace in Late Victorian Britain* (Edinburgh: Edinburgh University Press, 2011), 23.

11. Ibid.

12. Ibid., 3.

13. This argument is taken from Rhonda K. Garelick, *Rising Star: Dandyism, Gender, and Performance in the Fin de Siècle* (Princeton, NJ: Princeton University Press, 2021), 9.

14. Jules Barbey d'Aurevilly, *Of Dandyism and of George Brummell* (London: J. M. Dent, 1897), 74.

15. Quoted in Jennifer Birkett, *The Sins of the Fathers: Decadence in France 1870–1914* (London: Quartet Books, 1986), 10.

16. Quoted in Mary Warner Blanchard, *Oscar Wilde's America: Counterculture in the Gilded Age* (New Haven, CT: Yale University Press, 1998), 33.

17. Charles Baudelaire, *Baudelaire: Selected Writings on Art and Artists* (Cambridge: Cambridge University Press, 1981), 422.

18. Christopher Prendergast, *Paris and the Nineteenth Century* (Hoboken, NJ: Wiley, 1995).

19. Hugh Cunningham, *The Challenge of Democracy: Britain 1832–1918* (London: Routledge, 2014), 155.

20. Christopher G. Bates, *The Early Republic and Antebellum America: An Encyclopedia of Social, Political, Cultural, and Economic History* (New York: Routledge, 2015); "Total Population: New York City & Boroughs, 1900 to 2010," www1.nyc.gov/assets/planning/download/pdf/data-maps/nyc-population/historical-population/nyc_total_pop_1900-2010.pdf.

21. Émile Zola, *The Ladies' Paradise: A Realistic Novel* (London: Vizetelly, 1886), 378.

22. Nicholas Daly, *The Demographic Imagination and the Nineteenth-Century City* (Cambridge: Cambridge University Press, 2015).

23. Quoted in ibid., 116.

24. Quoted in ibid., 115.

25. Ibid., 114.

26. Charles Baudelaire, *Flowers of Evil and Other Works: A Dual-Language Book* (New York: Dover, 2013), 75.

27. Alfred Austin, *The Golden Age: A Satire* (London: Chapman and Hall, 1871), 66.

28. Honoré de Balzac, *Treatise on Elegant Living* (Cambridge, MA: Wakefield Press, 2010), ebook.

29. Joris K. Huysmans, *Against Nature* (New York: Dover, 2018), 6.

30. D'Aurevilly, *Dandyism*, 33.

31. Quoted in Edmund Wilson, *Axel's Castle: A Study of the Imaginative Literature of 1870–1930* (New York: Farrar, Straus & Giroux, 2019), ebook.

32. Quoted in Blanchard, *Oscar Wilde's America*, 7.

33. Oscar Wilde, *The Picture of Dorian Gray* (Guelph, Ontario: Broadview Press, 1998), 138.

34. Huysmans, *Against Nature*, 140.

35. Quoted in Garelick, *Rising Star*, 45.

36. Edmond and Jules de Goncourt, *Pages from the Goncourt Journals*, trans. Robert Baldick (New York: New York Review of Books, 2007), 38.

37. Auguste Villiers de l'Isle-Adam, *Tomorrow's Eve* (Champaign-Urbana: University of Illinois Press, 1982).

38. Ibid., 62.

39. Ibid., 118.

40. Huysmans, *Against Nature*, 20.

41. Alex Ross, "The Occult Roots of Modernism," *New Yorker*, June 19, 2017, www.newyorker.com/magazine/2017/06/26/the-occult-roots-of-modernism.

42. Joséphin Péladan, *Comment on devient mage* (Paris: Chamuel, 1892), 81, trans. Sasha Chaitow.

43. Quoted in Sasha Chaitow, "How to Become a Mage (or Fairy): Joséphin Péladan's Initiation for the Masses," *Pomegranate* 14, no. 2 (2012): 193.

44. Wilde, *Dorian Gray*, 50.

45. Octave Uzanne, *Barbey D'Aurevilly* (Paris: La Cité des Livres, 1927), 25, translation my own.

46. Melanie Hawthorne, *Rachilde and French Women's Authorship: From Decadence to Modernism* (Lincoln: University of Nebraska Press, 2001).

CHAPTER SEVEN: "I SHALL BE RULING THE WORLD FROM NOW ON"

1. Lucy Hughes-Hallett, *The Pike: Gabriele D'Annunzio, Poet, Seducer and Preacher of War* (London: Fourth Estate, 2013), 1.

2. Quoted in William Pfaff, *The Bullet's Song: Romantic Violence and Utopia* (New York: Simon & Schuster, 2004), 170.

3. Ibid., 160.

4. Hughes-Hallett, *The Pike*, 27.

5. Pfaff, *Bullet's Song*, 154–155.

6. See Giovanni Gullace, *Gabriele D'Annunzio in France: A Study in Cultural Relations*, 1st ed. (Syracuse, NY: Syracuse University Press, 1966), 79.

7. Quoted in Pfaff, *Bullet's Song*, 162.

8. Quoted in Hughes-Hallett, *The Pike*, 54.

9. Quoted in Pfaff, *Bullet's Song*, 175.

10. Quoted in Odon Por, *Fascism* (New York: Alfred A. Knopf, 1923), xxi.

11. Quoted in Hughes-Hallett, *The Pike*, 5.

12. Ibid., 85.

13. Quoted in Pfaff, *Bullet's Song*, 185.

14. Quoted in Hughes-Hallett, *The Pike*, 82.

15. Friedrich Nietzsche, *The Gay Science* (New York: Vintage, 1974), 301.

16. Friedrich Nietzsche, *Thus Spake Zarathustra* (London: Arcturus Publishing, 2019), ebook.

17. Friedrich Nietzsche, *On the Genealogy of Morals and Ecce Homo* (New York: Random House, 2010), 123.

18. Friedrich Nietzsche, *The Antichrist* (New York: Dover, 2018), 4.

19. Nietzsche, *Gay Science*, 232.

20. Nietzsche, *Gay Science*, 175.

21. Nietzsche, *Zarathustra*, 6.

22. Quoted in Richard Wolin, *The Seduction of Unreason: The Intellectual Romance with Fascism from Nietzsche to Postmodernism*, 2nd ed. (Princeton, NJ: Princeton University Press, 2019), 28.

23. Quoted in Jacob Golomb, *Nietzsche, Godfather of Fascism?: On the Uses and Abuses of a Philosophy* (Princeton, NJ: Princeton University Press, 2009), 241.

24. Ibid.

25. Quoted in Giuliana Pieri, "Gabriele D'Annunzio and the Self-Fashioning of a National Icon," *Modern Italy* 21, no. 4, https://doi.org/10.1017/mit.2016.49.

26. Luigi Russolo, ed., *Speed Destruction Noise War: Futurist Manifestos 1909–15* (n.p.: Elektron Ebooks, 2013), ebook.

27. Quoted in Pfaff, *Bullet's Song*, 31.

28. Patrick G. Zander, *Fascism Through History: Culture, Ideology, and Daily Life*, 2 vols. (Santa Barbara, CA: ABC-CLIO, 2020), 537.

29. Quoted in Pfaff, *Bullet's Song*, 42.

30. Quoted in Mabel Berezin, *Making the Fascist Self: The Political Culture of Interwar Italy* (Ithaca, NY: Cornell University Press, 2018), 50.

31. Quoted in Simonetta Falasca-Zamponi, *Fascist Spectacle: The Aesthetics of Power in Mussolini's Italy* (Berkeley: University of California Press, 2000), 21.

32. Ibid.

33. Quoted in Golomb, *Nietzsche*, 250.

34. Benito Mussolini, "Fascism," in *Princeton Readings in Political Thought: Essential Texts Since Plato*, rev. ed. (Princeton, NJ: Princeton University Press, 2018), 540.

35. Quoted in Walter L. Adamson, "Modernism and Fascism: The Politics of Culture in Italy, 1903–1922," *American Historical Review* 95, no. 2 (April 1990): 359.


## CHAPTER EIGHT: THE POWER OF *IT*

1. Quoted in James Robert Parish, *Prostitution in Hollywood Films: Plots, Critiques, Casts, and Credits for 389 Theatrical and Made-for-Television Releases* (Jefferson, NC: McFarland, 1992), 29.

2. Quoted in Matthew Rukgaber, *Nietzsche in Hollywood: Images of the Übermensch in Early American Cinema* (Albany: State University of New York Press, 2022), ebook.

3. Julie Grossman, *The Femme Fatale* (New Brunswick, NJ: Rutgers University Press, 2020), ebook.

4. Elinor Glyn, "It," *Hearst's International Combined with Cosmopolitan*, 1927, 64.

5. Ibid.

6. Elinor Glyn, *The Philosophy of Love* (Auburn, NY: Authors' Press, 1923), 128.

7. Quoted in Sharon Marcus, *The Drama of Celebrity* (Princeton, NJ: Princeton University Press, 2020), 55.

8. Quoted in Ty Burr, *Gods Like Us: On Movie Stardom and Modern Fame* (New York: Anchor, 2013), 11.

9. James Chapman, *Film and History* (Basingstoke, UK: Palgrave Macmillan, 2017), 119.

10. Quoted in Burr, *Gods Like Us*, 4.

11. Ibid., 5.

12. Quoted in ibid., 16.

13. Quoted in ibid., 28.

14. Quoted in ibid., 21.

15. Quoted in Richard deCordova, *Picture Personalities: The Emergence of the Star System in America* (Champaign-Urbana: University of Illinois Press, 2001), 98.

16. See Paul McDonald, *Hollywood Stardom* (Chichester, UK: Wiley-Blackwell, 2013).

17. Burr, *Gods Like Us*.

18. Quoted in Robert Staughton Lynd and Helen Merrell Lynd, *Middletown: A Study in American Culture* (New York: Harcourt, Brace, 1929), 161.

19. Quoted in Burr, *Gods Like Us*.

20. "Don't Pay Me a Cent If I Can't Give You a Magnetic Personality—5 Days Free Proof!," *Popular Mechanics* 45, no. 3 (March 1926): 19; see discussion of personal magnetism in Karen Sternheimer, *Celebrity Culture and the American Dream: Stardom and Social Mobility* (New York: Routledge, 2014), 60.

21. "Don't Pay Me a Cent."

22. Quoted in Joseph L. DeVitis and John Martin Rich, *The Success Ethic, Education, and the American Dream* (Albany: State University of New York Press, 1996), 59.

23. Orison Swett Marden, *How to Succeed* (self-pub., CreateSpace, 2013).

24. "Instantaneous Personal Magnetism," *Popular Mechanics*, March 1928, 99.

25. Quoted in Jennifer Scanlon, *Inarticulate Longings: The Ladies' Home Journal, Gender and the Promise of Consumer Culture* (New York: Routledge, 2020), 209.

26. Quoted in Roland Marchand, *Advertising the American Dream: Making Way for Modernity, 1920–1940* (Berkeley: University of California Press, 1985), 213.

27. Ibid.

28. Quoted in Sternheimer, *Celebrity Culture*, 49. The next two paragraphs are taken from Sternheimer's reporting (ibid., 98).

29. See ibid., 67.

30. Quoted in ibid., 71.

31. Quoted in Marchand, *Advertising the American Dream*, 11.

32. Ibid., 8.

33. *Address of President Coolidge Before the American Association of Advertising Agencies* (Washington, DC: US Government Printing Office, 1926), 7.

34. Ibid.


## CHAPTER NINE: "YOU BASICALLY JUST SAID YOU WERE"

1. Dotson Rader, "Twilight of the Tribe: The Wedding that Wasn't," *Village Voice*, July 31, 1969, www.villagevoice.com/2020/10/07/twilight-of-the-tribe-the-wedding-that-wasnt/.

2. Ibid.

3. Ibid.

4. Ibid.

5. Craig B. Highberger, *Superstar in a Housedress: The Life and Legend of Jackie Curtis* (New York: Open Road, 2015), 23.

6. For clarity, I will continue to use she/her pronouns to refer to Jackie, except when quoting contemporaries using other pronouns.

7. Highberger, *Superstar*, 2.

8. Ibid., 11.

9. Rader, "Twilight of the Tribe."

10. Ibid.

11. Highberger, *Superstar*, 40.

12. Ibid., 52.

13. Quoted in Kembrew McLeod, *The Downtown Pop Underground: New York City and the Literary Punks, Renegade Artists, DIY Filmmakers, Mad Playwrights, and Rock 'N' Roll Glitter Queens Who Revolutionized Culture* (New York: Abrams, 2018), 71.

14. Quoted in Highberger, *Superstar*, 80.

15. Quoted in ibid., 176.

16. Andy Warhol, *Andy Warhol: From A to B and Back Again* (New York: Whitney Museum of American Art, 2018), 70.

17. Sloan Wilson, *The Man in the Gray Flannel Suit* (New York: Hachette Books, 2009), ebook.

18. Quoted in Anthony Esler, *Bombs, Beards, and Barricades: 150 Years of Youth in Revolt* (New York: Stein and Day, 1972), 275; see also Galt MacDermot, *Vocal Selections from Hair: The American Tribal Love-Rock Musical*, lyrics by Gerome Ragni and James Rado (Van Nuys, CA: Alfred Music, 2009).

19. Jennifer H. Meadows and August E. Grant, *Communication Technology Update*, 10th ed. (Burlington, MA: Focal Press, 2006), 27.

20. Quoted in Andreas Killen, *1973 Nervous Breakdown: Watergate, Warhol, and the Birth of Post-Sixties America* (New York: Bloomsbury USA, 2008), 53.

21. Joe McGinniss, *The Selling of the President 1968* (New York: PocketBooks, 1970), 31.

22. Ibid., 194.

23. Ibid., 27.

24. Quoted in ibid., 28.

25. Daniel J. Boorstin, *The Image: A Guide to Pseudo-Events in America* (New York: Vintage, 2012), 9.

26. Quoted in Killen, *1973 Nervous Breakdown*, 139.

27. Quoted in ibid., 144.

28. Warhol, *From A to B*, 55.

29. Ibid., 54.

30. Ibid.

31. Candy Darling, *Candy Darling: Memoirs of an Andy Warhol Superstar* (New York: Open Road, 2015), 39.

32. Quoted in Killen, *1973 Nervous Breakdown*, 58; my account of the Loud family, as well as the critical sources quoted in the next few paragraphs, is taken from *1973 Nervous Breakdown*; see also *An American Family*, produced by Craig Gilbert, aired January 11–March 29, 1973, on WNET New York.

33. Killen, *1973 Nervous Breakdown*, 68.

34. Ibid., 73; see Roger Rosenblatt, "Residuals on an American Family," *New Republic*, November 23, 1974.

35. Margaret Mead, "As Significant as the Invention of Drama or the Novel," in *The Documentary Film Reader: History, Theory, Criticism*, ed. Jonathan Kahana (Oxford: Oxford University Press, 2016), 526.

36. Quoted in Killen, *1973 Nervous Breakdown*; original *Time*, February 27, 1973.

37. Killen, *1973 Nervous Breakdown*, 63.

38. Quoted in ibid., 62; original Abigail McCarthy, "'An American Family,' and 'The Family of Man,'" *Atlantic Monthly*, July 1973.

39. Killen, *1973 Nervous Breakdown*, 67.

40. Ibid., 69.

## CHAPTER TEN: "DO IT YOURSELF"

1. Ed Regis, "Meet the Extropians," *Wired*, October 1, 1994, www.wired.com/1994/10/extropians/.

2. Quoted in Mark O'Connell, *To Be a Machine: Adventures Among Cyborgs, Utopians, Hackers, and the Futurists Solving the Modest Problem of Death* (New York: Anchor, 2018), 37.

3. Max More, "The Principles of Extropianism," *Extropy* 6 (Summer 1990): 16.

4. Regis, "Meet the Extropians."

5. "EXTRO 1: The First Extropy Institute Conference on Transhumanist Thought" (poster, Sunnyvale, CA, April 30–May 1, 1994), http://fennetic.net/pub/extropy/extro1_ad.pdf.

6. Regis, "Meet the Extropians."

7. Max More, "Technological Self-Transformation: Expanding Personal Extropy," *Extropy* 10 (Winter/Spring 1993).

8. Ibid., 18.

9. J. Storrs Hall, "What I Want to Be When I Grow Up, Is a Cloud," *Extropy* 13 (1994), reprinted by the Kurzweil Library, July 6, 2001, www.kurzweilai.net/what-i-want-to-be-when-i-grow-up-is-a-cloud (web pages on file with author).

10. More, "Technological Self-Transformation," 18.

11. Ibid.

12. "Larry King Interviews Futurist FM-2030," video, YouTube, uploaded January 9, 2011, https://youtube/XkMVzEft7Og.

13. Regis, "Meet the Extropians."

14. Quoted in Fred Turner, *From Counterculture to Cyberculture: Stewart Brand, the Whole Earth Network, and the Rise of Digital Utopianism* (Chicago: University of Chicago Press, 2010), 43.

15. Quoted in Turner, *From Counterculture*, 37.

16. Theodore Roszak, *The Making of a Counter Culture: Reflections on the Technocratic Society and Its Useful Opposition* (New York: Anchor, 1969), 240.

17. Ibid., 328.

18. Quoted in Hsiao-Yun Chu and Roberto G. Trujillo, eds., *New Views on R. Buckminster Fuller* (Redwood City, CA: Stanford University Press, 2009), 157.

19. John Markoff, "Op-Ed: The Invention of Google Before Google—a Radical Mail-Order 'Catalog,'" *Los Angeles Times*, March 28, 2018, www.latimes.com/opinion/op-ed/la-oe-markoff-stewart-brand-whole-earth-catalog-20180328-story.html.

20. Turner, *From Counterculture*, 213.

21. Stewart Brand, "We Owe It All to the Hippies," *Time*, 1995.

22. Ibid.

23. John Perry Barlow, "Declaration for the Independence of Cyberspace" (Davos, Switzerland, February 8, 1996), Electronic Frontier Foundation, www.eff.org/cyberspace -independence.

24. Ibid.

25. Ibid.

26. Ibid.

27. Sidebar, *Extropy* 10 (Winter/Spring 1993): 22.

28. Richard Barbrook and Andy Cameron, "The Californian Ideology," in *Crypto Anarchy, Cyberstates, and Pirate Utopias*, ed. Peter Ludlow (Cambridge, MA: MIT Press, 2001), 376.

29. Ibid., 377.

30. Antonio Regalado, "Meet Altos Labs, Silicon Valley's Latest Wild Bet on Living Forever," *MIT Technology Review*, September 4, 2021, www.technologyreview.com/2021 /09/04/1034364/altos-labs-silicon-valleys-jeff-bezos-milner-bet-living-forever/.

31. Emily A. Vogels, "About One-in-Five Americans Use a Smart Watch or Fitness Tracker," Pew Research Center, January 9, 2020, www.pewresearch.org/fact-tank/2020/01 /09/about-one-in-five-americans-use-a-smart-watch-or-fitness-tracker/.

32. Quoted in "The Quantified Self: Data Gone Wild?" *PBS NewsHour*, September 28, 2013, www.pbs.org/newshour/show/the-quantified-self-data-gone-wild.

33. Blake Masters and Peter Thiel, *Zero to One: Notes on Startups, or How to Build the Future* (New York: Crown, 2014), 22.

34. Ibid., 81.

35. Ibid., 59.

36. Ibid., 60.

37. Carolyn Chen, *Work Pray Code: When Work Becomes Religion in Silicon Valley* (Princeton, NJ: Princeton University Press, 2022), 90.

38. Max More, "Transhumanism: Towards a Futurist Philosophy," *Extropy* 6 (Summer 1990): 6.

39. Ibid.

## CHAPTER ELEVEN: "BECAUSE I FELT LIKE IT"

1. Yvonne Villarreal, "'The Meeting that Changed the World': Inside the First Days of the Kardashian Empire," *Los Angeles Times*, June 3, 2021, www.latimes .com/entertainment-arts/tv/story/2021-06-03/keeping-up-with-the-kardashians-kim -kris-oral-history-pilot-episode.

2. Oliver Coleman, "The Making of a Reality Icon," *The Sun*, March 28, 2017, www .thesun.co.uk/living/3196659/this-is-the-real-story-behind-kim-kardashians-sex-tape-and -how-it-made-her-a-star/.

3. "Kim Drops Sex Tape Lawsuit, Gets a Big Load of Cash," TMZ, April 30, 2007, www.tmz.com/2007/04/30/kim-drops-sex-tape-lawsuit-gets-a-big-load-of-cash/.

4. "Kim Kardashian's 10 Year Anniversary for Sex Tape & the Money Keeps Rolling In," TMZ, April 7, 2017, www.tmz.com/2017/04/07/kim-kardashian-10-year-anniversary-sex-tape/.

5. Beth Allcock, "'No Holding Back': Kim Kardashian Admits She Made 2002 Sex Tape with Ray-J Because She Was 'Horny and Felt Like It,'" The Sun, June 6, 2021, www.the-sun.com/entertainment/3025470/kim-kardashian-sex-tape-ex-ray-j-horny-kuwtk/.

6. "Kardashians on Barbara Walters '10 Most Fascinating People,'" video, YouTube, uploaded December 15, 2011, www.youtube.com/watch?v=5YMV05HosIo.

7. Danielle Pergament, "Kim Kardashian and I Analyzed Each Other's Faces," Allure, August 2022, www.allure.com/story/kim-kardashian-cover-interview-august-2022.

8. Elizabeth Wagmeister, "'Money Always Matters': The Kardashians Tell All About Their New Reality TV Reign," Variety, March 9, 2022, https://variety.com/2022/tv/features/kardashians-hulu-kris-kim-khloe-1235198939/.

9. Pergament, "Kim Kardashian."

10. Jemima McEvoy, "Kim Kardashian Is $600 Million Richer After Shapewear Brand Skims Hits $3.2 Billion Valuation," Forbes, January 8, 2022, www.forbes.com/sites/jemimamcevoy/2022/01/28/kim-kardashian-is-600-million-richer-after-shapewear-brand-skims-hits-32-billion-valuation/.

11. Natalie Robehmed, "Kim Kardashian West, Mobile Mogul," Forbes, July 11, 2016, www.forbes.com/sites/natalierobehmed/2016/07/11/kim-kardashian-mobile-mogul-the-forbes-cover-story/.

12. Lauren O'Neill, "Goodbye to the Influencer Decade, and Thanks for Nothing," Vice, December 19, 2019, www.vice.com/en/article/vb55wa/instagram-influencers-history-2010s.

13. Jovita Trujillo, "See the Kardashian-Jenner's First Instagram Posts," Hola!, April 15, 2022, www.hola.com/us/celebrities/20220415331124/kim-khloe-kourtney-kardashian-kylie-kendall-jenner-first-instagram-posts-1/.

14. Huda Beauty (@hudabeauty), Instagram, www.instagram.com/hudabeauty/?hl=en.

15. Kayleen Schaefer, "How Bloggers Make Money on Instagram," Harper's Bazaar, May 20, 2015, www.harpersbazaar.com/fashion/trends/a10949/how-bloggers-make-money-on-instagram/.

16. Antonia Farzan, "Meet the 22-Year-Old Blogger Who Gets Paid up to $15,000 for a Single Instagram Post," Business Insider, May 22, 2015, www.businessinsider.com/fashion-blogger-who-gets-paid-15000-for-a-single-instagram-post-2015-5.

17. Edward Segal, "U.S. Freelance Workforce Continues to Grow, with No Signs of Easing: New Report," Forbes, December 8, 2021, www.forbes.com/sites/edwardsegal/2021/12/08/us-freelance-workforce-continues-to-grow-with-no-signs-of-easing-new-report/.

18. Tom Peters, "The Brand Called You," Fast Company, August 31, 1997, www.fastcompany.com/28905/brand-called-you.

19. Taylor Lorenz, "Rising Instagram Stars Are Posting Fake Sponsored Content," *The Atlantic*, December 18, 2018, www.theatlantic.com/technology/archive/2018/12/influencers-are-faking-brand-deals/578401/.

20. Hilary Sheinbaum, "What the Influencer Couple Has to Say About That Viral Proposal Scheme," *New York Times*, June 21, 2019, www.nytimes.com/2019/06/21/style/what-the-influencer-couple-has-to-say-about-that-viral-proposal-scheme.html.

21. Jacinda Santora, "Key Influencer Marketing Statistics You Need to Know for 2022," Influencer Marketing Hub, last modified August 1, 2022, https://influencermarketinghub.com/influencer-marketing-statistics/.

22. Taylor Locke, "86% of Young People Say They Want to Post Social Media Content for Money," CNBC, November 11, 2019, www.cnbc.com/2019/11/08/study-young-people-want-to-be-paid-influencers.html.

23. Scott Langdon, "Gen Z and the Rise of Influencer Culture," HigherVisibility, August 19, 2022, www.highervisibility.com/ppc/learn/gen-z-and-the-rise-of-influencer-culture/.

24. Brand Builders Group, "Personal Brands Drive More than 2/3 of All Americans to Spend More Money," PR Newswire, January 5, 2022, www.prnewswire.com/news-releases/personal-brands-drive-more-than-23-of-all-americans-to-spend-more-money-301454791.html.

25. Christopher Rosen, "How *The Apprentice* Brought Donald Trump Back to Life," *Vanity Fair*, September 29, 2020, www.vanityfair.com/hollywood/2020/09/donald-trump-the-apprentice-taxes.

26. Patrick Radden Keefe, "How Mark Burnett Resurrected Donald Trump as an Icon of American Success," *New Yorker*, December 27, 2018, www.newyorker.com/magazine/2019/01/07/how-mark-burnett-resurrected-donald-trump-as-an-icon-of-american-success.

27. Ibid.

28. Donald Trump, *The Art of the Deal* (New York: Random House, 2016).

29. Quoted in Carol George, *God's Salesman: Norman Vincent Peale and the Power of Positive Thinking* (New York: Oxford University Press, 2019), 114.

30. Norman Vincent Peale, *The Power of Positive Thinking* (Uttar Pradesh, India: Om Books International, 2016), 108.

31. Mark Fahey, "Donald Trump's Twitter Engagement Is Stronger Than Ever," CNBC, March 14, 2017, www.cnbc.com/2017/02/16/donald-trumps-twitter-engagement-is-stronger-than-ever.html; Aaron Mak, "Trump Was Losing Twitter Followers Until He Incited a Riot," *Slate*, January 12, 2021, https://slate.com/technology/2021/01/trump-twitter-ban-followers-capitol-riot.html.

32. Quoted in Michael Grynbaum and Rachel Abrams, "'Apprentice' Producer Denounces Trump but Won't Release Possibly Damning Tapes," *New York Times*, October 13, 2016, www.nytimes.com/2016/10/14/business/media/mark-burnett-apprentice-donald-trump.html.

33. Marisa Dellatto, "TikTok Hits 1 Billion Monthly Active Users," *Forbes*, September 27, 2021, www.forbes.com/sites/marisadellatto/2021/09/27/tiktok-hits-1-billion-monthly -active-users/?sh=d1f0a1b44b6e.

34. Ezra Marcus, "The 'E-Pimps' of OnlyFans," *New York Times*, May 16, 2022, www.nytimes.com/2022/05/16/magazine/e-pimps-onlyfans.html#:~:text=In%202019%2C %20there%20were%20reportedly,to%20more%20than%20a%20million.

## EPILOGUE: "HOW TO BE YOURSELF"

1. Cheryl Teh, "Influencer and Erstwhile Author Caroline Calloway Is Accused of Failing to Pay Over $40,000 in Rent: Lawsuit," *Insider*, March 21, 2022, www.insider.com /influencer-caroline-calloway-accused-of-not-paying-40000-in-rent-2022-3.

2. Constance Grady, "Caroline Calloway, Her 'One-Woman Fyre Fest,' and Her Ex–Best Friend Natalie, Explained," *Vox*, September 11, 2019, www.vox.com/culture/2019 /9/11/20860607/caroline-calloway-natalie-beach-explained.

3. Caroline Calloway (@carolinecaloway), "Let me help u, Emily, so you can focus on ur kids. I'm chaotic. I love my work. My work is writing, painting, photography, posting on social media, and living inside a Truman Show of my own making—performance art. Most ppl do not consider what I make to be art. More chaos ensues," Twitter, April 2, 2020, 7:27 p.m., https://twitter.com/carolinecaloway/status/1245764840913846273.

4. Gillian Friedman, "Jobless, Selling Nudes Online and Still Struggling," *New York Times*, January 13, 2021, www.nytimes.com/2021/01/13/business/onlyfans-pandemic-users .html.

5. Frederick Douglass, *The Essential Douglass: Selected Writings and Speeches*, ed. Nicholas Buccola (Indianapolis, IN: Hackett, 2016), 33.

# Index